Oracle DBA
Test 1 and Test 2
The Cram Sheet

This Cram Sheet contains the distilled, key facts about Oracle7 in the areas of SQL, PL/SQL, and database administration, which are the topics of the OCP-DBA Tests 1 and 2. Review this information last thing before you enter the test room, paying special attention to those areas you feel you need the most to review. You can transfer any of these facts from your head onto a blank piece of paper before beginning the exam.

INTERNAL STRUCTURES

1. Know these Oracle7 internal structures:
   - **Control files** Track database structures and ensure synchronicity of all database files via the system change number (SCN).
   - **Parameter file** Contains the initialization files that tell the Oracle server how to configure memory and internal resources as well as external file locations and process configurations.
   - **Alert log** Contains informational and error messages concerning the Oracle system and processes. It should be checked frequently, at least daily.
   - **Redo log files** Contain the transaction journals; they are critical for database recovery. Redo log files are copied to the archive logs if archive logging is enabled.
   - **Database datafiles** Make up the physical side of tablespaces. There are one or more datafiles per tablespace.
   - **Trace files** Generated by all background processes and, if tracing is enabled, by each session. Trace files contain statistics for the process and log process messages and errors.

THE ORACLE INSTANCE

2. The system global area (SGA) is made up of the database buffers, shared pool, log buffers, and request and response queues.

3. The database buffer cache is where all data must pass through to get to users and back to the database. It usually makes up the majority of the SGA size.

4. The shared pool, also known as the library caches, stores the parsed versions of stored objects.

5. The log buffers are used to store redo log entries prior to their being written to disk and usually make up the third largest section of the SGA.

6. An instance is made up of the SGA and a set of processes. The base set of processes consist of the SMON, PMON, DBWR, and LGWR.

7. The SMON process, known as the system monitor, cleans up sort memory areas and recovers instances after instance failures.

8. The PMON process, known as the process monitor, cleans up after failed processes.

9. The DBWR process, known as the dirty buffer writer (not database writer), writes dirty (used or changed) buffers from the SGA database buffers to the disk. DBWR also performs checkpoint writes if the CKPT process isn't available.

10. The LGWR process, known as the log writer, writes redo log entries from the log buffers to the redo logs.

11. The instance may have several optional processes: CKPT, ARCH, RECO, SNPnn, Dnnnn, Snnnn, and Pnnnn.

12. The CKPT process, known as the checkpoint process, relieves the DBWR process of its checkpointing duties, thus improving efficiency.

13. The ARCH process, known as the archiver, is only present when automatic archiving (**ARCHIVELOG** mode) is set. ARCH writes filled redo logs to the archive log location.

14. The RECO process, known as recoverer, is only present if distributed transactions are set. The only purpose of RECO is to recover failed distributed transactions.

15. The SNPnn process, known as the snapshot of job queue, is only set up if the **snapshot_processes** parameter or **job_queue** parameter is set to a nonzero value. The SNPnn processes (up to 9) wakeup at specified intervals, check the job tables, and if a job is due, run it.

16. Dnnnn processes, known as the distributor processes, monitor connections in the multithreaded environment and distribute them to the Snnnn (server) processes.

17. The Pnnnn processes, known as parallel query slaves, are used to perform parallel query operations and are only present if the parallel query operations are configured.

ORACLE STARTUP AND SHUTDOWN

18. To start up Oracle, the general procedure is:

    1. Start Server Manager (for example, on Unix: svrmgrl).

    2. Issue the **CONNECT INTERNAL** connection command.

    3. Issue **STARTUP** command with appropriate option:

       - **OPEN** The default option, does a **NOMOUNT**, **MOUNT**, and **OPEN EXCLUSIVE**.
       - **MOUNT** Starts instance processes but doesn't open the database for use.
       - **NOMOUNT** Only used for maintenance and testing.
       - **SHARED or PARALLEL** Only used if the database has the parallel option installed. Allows more than one instance to access the same database files.

    4. Startup proceeds from **NOMOUNT** to **MOUNT** to **OPEN** status.

19. To shut down an Oracle Instance, the usual procedure is:

    1. Start Server Manager (for example on Unix: svrmgrl).

    2. Issue the **CONNECT INTERNAL** connection command.

    3. Issue **SHUTDOWN** command with appropriate option:

       - **ABORT** Shutdowns regardless of logins.
       - **IMMEDIATE** Allows transactions to complete, log out users, and then shutdown.
       - **NORMAL** Waits for all users to exit, then shutdown.

DATA DICTIONARY

20. The data dictionary consists at lowest level of **X$** and **K$** C structs, not normally viewable or used by DBA.

21. The data dictionary has **V$** virtual views or tables, which contain variable data such as statistics.

22. The data dictionary has dollar tables ($), which actual contain database metadata about tables, views, indexes, and other database structures.

23. At the uppermost layer, the data dictionary has **DBA_** views about all objects, **ALL_** views about all objects a user can access, and the **USER_** views about all objects a user owns.

Are You Certifiable?

That's the question that's probably on your mind. The answer is: You bet! But if you've tried and failed or you've been frustrated by the complexity of the OCP program and the maze of study materials available, you've come to the right place. We've created our new publishing and training program, *Certification Insider Press*, to help you accomplish one important goal: to ace an exam without having to spend the rest of your life studying for it.

The book you have in your hands is part of our *Exam Cram* series. Each book is especially designed not only to help you study for an exam but also to help you understand what the exam is all about. Inside these covers you'll find hundreds of test-taking tips, insights, and strategies that simply cannot be found anyplace else. In creating our guides, we've assembled the very best team of certified trainers, professionals, and networking course developers.

Our commitment is to ensure that the *Exam Cram* guides offer proven training and active-learning techniques not found in other study guides. We provide unique study tips and techniques, memory joggers, custom quizzes, insights about trick questions, a sample test, and much more. In a nutshell, each *Exam Cram* guide is closely organized like the exam it is tied to.

To help us continue to provide the very best certification study materials, we'd like to hear from you. Write or email us (craminfo@coriolis.com) and let us know how our *Exam Cram* guides have helped you study, or tell us about new features you'd like us to add. If you send us a story about how an *Exam Cram* guide has helped you ace an exam and we use it in one of our guides, we'll send you an official *Exam Cram* shirt for your efforts.

Good luck with your certification exam, and thanks for allowing us to help you achieve your goals.

Keith Weiskamp
Publisher, Certification Insider Press

Oracle DBA
Test 1 and Test 2
SQL and PL/SQL • Database Administration

Oracle
Certified
Professional

Oracle DBA Test 1 And Test 2 Exam Cram

Limits of Liability and Disclaimer of Warranty

The author and publisher of this book have used their best efforts in preparing the book and the programs contained in it. These efforts include the development, research, and testing of the theories and programs to determine their effectiveness. The author and publisher make no warranty of any kind, expressed or implied, with regard to these programs or the documentation contained in this book.

The author and publisher shall not be liable in the event of incidental or consequential damages in connection with, or arising out of, the furnishing, performance, or use of the programs, associated instructions, and/or claims of productivity gains.

Trademarks

Trademarked names appear throughout this book. Rather than list the names and entities that own the trademarks or insert a trademark symbol with each mention of the trademarked name, the publisher states that it is using the names for editorial purposes only and to the benefit of the trademark owner, with no intention of infringing upon that trademark.

The Coriolis Group, Inc.
An International Thomson Publishing Company
14455 N. Hayden Road, Suite 220
Scottsdale, Arizona 85260

602/483-0192
FAX 602/483-0193
http://www.coriolis.com

Library of Congress Cataloging-in-Publication Data
Ault, Michael R.
    Oracle DBA test 1 and test 2 exam cram / by Michael R. Ault
        p.   cm.
    Includes index.
    ISBN 1-57610-262-9
    1. Relational databases--Examinations--Study guides.   2. Oracle
(Computer file)   I. Title.
QA76.9.D3A9395   1998
005.75'65--dc21   98-16072
                                                           CIP

Printed in the United States of America
10 9 8 7 6 5 4 3 2 1

Publisher
Keith Weiskamp

Acquisitions Editor
Shari Jo Hehr

Marketing Specialist
Cynthia Caldwell

Project Editor
Jeff Kellum

Production Coordinator
Jon Gabriel

Cover Design
Anthony Stock

Layout Design
April Nielsen

an International Thomson Publishing company

Albany, NY • Belmont, CA • Bonn • Boston • Cincinnati • Detroit • Johannesburg • London • Madrid
Melbourne • Mexico City • New York • Paris • Singapore • Tokyo • Toronto • Washington

About The Author

Michael R. Ault has been working in the data processing field since 1974 and with Oracle since 1990. Mike has attended numerous Oracle and university classes dealing with all areas of Oracle database administration and development and holds five Oracle masters certificates. Mike began his certification history with the Oracle Corporation test based Oracle6 certification, continued it as one of the developers and recipients of the Chauncy Oracle7 certification exam, and is currently an Oracle7.3 Oracle Certified Professional. Mike has written several books, including *Oracle 7.0 Administration & Management* (John Wiley & Sons), *Oracle8 Administration and Management* (John Wiley & Sons), and *Oracle8 Black Book* (Coriolis Group Books). Mike has written numerous articles for *Oracle* magazine, *DBMS Magazine*, and *OREVIEW* magazine and is a frequent presenter at ECO, IOUG-A, and Oracle Open World conferences. Mike also SYSOPS for the CompuServe ORAUSER forum and the RevealNet, Inc., Web page's DBA Pipeline at http://www.revealnet.com/. Mike is also the primary author for the Oracle Administrator Knowledge Base product from RevealNet, Inc.

Acknowledgments

I would like to thank the folks at SelfTest Software, especially Mr. John C. Phillips, who provided me access to the fine example test questions that Self Test Software provides for the Oracle examinations. I would also like to acknowledge the contributions from Michelle Berard, Barbara Pascavage, and Paul Collins, without whose help I couldn't have finished this book. I would also like to thank Jeff Kellum and Shari Jo Hehr from The Coriolis Group for their unwavering confidence as well as their gentle kicks from behind. Finally, I want to thank the unsung heroes at any publishing house, the proofreaders, page markup folks, and the ones who do all the odd, complex jobs that take a bunch of electronic ghosts and convert them into a book.

Table Of Contents

Introduction

Welcome to *Oracle DBA Exam Cram: Test 1 and Test 2*. This book will help you get ready to take—and pass—the first two of the four-part Oracle Certified Professional-Oracle Certified Database Administrator (OCP-DBA) track series of exams. In this introduction, I introduce Oracle's certification programs in general, and talk about how the *Exam Cram* series can help you prepare for Oracle's certification exams.

Exam Cram books help you understand and appreciate the subjects and materials you need to pass Oracle certification exams. The books are aimed strictly at test preparation and review. They do not teach you everything you need to know about a topic. Instead, I present and dissect the questions and problems that you're likely to encounter on a test. Nevertheless, to completely prepare yourself for any Oracle test, I recommend that you begin your studies with some classroom training or that you read one of the many DBA guides available from Oracle and third-party vendors. I also strongly recommend that you install, configure, and fool around with the software or environment that you'll be tested on, because nothing beats hands-on experience and familiarity when it comes to understanding the questions you're likely to encounter on a certification test. Book learning is essential, but hands-on experience is the best teacher of all!

The Oracle Certified Professional (OCP) Program

The OCP program for DBA certification currently includes four separate tests. I cover the first two in this first book in the series. A brief description of each test follows:

➤ **Test 1: Introduction to Oracle: SQL And PL/SQL** This test is the base test for the series. Knowledge tested in Test 1 will also be used in all other tests in the DBA series. Test 1 tests knowledge of SQL and PL/SQL language constructs, syntax, and usage. Test 1 covers Data Definition Language (DDL), Data Manipulation Language (DML), and Data Control Language (DCL). Also covered in Test 1 are basic data modeling and database design and basic Oracle Procedure Builder usage.

➤ **Test 2: Oracle7: Database Administration** Test 2 deals with all levels of database administration in Oracle7 (primarily version 7.3 and above). Topics include architecture, startup and shutdown, database creation, managing database internal and external constructs (such as redo logs, rollback segments, and tablespaces), and all other Oracle structures. Database auditing, use of National Language Support (NLS) features, and use of SQL*Loader and other utilities are also covered.

➤ **Test 3: Oracle7: Backup And Recovery Workshop** Test 3 covers one of the most important parts of the Oracle DBA's job: database backup and recovery operations. Test 3 tests knowledge in backup and recovery motives, architecture as it relates to backup and recovery, backup methods, failure scenarios, recovery methodologies, archive logging, supporting 24x7 shops, troubleshooting, and use of Oracle7's standby database features.

➤ **Test 4: Oracle7: Performance Tuning Workshop** Test 4 covers all aspects of tuning an Oracle7 database. Topics in both application and database tuning are covered. The test tests knowledge in diagnosis of tuning problems, database optimal configuration, shared pool tuning, buffer cache tuning, Oracle block usage, tuning rollback segments and redo mechanisms, monitoring and detection lock contention, tuning sorts, tuning in OLTP, DSS and mixed environments, and load optimization.

To obtain an OCP certificate in database administration, an individual must pass all four exams. You do not have to take the tests in any particular order. However, it is usually better to take the examinations in order because the knowledge tested builds from each exam. The core exams require individuals to demonstrate competence with all phases of Oracle7 database lifetime activities.

It's not uncommon for the entire process to take a year or so, and many individuals find that they must take a test more than once to pass. The primary goal of the *Exam Cram* series is to make it possible, given proper study and preparation, to pass all of the OCP-DBA tests on the first try.

Finally, certification is an ongoing activity. Once an Oracle product becomes obsolete, OCP-DBAs (and other OCPs) typically have a six-month time frame in which they can become recertified on current product versions. (If an individual does not get recertified within the specified time period, his certification becomes invalid.) Because technology keeps changing and new products continually supplant old ones, this should come as no surprise.

The best place to keep tabs on the OCP program and its various certifications is on the Oracle Web site. The current root URL for the OCP program is at http://education.oracle.com/certification. Oracle's certification Web site changes frequently, so if this URL doesn't work, try using the Search tool on Oracle's site (www.oracle.com) with either "OCP" or the quoted phrase "Oracle Certified Professional Program" as the search string. This will help you find the latest and most accurate information about the company's certification programs.

Taking A Certification Exam

Alas, testing is not free. You'll be charged $125 for each test you take, whether you pass or fail. In the United States and Canada, tests are administered by Sylvan Prometric. Sylvan Prometric can be reached at 1-800-755-3926 or 1-800-891-EXAM, any time from 7:00 A.M. to 6:00 P.M., Central Time, Monday through Friday. If you can't get through at this number, try 1-612-896-7000 or1-612-820-5707.

To schedule an exam, call at least one day in advance. To cancel or reschedule an exam, you must call at least one day before the scheduled test time (or you may be charged the $125 fee). When calling Sylvan Prometric, please have the following information ready for the telesales staffer who handles your call:

➤ Your name, organization, and mailing address.

➤ The name of the exam you want to take.

➤ A method of payment. (The most convenient approach is to supply a valid credit card number with sufficient available credit. Otherwise, payments by check, money order, or purchase order must be received before a test can be scheduled. If the latter methods are required, ask your order-taker for more details.)

An appointment confirmation will be sent to you by mail if you register more than five days before an exam, or will be sent by fax if less than five days before the exam. A Candidate Agreement letter, which you must sign to take the examination, will also be provided.

On the day of the test, try to arrive at least 15 minutes before the scheduled time slot. You must bring and supply two forms of identification, one of which one must be a photo ID.

All exams are completely closed book. In fact, you will not be permitted to take anything with you into the testing area; you will be furnished with a blank sheet of paper and a pen. I suggest that you immediately write down the most critical information about the test you're taking on the sheet of paper. (*Exam Cram* books provide a brief reference—The Cram Sheet, located inside the front of this book—that lists the essential information from the book in distilled form.) You will have some time to compose yourself, to record this critical information, and even to take a sample orientation exam before you begin the real thing. I suggest you take the orientation test before taking your first exam; they're all more or less identical in layout, behavior, and controls, so you probably won't need to do this more than once.

When you complete an Oracle certification exam, the testing software will tell you whether you've passed or failed. All tests are scored on a basis of 800 to 850 points depending on the mix of questions and results are broken into several topical areas. Whether you pass or fail, I suggest you ask for—and keep—the detailed report that the test administrator prints for you. You can use the report to help you prepare for another go-round, if necessary, and even if you pass, the report shows areas you may need to review to keep your edge. If you need to retake an exam, you'll have to call Sylvan Prometric, schedule a new test date, and pay another $125.

Tracking OCP Status

Oracle generates transcripts that indicate the exams you have passed and your corresponding test scores. After you pass the necessary set of four exams, you'll be certified as a DBA. Official certification normally takes anywhere from four to six weeks (generally within 30 days), so don't expect to get your credentials overnight. Once certified, you will receive a package, which includes a Welcome Kit that contains a number of elements:

➤ An OCP-DBA certificate, suitable for framing, along with an OCP program membership card and lapel pin.

➤ A license to use the OCP logo, thereby allowing you to use the logo in advertisements, promotions, documents, and on letterhead, business cards, and so on. An OCP logo sheet, which includes camera-ready artwork, comes with the license. (Note: Before using any of the artwork, individuals must sign and return a licensing agreement that indicates they'll abide by its terms and conditions.)

Many people believe that the benefits of OCP certification go well beyond the perks that Oracle provides to newly anointed members of this elite group. I am starting to see more job listings that request or require applicants to have an OCP-DBA certification, and many individuals who complete the program can qualify for increases in pay and/or responsibility. As an official recognition of hard work and broad knowledge, OCP certification is a badge of honor in many IT organizations.

How To Prepare For An Exam

At a minimum, preparing for OCP-DBA exams requires that you obtain and study the following materials:

➤ The Oracle7 Server version 7.3 Documentation Set on CD-ROM.

➤ The exam prep materials, practice tests, and self-assessment exams on the Oracle certification page (education.oracle.com/certification). Find the materials, download them, and use them!

➤ This *Exam Cram* book. It's the first and last thing you should read before taking the first two exams.

In addition, you'll probably find any or all of the following materials useful in your quest for Oracle7 DBA expertise:

➤ **OCP Resource Kits** Oracle Corporation has a CD-ROM with example questions and materials to help with the exam, generally, these are provided free by requesting them from your Oracle representative. They have also been offered free for the taking at most Oracle conventions, such as IOUGA-Alive! and Oracle Open World.

➤ **Classroom Training** Oracle, TUSC, LearningTree, and many others offer classroom and computer based training-type material that you will find useful to help you prepare for the exam. But a word of warning, these classes are fairly expensive (in the range of $300 per day of training). However, they do offer a condensed form of learning to help you "brush up" on your Oracle knowledge. The tests are closely tied to the classroom training provided by Oracle, so I would suggest at least taking the introductory classes to get the Oracle-specific (and classroom-specific) terminology under your belt.

➤ **Other Publications** You'll find direct references to other publications and resources in this book, and there's no shortage of materials available about Oracle7 DBA topics. To help you sift through some of the publications out there, I end each chapter with a "Need To Know More?" section that provides pointers to more complete and exhaustive resources covering the chapter's subject matter. This tells you where to look for further details.

➤ **The Oracle Support CD-ROM** Oracle provides a Support CD-ROM on a quarterly basis. This CD-ROM contains useful white papers, bug reports, technical bulletins, and information about release-specific bugs, fixes, and new features. Contact your Oracle representative for a copy.

➤ **The Oracle Administrator and PL/SQL Developer** These are online references from RevealNet, Inc, an Oracle and database online reference provider. These online references provide instant look-up on thousands of database and developmental topics and are an invaluable resource for study and learning about Oracle. Demo copies can be downloaded from http://www.revealnet.com/. Also available at the RevealNet Web site are the DBA and PL/SQL Pipelines, online discussion groups where you can obtain expert information from Oracle DBAs worldwide. The costs of these applications run about $400 each (current pricing is available on the Web site) and are worth every cent.

These required and recommended materials represent a nonpareil collection of sources and resources for Oracle DBA topics and software. In the section that follows, I explain how this book works, and give you some good reasons why this book should also be on your required and recommended materials list.

About This Book

Each topical *Exam Cram* chapter follows a regular structure, along with graphical cues about especially important or useful material. Here's the structure of a typical chapter:

➤ **Opening Hotlists** Each chapter begins with lists of the terms, tools, and techniques that you must learn and understand before you can be fully conversant with the chapter's subject matter. I follow the hotlists with one or two introductory paragraphs to set the stage for the rest of the chapter.

➤ **Topical Coverage** After the opening hotlists, each chapter covers a series of at least four topics related to the chapter's subject. Throughout this section, I highlight material most likely to appear on a test using a special Study Alert layout, like this:

> This is what a Study Alert looks like. Normally, a Study Alert stresses concepts, terms, software, or activities that will most likely appear in one or more certification test questions. For that reason, I think any information found offset in Study Alert format is worthy of unusual attentiveness on your part. Indeed, most of the facts appearing in The Cram Sheet appear as Study Alerts within the text.

Occasionally in *Exam Crams*, you'll see tables called "Vital Statistics." The contents of Vital Statistics tables are worthy of an extra once-over. These tables contain informational tidbits that might show up in a test question.

Even if material isn't flagged as a Study Alert or included in a Vital Statistics table, *all* the contents of this book are associated, at least tangentially, to something test-related. This book is lean to focus on quick test preparation; you'll find that what appears in the meat of each chapter is critical knowledge.

I have also provided tips that will help build a better foundation of data administration knowledge. Although the information may not be on the exam, it is highly relevant and will help you become a better test-taker.

This is how tips are formatted. Keep your eyes open for these, and you'll become a test guru in no time!

➤ **Exam Prep Questions** This section presents a series of mock test questions and explanations of both correct and incorrect answers. I also try to point out especially tricky questions by using a special icon, like this:

Ordinarily, this icon flags the presence of an especially devious question, if not an outright trick question. Trick questions are calculated to "trap" you if you don't read them carefully, and more than once at that. Although they're not ubiquitous, such questions make regular appearances in the Oracle exams. That's why I say exam questions are as much about reading comprehension as they are about knowing DBA material inside out and backward.

➤ **Details And Resources** Every chapter ends with a section entitled "Need To Know More?". This section provides direct pointers to Oracle and third-party resources that offer further details on the chapter's subject matter. In addition, this section tries to rate the quality and thoroughness of each topic's coverage. If you find a resource you like in this collection, use it; but don't feel compelled to use all these resources. On the other hand, I recommend only resources I use on a regular basis, so none of my recommendations will be a waste of your time or money.

The bulk of the book follows this chapter structure slavishly, but there are a few other elements that I would like to point out. There is one appendix: a reasonably exhaustive glossary of DBA-specific and general Oracle terminology related to this book. Finally, look for The Cram Sheet, which appears inside the front of this *Exam Cram* book. It is a valuable tool that represents a condensed and compiled collection of facts, figures, and tips that I think you should memorize before taking the test. Because you can dump this information out of your head onto a piece of paper before answering any exam questions, you can master this information by brute force—you need to remember it only long enough to write it down when you walk into the test room. You might even want to look at it in the car or in the lobby of the testing center just before you walk in to take the test.

How To Use This Book

If you're prepping for a first-time test, I've structured the topics in this book to build on one another. Therefore, some topics in later chapters make more sense after you've read earlier chapters. An example would be that Chapter 13, "Database Administration," assumes that you have mastered the material in Chapters 2 through 10 (Chapters 11 and 12 are the sample test and answer key for "Introduction to Oracle: SQL and PL/SQL). That's why I suggest you read this book from front to back for your initial test preparation.

 You must study the information in Chapters 2 though 10 as well as the data in Chapter 13 to properly prepare for the Database Administration sample test in Chapter 14.

If you need to brush up on a topic or you have to bone up for a second try, use the index or table of contents to go straight to the topics and questions that you need to study. Beyond the tests, I think you'll find this book useful as a tightly focused reference to some of the most important aspects of topics associated with being a DBA, as implemented under Oracle7.

Given all the book's elements and its specialized focus, I've tried to create a tool that you can use to prepare for—and pass—the Oracle OCP-DBA set of examinations. Please share your feedback on the book with me, especially if you have ideas about how I can improve it for future test-takers. I'll consider everything you say carefully, and I try respond to all suggestions. You can reach me via email at mikerault@compuserve.com. Please remember to include the title of the book in your message; otherwise, I'll be forced to guess which book of mine you're making a suggestion about.

For up-to-date information on certification, online discussion forums, sample tests, content updates, and more, visit the Certification Insider Press Web site at www.certificationinsider.com.

Thanks, and enjoy the book!

Oracle OCP Certification Tests

Terms you'll need to understand:

✓ Radio button

✓ Checkbox

✓ Exhibit

✓ Multiple-choice question formats

✓ Careful reading

✓ Process of elimination

Techniques you'll need to master:

✓ Preparing to take a certification exam

✓ Practicing (to make perfect)

✓ Making the best use of the testing software

✓ Budgeting your time

✓ Saving the hardest questions until last

✓ Guessing (as a last resort)

As experiences go, test-taking is not something that most people anticipate eagerly, no matter how well they're prepared. In most cases, familiarity helps ameliorate test anxiety. In plain English, this means you probably won't be as nervous when you take your third or fourth Oracle certification exam as you will be when you take your first one.

But no matter whether it's your first test or your tenth, understanding the exam-taking particulars (how much time to spend on questions, the setting you'll be in, and so on) and the testing software will help you concentrate on the material rather than on the environment. Likewise, mastering a few basic test-taking skills should help you recognize—and perhaps even outfox—some of the tricks and gotchas you're bound to find in some of the Oracle test questions.

In this chapter, I'll explain the testing environment and software, as well as describe some proven test-taking strategies you should be able to use to your advantage.

The Testing Situation

When you arrive at the Sylvan Prometric Testing Center where you scheduled your test, you'll need to sign in with a test coordinator. He or she will ask you to produce two forms of identification, one of which must be a photo ID. Once you've signed in and your time slot arrives, you'll be asked leave any books, bags, or other items you brought with you, and you'll be escorted into a closed room. Typically, that room will be furnished with anywhere from one to half a dozen computers, and each workstation is separated from the others by dividers designed to keep you from seeing what's happening on someone else's computer.

You'll be furnished with a pen or pencil and a blank sheet of paper, or in some cases, an erasable plastic sheet and an erasable felt-tip pen. You're allowed to write down any information you want on this sheet, and you can write stuff on both sides of the page. I suggest that you memorize as much as possible of the material that appears on The Cram Sheet (in the front of this book), and then write that information down on the blank sheet as soon as you sit down in front of the test machine. You can refer to the sheet any time you like during the test, but you'll have to surrender it when you leave the room.

Most test rooms feature a wall with a large window. This allows the test coordinator to monitor the room, to prevent test-takers from talking to one another, and to observe anything out of the ordinary that might go on. The test coordinator will have preloaded the Oracle certification test you've signed up for and you'll be permitted to start as soon as you're seated in front of the machine.

All Oracle certification exams permit you to take up to a certain maximum amount of time (usually 90 minutes) to complete the test (the test itself will tell you, and it maintains an on-screen counter/clock so that you can check the time remaining any time you like). Each exam consists of between 60 and 70 questions, randomly selected from a pool of questions.

Unfortunately, because there are different versions of each test, it is impossible to give you a specific passing grade. Your passing score is determined by the version of the test you receive.

All Oracle certification exams are computer generated and use a multiple-choice format. Although this might sound easy, the questions are constructed not just to check your mastery of basic facts and figures about Oracle7 DBA topics, but also require you to evaluate one or more sets of circumstances or requirements. Often, you'll be asked to give more than one answer to a question; likewise, you may be asked to select the best or most effective solution to a problem from a range of choices, all of which technically are correct. The tests are quite an adventure, and they involve real thinking. This book will show you what to expect and how to deal with the problems, puzzles, and predicaments you're likely to find on the tests, in particular Test 1 and Test 2, "Introduction to Oracle: SQL and PL/SQL" and "Oracle7: Database Administration," respectively.

Test Layout And Design

A typical test question is depicted in Question 1. It's a multiple-choice question that requires you to select a single correct answer. Following the question is a brief summary of each potential answer and why it was either right or wrong.

Question 1

You issue this SQL*Plus command:

```
SAVE my_file REPLACE
```

What task has been accomplished?

- ○ a. A new file was created.
- ○ b. An existing file was replaced.
- ○ c. The command was continued to the next line of the SQL prompt.
- ○ d. No task was accomplished because a file extension was not designated.

The correct answer is b. The **SAVE** command has the one option, **REPLACE**. **SAVE** without **REPLACE** requires that the file not exist; **SAVE** with **RE-PLACE** replaces an existing file. No file extension is required, the default is platform-specific but is usually .lst or .lis. Answer a is incorrect because we specified the **REPLACE** option. With just a **SAVE**, a new file is created; with a **SAVE...REPLACE** an existing file is replaced. Answer c is incorrect because the continuation of a line is done automatically when you hit the Return key. Answer d is incorrect because if we don't specify a suffix, a default one is added.

This sample question corresponds closely to those you'll see on Oracle certification tests. To select the correct answer during the test, you would position the cursor over the radio button next to answer b and click the mouse to select that particular choice. The only difference between the certification test and this question is that the real questions are not immediately followed by the answers.

Next, I'll examine a question that requires choosing multiple answers. This type of question provides checkboxes, rather than radio buttons, for marking all appropriate selections.

Question 2

Which three ways can the SQL buffer be terminated?

- ❑ a. Enter a slash (/).
- ❑ b. Press Return (or Enter) once.
- ❑ c. Enter an asterisk (*).
- ❑ d. Enter a semicolon (;).
- ❑ e. Press Return (or Enter) twice.
- ❑ f. Press Esc twice.

The correct answers for this question are a, d, and e. A slash (/) is usually used for termination of PL/SQL blocks, procedures, and functions, but it can also be used for SQL commands. A semicolon (;) is generally used for terminating SQL commands. Pressing the Return key (or the Enter key on many keyboards) twice in succession will also tell the buffer your command is complete but will not execute it. Most of the time the slash or semicolon will also result in execution of the previous command (except within a PL/SQL block), a subsequent entry of the slash, the semicolon, or an "r" (short for run) will be required to execute the command(s) terminated with a double Return.

For this type of question, one or more answers must be selected to answer the question correctly. For Question 2, you would have to position the cursor over the checkboxes next to items a, d, and e to obtain credit for a correct answer.

These two basic types of questions can appear in many forms. They constitute the foundation on which all the Oracle certification exam questions rest. More complex questions may include so-called "exhibits," which are usually tables or data-content layouts of one form or another. You'll be expected to use the information displayed in the exhibit to guide your answer to the question.

Other questions involving exhibits may use charts or diagrams to help document a workplace scenario that you'll be asked to troubleshoot or configure. Paying careful attention to such exhibits is the key to success—be prepared to toggle between the picture and the question as you work. Often, both are complex enough that you might not be able to remember all of either one.

Using Oracle's Test Software Effectively

A well-known test-taking principle is to read over the entire test from start to finish first, but to answer only those questions that you feel absolutely sure of on the first pass. On subsequent passes, you can dive into more complex questions, knowing how many such questions you have to deal with.

Fortunately, Oracle test software makes this approach easy to implement. At the bottom of each question, you'll find a checkbox that permits you to mark that question for a later visit. (Note that marking questions makes review easier, but you can return to any question by clicking the Forward and Back buttons repeatedly until you get to the question.) As you read each question, if you answer only those you're sure of and mark for review those that you're not, you can keep going through a decreasing list of open questions as you knock the trickier ones off in order.

There's at least one potential benefit to reading the test over completely before answering the trickier questions: Sometimes, you find information in later questions that sheds more light on earlier ones. Other times, information you read in later questions might jog your memory about Oracle7 DBA facts, figures, or behavior that also will help with earlier questions. Either way, you'll come out ahead if you defer those questions about which you're not absolutely sure of the answer(s).

Keep working on the questions until you are absolutely sure of all your answers or until you know you'll run out of time. If there are still unanswered questions, you'll want to zip through them and guess. No answer guarantees no credit for a question, and a guess has at least a chance of being correct. This strategy only works because Oracle scores blank answers and incorrect answers as equally wrong.

 At the very end of your test period, you're better off guessing than leaving questions blank or unanswered.

Taking Testing Seriously

The most important advice I can give you about taking any Oracle test is this: Read each question carefully. Some questions are deliberately ambiguous; some use double negatives; others use terminology in incredibly precise ways. I've taken numerous practice tests and real tests myself, and in nearly every test I've missed at least one question because I didn't read it closely or carefully enough.

Here are some suggestions on how to deal with the tendency to jump to an answer too quickly:

➤ Make sure you read every word in the question. If you find yourself jumping ahead impatiently, go back and start over.

➤ As you read, try to restate the question in your own terms. If you can do this, you should be able to pick the correct answer(s) much more easily.

➤ When returning to a question after your initial read-through, reread every word again—otherwise, the mind falls quickly into a rut. Sometimes seeing a question afresh after turning your attention elsewhere lets you see something you missed before, but the strong tendency is to see what you've seen before. Try to avoid that tendency at all costs.

➤ If you return to a question more than twice, try to articulate to yourself what you don't understand about the question, why the answers don't appear to make sense, or what appears to be missing. If you chew on the subject for a while, your subconscious might provide the details that are lacking, or you may notice a "trick" that will point to the right answer.

Above all, try to deal with each question by thinking through what you know about being an Oracle7 DBA, utilities, characteristics, behaviors, facts, and figures involved. By reviewing what you know (and what you've written down on your information sheet), you'll often recall or understand things sufficiently to determine the answer to the question.

Question-Handling Strategies

Based on the tests I've taken, a couple of interesting trends in the answers have become apparent. For those questions that take only a single answer, usually two or three of the answers will be obviously incorrect, and two of the answers will be plausible. But, of course, only one can be correct. Unless the answer leaps out at you (and if it does, reread the question to look for a trick; sometimes those are the ones you're most likely to get wrong), begin the process of answering by eliminating those answers that are obviously wrong.

Things to look for in the "obviously wrong" category include spurious command choices or table or view names, nonexistent software or command options, and terminology you've never seen before. If you've done your homework for a test, no valid information should be completely new to you. In that case, unfamiliar or bizarre terminology probably indicates a totally bogus answer. As long as you're sure what's right, it's easy to eliminate what's wrong.

Numerous questions assume that the default behavior of a particular Oracle utility (such as SQL*Plus or Procedure Builder) is in effect. It's essential, therefore, to know and understand the default settings for Procedure Builder, SQL*Plus, SQL*Loader, and Server Manager utilities. If you know the defaults and understand what they mean, this knowledge will help you cut through many Gordian knots.

Likewise, when dealing with questions that require multiple answers, you must know and select all of the correct options to get credit. This, too, qualifies as an example of why "careful reading" is so important.

As you work your way through the test, another counter that Oracle thankfully provides will come in handy—the number of questions completed and questions outstanding. Budget your time by making sure that you've completed one-fourth of the questions one-quarter of the way through the test period (between 13 and 17 questions in the first 22 or 23 minutes). Check again three-quarters of the way through (between 39 and 51 questions in the first 66 to 69 minutes).

If you're not through after 85 minutes, use the last 5 minutes to guess your way through the remaining questions. Remember, guesses are potentially more valuable than blank answers, because blanks are always wrong, but a guess might turn out to be right. If you haven't a clue with any of the remaining questions, pick answers at random, or choose all a's, b's, and so on. The important thing is to submit a test for scoring that has an answer for every question.

Mastering The Inner Game

In the final analysis, knowledge breeds confidence, and confidence breeds success. If you study the materials in this book carefully and review all of the questions at the end of each chapter, you should be aware of those areas where additional studying is required.

Next, follow up by reading some or all of the materials recommended in the "Need To Know More?" section at the end of each chapter. The idea is to become familiar enough with the concepts and situations that you find in the sample questions to be able to reason your way through similar situations on a real test. If you know the material, you have every right to be confident that you can pass the test.

Once you've worked your way through the book, take the practice tests in Chapters 11 and 14. These tests will provide a reality check and will help you identify areas you need to study further. Make sure you follow up and review materials related to the questions you miss before scheduling a real test. Only when you've covered all the ground and feel comfortable with the whole scope of the practice tests, should you take a real test.

 If you take my practice tests (Chapter 11 and Chapter 14) and don't score at least 75 percent correct, you'll want to practice further. At a minimum, download the practice tests and the self-assessment tests from the Oracle Education Web site's download page (its location appears in the next section). If you're more ambitious or better funded, you might want to purchase a practice test from one of the third-party vendors that offers them. I've had good luck with tests from Self Test Software (the vendor who supplies the practice tests). See the next section in this chapter for contact information.

Armed with the information in this book, and with the determination to augment your knowledge, you should be able to pass the certification exam. But if you don't work at it, you'll spend the test fee more than once before you finally do pass. If you prepare seriously, the execution should go flawlessly. Good luck!

Additional Resources

By far, the best source of information about Oracle certification tests comes from Oracle itself. Because its products and technologies—and the tests that go with them—change frequently, the best place to go for exam-related information is online.

If you haven't already visited the Oracle certification pages, do so right now. As I'm writing this chapter, the certification home page resides at http://education.oracle.com/certification/ (see Figure 1.1).

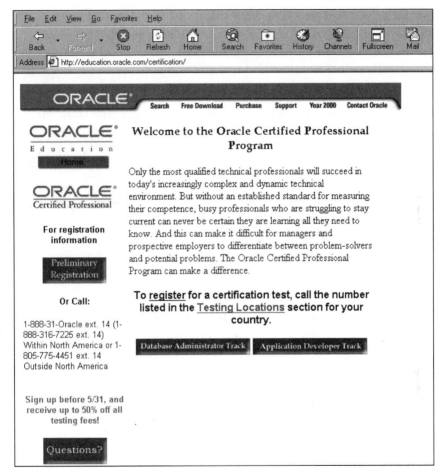

Figure 1.1   The Oracle certification page should be your starting point for further investigation of the most current exam and preparation information.

Note: It might not be there by the time you read this, or it may have been replaced by something new and different, because things change regularly on the Oracle site. Should this happen, please read the section titled "Coping With Change On The Web," later in this chapter.

The menu options in the left column of the page point to the most important sources of information in the certification pages. Here's what to check out:

➤ **Step-by-Step** Use this to jump to a step-by-step guide on how to prepare for and take the OCP tests.

➤ **Managers and Candidates** These sections provide facts that managers should know about why their employees should be Oracle certified and facts that candidates should know about the exams.

➤ **Program Guide** This is a detailed section that provides many jump points to test-related topics as well as everything you need know but didn't know to ask.

➤ **Assessment Tests** This section provides a download of the latest copy of the assessment test after you fill out an online questionnaire.

Of course, these are just the high points of what's available in the Oracle certification pages. As you browse through them—and I strongly recommend that you do—you'll probably find other things I didn't mention here that are every bit as interesting and compelling.

Coping With Change On The Web

Sooner or later, all the specifics I've shared with you about the Oracle certification pages, and all the other Web-based resources I mention throughout the rest of this book, will go stale or be replaced by newer information. In some cases, the URLs you find here might lead you to their replacements; in other cases, the URLs will go nowhere, leaving you with the dread "404 File Not Found" error message.

When that happens, please don't give up. There's always a way to find what you want on the Web—if you're willing to invest some time and energy. To begin with, most large or complex Web sites—and Oracle's qualifies on both counts—offer a search engine. As long as you can get to Oracle's home page (and I'm sure that it will stay at www.oracle.com for a long while yet), you can use this tool to help you find what you need.

The more particular or focused you can make a search request, the more likely it is that the results will include information you can use. For instance, you can search the string "training and certification" to produce a lot of data about the subject in general, but if you're looking for the Preparation Guide for the Oracle DBA tests, you'll be more likely to get there quickly if you use a search string such as this:

```
"DBA" AND "preparation guide"
```

Likewise, if you want to find the training and certification downloads, try a search string such as this one:

```
"training and certification" AND "download page"
```

Finally, don't be afraid to use general search tools such as www.search.com, www.altavista.com, or www.excite.com to search for related information. Even though Oracle offers the best information about its certification exams online, there are plenty of third-party sources of information, training, and assistance in this area that do not have to follow a party line like Oracle does. The bottom line is this: If you can't find something where the book says it lives, start looking around. If worse comes to worse, you can always email me! I just might have a clue. My email address is mikerault@compuserve.com.

Third-Party Test Providers

There are third-party companies that provide example assessment tests. I suggest obtaining and taking as many of these as you can so that you become completely familiar and confident with test taking. Among these third-party providers are:

➤ **RevealNet, Inc.** In the Oracle Administrator program, there is a complete review section for the DBA examination with example test questions. A fully functional 15-day demo can be downloaded from the Web site free of charge. The company is reached through its Web site at http://www.revealnet.com/. You can also call RevealNet at 1-800-738-3254 or 202-234-8557. RevealNet's address is: RevealNet, Inc., 3016 Cortland Place NW, Washington DC, 20008.

➤ **Self Test Software** Self Test also offers sample Oracle tests for all four of the OCP-DBA tests. Self Test is located at 4651 Woodstock Road, Suite 203-384, Roswell, GA, 30075. The company can be reached by phone at 770-641-9719 or 1-800-200-6446, and by fax at 770-641-1489. Visit Self Test's Web site at http://www.stsware.com; you can even order the software online.

Oracle
Internal Structures

. . . .

Terms you'll need to understand:

√ Cache

√ Buffer

√ SGA

√ Table

√ Index

√ UGA

√ Rollback

√ PGA

Techniques you'll need to master:

√ Understanding the structures of the SGA

√ Understanding the interrelations of Oracle processes

√ Understanding the physical structure of an Oracle database

√ Tuning the Oracle internal processes

The Oracle internal structures are the underpinnings upon which you will hang all other DBA knowledge. An intimate and complete understanding of how the Oracle internals and the Oracle processes interact with each other is vital to your success as a DBA.

In this chapter, I'll explain the Oracle internal structures, the Oracle data dictionary, and the Oracle processes (SMON, PMON, DBWR, LGWR, ARCH, CKPT, Dnnnn, Snnnn, SNPnn), their purpose, failure modes, and tuning suggestions.

The Oracle Concepts Of Database And Instance

In an Oracle configuration, the base set of files, datafiles, redo logs, control files, and parameter files make up the database, and one or more sets of operating system processes and shared memory areas (each known as a shared global area [SGA]) make up an Oracle instance. Figure 2.1 shows the relation of these files and processes to the SGA (or SGAs, in the case of Oracle parallel server).

The diagram of the Oracle processes, files, and SGA relations is vital to understanding the interrelations of these objects.

 You should be able to reproduce at least a general facsimile of this diagram at will.

Likewise, an understanding of the internal structures of the SGA is also vital to an Oracle DBA in day-to-day operations.

Oracle Database Files

Oracle files are used for storage of data, for transaction information, or for parameter values. Oracle data is stored in files known as *datafiles*. The tablespace, a logical unit of storage in Oracle, maps to one or more datafiles. Each Oracle instance must have the following:

➤ At least a single datafile for the **SYSTEM** tablespace

➤ A control file to maintain transaction control numbers and datafile information

➤ Two redo log files to contain transaction redo information

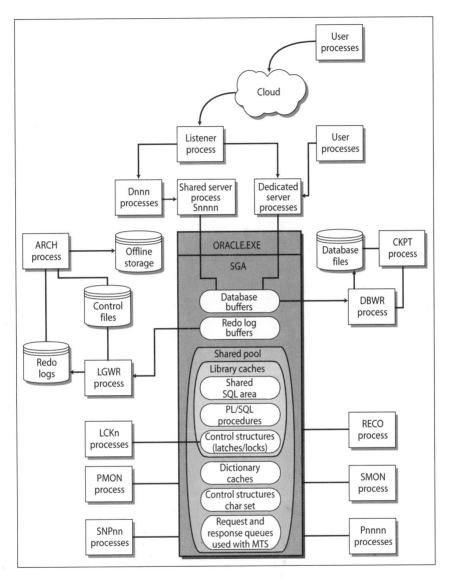

Figure 2.1   The Oracle version 7.x SGA structure.

➤ A parameter file to specify constants used to initialize the Oracle system

Therefore, the minimal Oracle installation consists of a set of five files and the Oracle executables.

Once Oracle starts up, it creates more files. These files fall into either event or trace logging categories. Oracle opens a single alert log that tracks overall instance status, and it starts trace files for all baseline Oracle processes. There'll be a minimum of four baseline Oracle processes—PMON, SMON, DBWR, and LGWR—with a possible fifth, RECO, if the distributed option is loaded. The trace files will generally contain process startup information and will only contain more if there are errors with their process. Periodically check the contents of the location specified for trace files and clean out any old ones. The alert log should be checked frequently during the database operation (in Unix, I place a **tail -f** against all monitored database alert logs and have them in their own windows on my monitoring screen). Some errors, such as the archive logging process getting stuck or redo log corruption in a mirrored set, will only show up here.

If the database has more tablespaces than just the **SYSTEM** tablespace (and it should), additional datafiles will exist, at least one for each additional tablespace. If there are optional processes started (such as ARCH, CKPT, Snnnn and Dnnnn, and SNPnn), they, too, will have trace files started for them. In most installations, there'll be a minimum of three redo log groups of two mirrored files each, generally more.

As a minimum, the following tablespaces should be created in any instance:

➤ **USERS**

➤ **TEMP**

➤ **RBS**

➤ **TOOLS**

➤ **SYSTEM** (the required tablespace)

At least two additional tablespaces, **APL_DATA** and **APL_INDEX** (or ones named for the specific application), are usually created, as well as those mentioned previously. In complex databases (especially parallel server databases), some tables may be placed in their own tablespace, adding to the number of required datafiles. Figure 2.2 provides an example layout for an Oracle database. The only datafile required for instance startup is the **SYSTEM** tablespace, but other tablespaces are the logical repository for physically grouped data.

The **SYSTEM** tablespace should never be used for mundane, day-to-day storage of common indexes and tables. It's the strict domain of the data dictionary tables and indexes. Being the only required tablespace, if the **SYSTEM** tablespace is somehow taken offline, the instance will immediately shut down.

A tablespace used for rollback segments should also *only* be used for rollback segments, just as a temporary tablespace, such as **TEMP**, should only

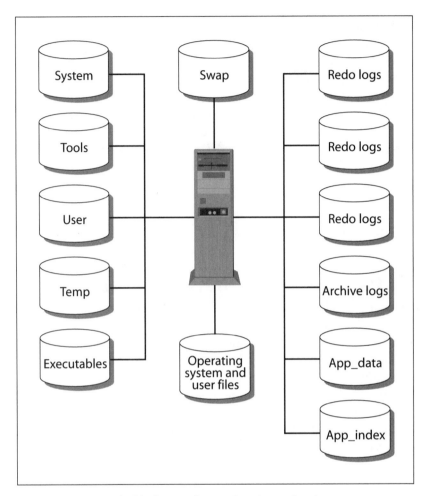

Figure 2.2   Example file layout for an Oracle7.x database.

be used for temporary segments. In the absence of any application tablespaces for tables or indexes, the **USER** tablespace should be used for these items.

Loss of any of the datafiles will keep the instance from starting up if it's shut down. Loss of a datafile while the datafile is active will result in several possible scenarios, depending on which datafile is lost. Loss of any datafile is considered a media failure, and recovery can be either incomplete or complete, depending on the file lost.

Control files, parameter files, redo logs, and datafiles make up the physical database.

The Control Files

The control files contain information on all physical database files (the database physical structure) and their current transaction state. The control files are read to mount and open the database, and transaction numbers are recorded for each datafile. If the control files and datafiles are out of sync, the database will not start up and will report either that recovery is needed or that the datafiles are out of sync with the control files. Control files are required for database start up and recovery. The database is required to have one control file, however, Oracle (and simple prudence) recommends a minimum of two control files on separate physical disks or on separate disk farms in a RAID configuration.

Note: Call me paranoid; I usually configure three control files.

The Parameter File (init<SID>.ora)

Although not considered to be a part of the database because the Oracle processes don't write to it, the parameter file contains the initialization parameters that instruct the Oracle instance on how to set itself up with buffers, processes, caches, and the like. The parameter file is read while starting the instance during the mount and open phases of startup. Thus, the parameter file sizes all SGA components either through direct parameter values or indirectly from calculations based on parameter values specified in the parameter file. The DBA is responsible for tuning the database using the initialization parameters. There are over 160 of these initialization parameters; depending on the version of Oracle, there will be more or less. Oracle8 contains 193 parameters; Oracle7.3 houses 168 parameters. The parameters for Oracle7.3 are listed in Table 2.1.

Table 2.1	The parameters for Oracle7.3.	
Name	**Value**	**Description**
always_anti_join	NESTED_LOOPS	Always use this antijoin when possible
async_read	TRUE	Enable Async Read
async_write	TRUE	Enable DBWR Async Write
audit_file_dest	?/rdbms/audit	Directory in which auditing files are to reside

(continued)

Table 2.1   The parameters for Oracle7.3 *(continued)*.

Name	Value	Description
audit_trail	NONE	Enable system auditing
b_tree_bitmap_plans	FALSE	Enable the use of bitmap plans for tables with only B-tree indexes
background_core_dump	FULL	Core file size for background processes
background_dump_dest	/oracle14/ORCHATP1 /admin/bdump	Detached process dump directory
bitmap_merge_area_size	1048576	Maximum memory allow for BITMAP MERGE
blank_trimming	FALSE	Blank trimming semantics parameter
cache_size_threshold	14400	Maximum size (in blocks) of table or piece to be cached
ccf_io_size	131072	Number of bytes per write when creating contiguous file
checkpoint_process	TRUE	Create a separate checkpoint process
cleanup_rollback_entries	20	Number of undo entries to apply per transaction cleanup
close_cached_open _cursors	FALSE	Close cursors cached by PL/SQL at each commit
commit_point_strength	1	Bias this node has toward not preparing in a two-phase commit
compatible	7.3.2.0	Database will be completely compatible with this software version
compatible_no_recovery	FALSE	Database will be compatible unless crash or media recovery is needed
control_files	/oracle13/ORCHATP1 /control /cntrlORCHATP1 01.dbf, /oracle15/ORCHATP1 /control /cntrlORCHATP102.dbf, /oracle11/ORCHATP1 /control /cntrlORCHATP103.dbf	Control file names list

(continued)

Table 2.1 The parameters for Oracle7.3 *(continued)*.

Name	Value	Description
core_dump_dest	/oracle14/ORCHATP1/admin/cdump	Core dump directory
cpu_count	6	Number of CPUs for this instance
create_bitmap_area_size	8388608	Size of create bitmap buffer for bitmap index
cursor_space_for_time	FALSE	Use more memory to get faster execution
db_block_buffers	144000	Number of database blocks cached in memory
db_block_checkpoint_batch	8	Maximum number of blocks to checkpoint in a database writer I/O
db_block_checksum	FALSE	Store checksum in database blocks and check during reads
db_block_lru_extended_statistics	0	Maintain buffer cache LRU statistics for last n blocks discarded
db_block_lru_latches	3	Number of LRU latches
db_block_lru_statistics	FALSE	Maintain buffer cache LRU hits-by-position statistics (slow)
db_block_size	8192	Size of database block in bytes
db_domain	WORLD	Directory part of global database name stored with CREATE DATABASE
db_file_multiblock_read_count	16	Database block to be read each I/O
db_file_simultaneous_writes	4	Maximum simultaneous (overlapped) writes per database file
db_file_standby_name_convert		Datafile name convert pattern and string for standby database
db_files	1022	Maximum allowable number of database files
db_name	ORCHATP1	Database name specified in CREATE DATABASE
db_writers	1	Number of database writer processes
dblink_encrypt_login	FALSE	Enforce password for distributed login always be encrypted

(continued)

Table 2.1   The parameters for Oracle7.3 *(continued)*.

Name	Value	Description
delayed_logging _block_cleanouts	TRUE	Turn on delayed-logging block cleanouts feature
discrete_transactions _enabled	FALSE	Enable OLTP mode
distributed_lock_timeout	60	Number of seconds a distributed transaction waits for a lock
distributed_recovery _connection_hold_time	200	Number of seconds RECO holds outbound connections open
distributed_transactions	31	Maximum number of concurrent distributed transactions
dml_locks	200	DML locks—one for each table modified in a transaction
enqueue_resources	265	Resources for enqueues
event		Debug event control—default null string
fixed_date		Fixed SYSDATE value
gc_db_locks	144000	Number of database locks (DFS)
gc_files_to_locks		Mapping between file numbers and hash buckets
gc_freelist_groups	50	Number of freelist groups locks (DFS)
gc_lck_procs	1	Number of background parallel server lock processes to start
gc_releasable_locks	144000	Number of releasable database locks (DFS)
gc_rollback_locks	20	Number of undo locks (DFS)
gc_rollback_segments	20	Number of undo segments
gc_save_rollback_locks	20	Number of save undo locks (DFS)
gc_segments	10	Number of segment headers
gc_tablespaces	5	Number of tablespaces
global_names	FALSE	Enforce that database links have same name as remote database
hash_area_size	0	Size of in-memory hash work area
hash_join_enabled	TRUE	Enable/disable hash join

(continued)

Table 2.1   The parameters for Oracle7.3 *(continued)*.

Name	Value	Description
hash_multiblock_io_count	8	Number of blocks hash join will read/write at once
ifile		Include file in init.ora
instance_number	0	Instance number
job_queue_interval	600	Wake-up interval in seconds for job queue processes
job_queue_keep _connections	FALSE	Keep network connections between execution of jobs
job_queue_processes	2	Number of job queue processes to start
license_max_sessions	0	Maximum number of non-system user sessions allowed
license_max_users	0	Maximum number of named users that can be created in the database
license_sessions_warning	0	Warning level for number of non-system user sessions
log_archive_buffer_size	32	Size of each archival buffer in log file blocks
log_archive_buffers	5	Number of buffers to allocate for archiving
log_archive_dest	/oracle31/ ORCHATP1/arch/log/	Archival destination text string
log_archive_format	%t_%s.arch	Archival destination format
log_archive_start	TRUE	Start archival process on SGA initialization
log_block_checksum	FALSE	Calculate checksum for redo blocks when writing
log_buffer	3145728	Redo circular buffer size
log_checkpoint_interval	31457280	Indicates number of redo blocks for checkpoint threshold
log_checkpoint_timeout	0	Maximum time interval in seconds between checkpoints
log_checkpoints_to_alert	FALSE	Log checkpoint begin/end to alert file
log_file_standby _name_convert		Log file name convert pattern and string for standby database

(continued)

Table 2.1   The parameters for Oracle7.3 *(continued)*.

Name	Value	Description
log_files	255	Maximum allowable number of log files
log_simultaneous_copies	6	Number of simultaneous copies into redo buffer (number of copy latches)
log_small_entry_max_size	80	Redo entries larger than this will acquire the redo copy latch
max_commit _propagation_delay	90000	Maximum age of new snapshot in .01 seconds
max_dump_file_size	10240	Maximum size (in blocks) of dump file
max_enabled_roles	20	Maximum number of roles a user can have enabled
max_rollback_segments	30	Maximum number of rollback segments in SGA cache
max_transaction _branches	8	Maximum number of branches per distributed transaction
mts_dispatchers	NULL	Specifications of dispatchers
mts_listener_address	(address= (protocol=ipc) (key=%s))	Address(es) of network listener
mts_max_dispatchers	0	Maximum number of dispatchers
mts_max_servers	0	Maximum number of servers
mts_multiple_listeners	FALSE	Are multiple listeners enabled?
mts_servers	0	Number of servers to start up
mts_service	ORCHATP1	Service supported by dispatchers
nls_currency	NULL	NLS local currency symbol
nls_date_format	NULL	NLS Oracle date format
nls_date_language	NULL	NLS date language name
nls_iso_currency	NULL	NLS ISO currency territory name
nls_language	AMERICAN	NLS language name
nls_numeric_characters	NULL	NLS numeric characters
nls_sort	NULL	NLS linguistic definition name
nls_territory	AMERICA	NLS territory name

(continued)

Table 2.1   **The parameters for Oracle7.3 *(continued)*.**

Name	Value	Description
open_cursors	50	Maximum number of cursors per process
open_links	4	Maximum number of open links per process
optimizer_mode	CHOOSE	Optimizer mode
optimizer_percent _parallel	0	Optimizer percent parallel
oracle_trace_collection _name	oracle7	Oracle TRACE default collection name
oracle_trace_collection _path	?/rdbms/log	Oracle TRACE collection path
oracle_trace_collection _size	5242880	Maximum size of Oracle TRACE collection file
oracle_trace_enable	FALSE	Oracle TRACE instancewide enable/disable
oracle_trace_facility_name	oracle7	Oracle TRACE default facility name
oracle_trace_facility_path	?/rdbms/admin	Oracle TRACE facility path
os_authent_prefix	ops$	Prefix for auto-logon accounts
os_roles	FALSE	Retrieve roles from the operating system
parallel_default_max _instances	0	Default maximum number of instances for parallel query
parallel_max_servers	5	Maximum parallel query servers per instance
parallel_min_percent	0	Minimum percent of threads required for parallel query
parallel_min_servers	0	Minimum parallel query servers per instance
parallel_server_idle_time	5	Idle time before parallel query server dies
partition_view_enabled	FALSE	Enable/disable partitioned views
post_wait_device	/devices/pseudo/ pw@0:pw	Name of post-wait device
pre_page_sga	FALSE	Prepage SGA for process
processes	100	Maximum number of user processes

(continued)

Table 2.1   The parameters for Oracle7.3 *(continued)*.

Name	Value	Description
recovery_parallelism	0	Number of server processes to use for parallel recovery
reduce_alarm	FALSE	Reduce alarm
remote_dependencies _mode	timestamp	Remote-procedure-call dependencies mode parameter
remote_login_passwordfile	NONE	Password file usage parameter
remote_os_authent	FALSE	Allow unsecure remote clients to use auto-logon accounts
remote_os_roles	FALSE	Allow unsecure remote clients to use OS roles
resource_limit	TRUE	Master switch for resource limit
rollback_segments	r01, r02, r03, r04, r05, r06, r07, r08, r09, r10	Undo segment list
row_cache_cursors	10	Number of cached cursors for row cache
row_locking	always	Row locking
sequence_cache_entries	12	Number of sequence cache entries
sequence_cache_hash _buckets	11	Number of sequence cache hash buckets
serializable	FALSE	Serializable
session_cached_cursors	0	Number of cursors to save in the session cursor cache
sessions	115	User and system sessions
shadow_core_dump	FULL	Core file size for shadow processes
shared_pool_reserved _min_alloc	5000	Minimum allocation size in bytes for reserved area of shared pool
shared_pool_reserved_size	0	Size in bytes of reserved area of shared pool
shared_pool_size	262144000	Size in bytes of shared pool
snapshot_refresh_interval	60	Wake-up interval in seconds for job queue processes
snapshot_refresh_keep _connections	FALSE	Keep network connections between execution of jobs
snapshot_refresh _processes	0	Number of job queue processes to start

(continued)

Table 2.1   The parameters for Oracle7.3 *(continued)*.

Name	Value	Description
sort_area_retained_size	5242880	Size of in-memory sort work area retained between fetch calls
sort_area_size	20971520	Size of in-memory sort work area
sort_direct_writes	TRUE	Use direct write
sort_read_fac	5	Multiblock read factor for sort
sort_spacemap_size	512	Size of sort disk area space map
sort_write_buffer_size	65536	Size of each sort direct write buffer
sort_write_buffers	4	Number of sort direct write buffers
spin_count	2000	Number of times to spin on latch miss
sql92_security	FALSE	Require select privilege for searched update/delete
sql_trace	FALSE	Enable SQL trace
temporary_table_locks	115	Temporary table locks
text_enable	FALSE	Enable text searching
thread	0	Redo thread to mount
timed_statistics	TRUE	Maintain internal timing statistics
transactions	126	Maximum number of concurrent active transactions
transactions_per _rollback_segment	71	Number of active transactions per rollback segment
use_ism	TRUE	Enable shared page table— Intimate Shared Memory
use_post_wait_driver	FALSE	Use post-wait driver
use_readv	FALSE	Use readv for multiblock read
user_dump_dest	/oracle14/ORCHATP1 /admin/udump	User process dump directory
utl_file_dir		utl_file accessible directories list
v733_plans_enabled	FALSE	Enable/disable several performance features introduced in Oracle7.3.3

The Alert Log (alert_<SID>.log)

The alert log contains informational, warning, and error messages dealing with the Oracle core processes and the SGA. Additionally, the alert log contains a history of any physical changes to the database, such as the addition or status change of datafiles, redo logs, or rollback segments. The use of optional initialization parameters information concerning checkpoints can also be recorded in the alert log.

The alert log is the only location where errors, such as detection of a corrupted member of a mirrored redo log or the filling of the archive log destination (archiver stuck), are reported. Other informational messages useful for tuning (such as excessive archive waits for a checkpoint or waits due to the redo logs writing to archive) are also reported in the alert log. Oracle recommends that the log be checked at least once a day. I usually keep an active **tail -f** session in Unix going for each database I monitor (on a Windows 95 or X-Windows monitor) so that I will know at a glance if anything odd is going on.

The alert log is continuously being written to, and, thus, it continuously grows in size. If the disk location of the alert log fills up, the instance will slow down or stop until space is made available. Periodically compress and archive the alert log, or, if it contains no important information, remove it. The instance will re-create it if it's not present.

The Redo Log Files

The redo log files are set up at instance creation. A minimum of two one-member groups in a single thread is required for instance startup. I usually run three or more groups of two-mirrored members, with each member being placed on a separate disk or separately controlled disk farm, if possible, to reduce contention. In most cases, I've found five groups optimal to prevent checkpoint and archiver wait errors. The redo logs hold records used for recovery purposes, and they contain information on all data modifying transactions that occur in the database, unless these transactions have been run as nonrecoverable. The LGWR process writes data on changes from the redo log buffers to the redo logs. A **COMMIT** is not considered complete until the LGWR signals that all redo log entries have been written to disk. Remember, the redo log buffer is a part of the SGA.

Database Datafiles

The Oracle system uses logical and physical storage. *Logical storage* uses the concept of tablespaces. A tablespace is physically implemented through one or more datafiles. Datafiles are subdivided into segments that are subdivided into extents, which may be of several types, depending on what they store or their usage. Here is a list of possible segments:

➤ Table segment

➤ Index segment

➤ Rollback segment

➤ Temporary segment

A single segment extent cannot span multiple datafiles and must be contiguous.

The table segment contains data that corresponds to a table object in the database. This will usually be the most common type of segment because it stores the actual data contained in the database.

The index segment contains table index information. The index segment will contain data and **ROWID** pointers and will be stored as a B-tree (the most common), a cluster (either B-tree or hash), or a bitmapped format, depending on the type of index object the segment is assigned to.

The rollback segment contains records of changes for multiple transactions. Each transaction gets assigned to a single rollback segment extent. The most costly statement in terms of rollback segment space usage is an update because it must capture both the before and the after image; the least expensive is a delete because the rollback only captures the deleted **ROWID**s.

The Trace Files (*.trc)

The trace files are created either at process startup, when a process abnormally exits, or if certain errors occur in a process. Trace files are forced to be generated by setting initialization parameters, enabling session tracing, or by turning on tracing at the process level with the **ALTER SESSION** command. Traces are used to track internal process errors and to track what a user process actually does in the case of session traces. A special type of trace called a *core dump* is used for severe errors; it's a dump of the state of the memory in the memory core area of the SGA.

Session tracing should be used to capture information for tuning session SQL processes. Using a trace file and the TKPROF utility, all of a process's SQL statements can be analyzed and the statements' execution plans generated. Trace files are placed in the locations specified in the initialization file using the following parameters:

➤ BACKGROUND_DUMP_DEST

➤ CORE_DUMP_DEST

➤ USER_DUMP_DEST

Trace file sizes are limited by the **MAX_DUMP_FILE_SIZE** initialization parameter. The trace file and core dump destinations should be monitored for space usage, and periodically the files should be cleaned out.

In some earlier versions of Oracle7, frequent core dumps were a problem. Because core dumps take up a large amount of disk space, be sure to monitor for these in development environments. (Any abnormal termination of a C process using Oracle may result in a core dump, as will abnormal terminations of other third-party tools, such as Visual Basic and PowerBuilder.) If the locations for these dump files fill up, it could result in the instance stalling when it attempts to write to a trace file.

The Oracle Instance

Oracle defines the Oracle instance as the shared global area (SGA) and the required background processes. The base processes are SMON, PMON, DBWR, and LGWR. Optional processes include CKPT (not optional on Oracle8 databases), ARCH, RECO (required on distributed databases), LCKn (where n is 0 to 9, one per parallel instance required), Dnnnn (dispatcher process for multithreaded server [MTS]), Snnnn (server process for MTS), Pnnnn (parallel query slave process for parallel query option [PQO]), and SNPnn (snapshot/job queue processes). The combination of the SGA and processes is the instance. If any of the required processes dies, the Oracle instance dies. Loss of optional processes, such as ARCH, RECO, LCKn, or the server or dispatcher processes, may result in instance failure. This type of failure is an instance failure and is automatically recovered on the next startup or by one of the other instances in a parallel server configuration as soon as the failed instance's heartbeat loss is detected.

The SGA And Its Contents

The SGA is made up of several memory components, and the largest of these is usually the database base buffer cache, followed by the shared pool area, and the redo log buffers. The shared pool consists of the shared SQL area (also known as the library cache) where SQL and PL/SQL statements are kept, the data dictionary cache where data dictionary-related entries are kept, control structures (latches and locks), control structures (such as character set data, and, if MTS is being used, request and response queues). Figure 2.1 (shown earlier) graphically depicts these SGA components and their relationship to the Oracle datafiles. The SGA also contains the sort extent pool in non-MTS instances; in MTS instances the user global area (UGA) contains the sort extent pool.

The Data Base Buffer Cache

The major SGA component is the database buffers. The database buffers are controlled by the initialization parameters **DB_BLOCK_SIZE** and

DB_BLOCK_BUFFERS. The **DB_BLOCK_SIZE** sets the size of database blocks used in all other components of the SGA. The **DB_BLOCK_SIZE** is a multiple of the operating system block size, which is usually a multiple of 512 bytes. On most systems, the **DB_BLOCK_SIZE** is a minimum of 2K.

Oracle is now suggesting that **DB_BLOCK_SIZE** be set to the maximum allowed on the operating system you use. Most experts disagree and suggest **DB_BLOCK_SIZE** be set according to how data is accessed on your system, a much more sensible suggestion.

The **DB_BLOCK_BUFFERS** parameter is used to tell the Oracle kernel how large to set the area that stores data read from disk. Generally, the **DB_BLOCK_BUFFERS** parameter is set to at least 30 to 40 percent of the shared memory segment allowed on your platform or of the total available physical memory. An SGA that is sized too large can result in excessive paging and swapping. If a recent change was made to SGA size and performance degrades, check for swapping and paging of the Oracle process.

The database buffer area is set up into the dirty list (buffers that have been modified and are waiting to be written to disk) and the least recently used (LRU) list. Free buffers are buffers that have not been modified and are available for use. If an Oracle server (user) process attempts to move a buffer to the dirty list and the list is full, it signals DBWR and DBWR writes the dirty buffers back to disk, placing them on the free list. The only action that adds blocks to the database buffer cache is a read by a server process at the request of a user. The database buffer cache stores copies of data blocks and is shared by all users.

The Shared Pool

The next largest component of the SGA is the shared pool. The shared pool is controlled in size by the initialization parameter **SHARED_POOL_SIZE**. The parameter **SHARED_POOL_SIZE** is set in bytes and is generally set to 10 to 20 percent of available memory, although, in some heavy ad hoc environments, it can be much larger. The shared pool holds the parsed SQL and PL/SQL code in the area known as the shared SQL area or library caches.

In dedicated server environments, the shared pool can be smaller than the equivalent multithreaded server (MTS) environment. This happens because, in a dedicated server system, the sort areas used by each process are kept in the user's process global area (PGA), whereas in an MTS environment, the UGA of the shared pool holds the sort areas. In both environments, the temporary extents used for sorting are tracked using the sort extent pool (SEP), which is a part of the shared pool. Any time a process needs a temporary segment for sorting, it checks the SEP first before allocating a new segment.

Other Shared Global Area Sections

The rest of the SGA is set with other initialization parameters such as:

➤ LOG_ARCHIVE_BUFFER_SIZE Sets the size of each archival buffer in log file blocks (equivalent to operating system blocks).

➤ LOG_ARCHIVE_BUFFERS Sets the number of LOG_ARCHIVE_BUFFER_SIZE section of memory to allocate for archive log writing.

➤ LOG_BUFFER Sets the size of the redo circular buffer.

The PCM Cache In Parallel Server

In the parallel server-enabled database, the parameters GC_FILES_TO_LOCKS and GC_DB_LOCKS can control a large, if not the largest, section of SGA in the parallel server configuration. The parallel cache management (PCM) lock cache is controlled by the GC_FILES_TO_LOCKS parameter, which maps the PCM locks to database block buffer size sets of datafile blocks. Although the GC_DB_LOCKS sets the maximum number of PCM locks, the locks aren't mapped to an actual cache site until they are mapped to datafile blocks using the GC_FILES_TO_LOCKS parameter. Each cache entry can take up to 115 bytes of memory storage in the SGA; this memory isn't taken from other SGA components but is additive.

The PGA And Its Contents

The PGA contains the user's session variables (session information) and arrays (stack space). Each user is assigned a PGA and, in multithreaded server systems, a UGA. The OPEN_LINKS, DB_FILES, and LOG_FILES parameters determine the PGA size. Though not a defined part of the SGA, the user's PGA interacts intimately with the SGA.

The OPEN_LINKS parameter determines the number of database links that each process can use simultaneously. The DB_FILES parameter sets the soft limit for the number of database files that can be simultaneously accessed by the database. (The actual limit is set by the database build parameter MAX_DATABASE_FILES). The LOG_FILES parameter sets the soft limit on the maximum number of log files (redo logs) available for the system (the actual maximum is set by the database build parameters MAX_LOG_FILES and MAX_LOG_GROUPS).

The Oracle Instance Processes

As stated earlier, the instance consists not only of the SGA and its components but also of the set of processes that interact with the SGA of which there are four: SMON, PMON, LGWR, and DBWR, along with numerous other optional processes.

 You must know all there is to know about the base Oracle processes and their interactions. Be sure to study the following sections carefully!

SMON Process

The SMON (Server Monitor) process monitors the Oracle instance and recovers temporary segment space when it is no longer needed. It coalesces contiguous areas of free space in database tablespaces, where the default storage parameter, **PCTINCREASE**, is set to zero, and recovers dead transactions skipped during crash and instance recovery because of file-read or offline errors. These transactions are eventually recovered by SMON when the tablespace or file is brought back online. If SMON dies, the instance will crash, requiring instance recovery on restart.

PMON Process

The PMON (Process Monitor) process cleans up failed transactions. This cleanup involves clearing out cache entries, releasing locks, and freeing other process resources. If MTS is being used, PMON watches for dead dispatcher and server processes and restarts them as needed. If PMON dies, the instance will crash, requiring instance recovery on startup. When an instance crashes and is restarted, PMON will roll back any uncommitted transactions, using the information in the rollback segments.

DBWR Process

The DBWR (Dirty Buffer Writer) process writes modified (or dirty) blocks from the database buffer cache to the disk files. Blocks aren't written on commit, only the rollback segment segments and header are affected by a commit. In general, DBWR writes only when more data needs to be read into the SGA and too few database buffers are free. The least recently used data is written to the datafiles first. DBWR's entire purpose in cyberlife is to manage the database buffer cache so the server processes can always find free buffers.

In Oracle7.3, if blocks have their lock bit set (that is, they were modified by a transaction) as they're written out of the cache, DBWR resets their lock bits back to unlocked status. In versions earlier than 7.3, the blocks were written as is, and the next process to read them reset the lock bits. A dirty buffer is any buffer that has had any of its bits twiddled. Even if the lock bit is only turned on and no other changes are performed, the block must be rewritten to disk. Writes are always deferred, if needed, to optimize system I/O.

Remember, DBWR only writes, it does no reading other than from cache; the dedicated and MTS server processes do all reading of disks. It's the only process that writes changed blocks from the database buffer cache to disk.

DBWR behavior is controlled by initialization parameters, and the initialization parameter **ASYNC_WRITE** tells DBWR to enable asynchronous writing to database files on systems that allow this to be switched. On systems in which asynchronous writes are the normal mode, **ASYNC_WRITE** isn't required to be set. The **DB_WRITERS** parameter controls the number of DBWR processes started at instance startup. On systems where multithreaded processes are used for the DBWR process, multiple DBWR processes are not needed.

LGWR And CKPT Processes

The LGWR (Log Writer) process writes out the redo buffer to the redo logs on a commit. At specific times, all modified database buffers in the SGA are written to the datafiles by DBWR; this event is called a *checkpoint*. The LGWR process is responsible for signaling DBWR at checkpoints and updating all the datafiles and control files of the database to indicate the most recent checkpoint. If the CKPT (Checkpoint) process (optional in Oracle7.x and mandatory in Oracle8) is present, the checkpoint responsibilities of LGWR are assumed by the CKPT process. The CKPT process is controlled by the **CHECKPOINT_ PROCESS** initialization parameter in versions earlier than 8.0. The LGWR process also allows for recovery of committed data in the database buffer cache at the time of an instance failure.

If the LGWR or CKPT process needs a file that the DBWR process is checkpointing, it waits until DBWR completes the checkpoint operation.

I always start the CKPT process. Oracle found it so useful that they have made it part of the standard set of processes in Oracle8, and it's no longer optional. Anything to reduce contention will improve performance.

ARCH Process

The ARCH (Archiver) process is responsible for copying filled redo log files to the archive log destination. The ARCH process is only present if archive logging is enabled for the instance. If the archive log destination is full, the archive log process will silently hang, only reporting a problem to new logins and the alert log. No redo log will be reused until it has been archived if archive logging is in effect for the database. The **ARCHIVE_LOG_START** parameter must be set to **TRUE** and the **ARCHIVELOG** mode must be set in the database for archive logging to be in effect. If only the **ARCHIVELOG** mode is set via the **ALTER DATABASE** command, database processing will continue until all available redo logs are filled, then Oracle will hang with an error in the alert log, indicating that all online redo logs need archiving. If the ARCH process abnormally terminates, the database will continue operation until all online redo logs are filled before it will hang.

RECO Process

The RECO (Recover) process recovers failed distributed transactions and is only present if the distributed database option is installed in the database system. The RECO process is started only if the **DISTRIBUTED_TRANSACTIONS** initialization parameter is set to a value greater than zero. For databases with the distributed option, the default for **DISTRIBUTED_TRANSACTIONS** is 32, so if you want to disable the RECO process, you must explicitly set this parameter to zero in the parameter file.

SNPnn Process

The SNPnn (Snapshot) process (where nn is an integer) was initially used strictly for snapshot processing. When job queues were added to the Oracle system, the SNPnn processes were also tasked with checking and executing jobs for the job queues. A failed snapshot process may inhibit job queue or snapshot processing and will generate a trace file but, otherwise, will not affect Oracle instance operation. Snapshot processes (or job queue processes) failure will result in an alert log entry.

The job queue processes are controlled by the **JOB_QUEUE_PROCESSES**, **JOB_QUEUE_INTERVAL**, and **JOB_QUEUE_KEEP_CONNECTIONS** (in some installations, these may begin with **SNAPSHOT** instead of **JOB**) initialization parameters. The **JOB_QUEUE_PROCESSES** sets the number of SNPnn processes created at instance startup. The **JOB_QUEUE_ INTERVAL** parameter sets the wakeup interval for the processes (how often they wake up and check the job and snapshot queue tables). The **JOB_QUEUE_KEEP_CONNECTIONS** initialization parameter tells the snapshot refresh process to keep database links open between process runs.

Dnnnn And Snnnn Processes

The Dnnnn (Dispatcher) process (nnnn is a sequential number) distributes instance attachments to Snnnn (Server) processes. Snnnn processes take the place of dedicated servers for user connections in MTS-enabled systems. Dnnnn and Snnnn processes are only present in MTS systems. In some Oracle versions, abnormal or forced termination of a Pnnnn process can result in instance termination; this is a known Oracle bug.

The Dnnnn and Snnnn processes are controlled by the **MTS_DISPATCHERS,** **MTS_MAX_DISPATCHERS, MTS_SERVERS,** and **MTS_MAX_ SERVERS** initialization parameters. The **MTS_DISPATCHERS** and **MTS_SERVERS** parameters set the minimum number of Dnnnn and Snnnn processes created at instance startup. The **MTS_MAX_DISPATCHERS** and **MTS_MAX_SERVERS** parameters set the maximum number of Dnnnn and Snnnn processes allowed to be automatically started as needed.

In an MTS system, the SQLNET listener process determines if a user connection should be dedicated or should use a shared server process. If the listener determines that a shared connection is appropriate, it gives the user process the address of a dispatcher process.

In a dedicated server environment, both the Dnnnn and Snnnn processes are combined and a single process is started for each user; this single process is simply called a server process. This dedicated environment is also referred to as being a single-tasked or combined user and server process environment.

Pnnnn Processes

Pnnnn (Parallel Query Slave) processes (nnnn is a sequential number) are started and stopped by the parallel query server. A single parallel query can result in dozens of Pnnnn processes, depending on table size and number of processors and disks, as well as initialization parameters. Loss of a Pnnnn process may result in a failed query but, otherwise, shouldn't affect instance operations.

The Pnnnn processes are controlled by the initialization parameters **PARALLEL_MIN_SERVERS, PARALLEL_MAX_SERVERS, PAR- ALLEL_MIN_PERCENT,** and **PARALLEL_SERVER_IDLE_TIME.** The **PARALLEL_MIN_SERVERS** parameter sets the minimum number of parallel query slave processes to start at instance startup. The **PAR- ALLEL_MAX_SERVERS** parameter is used to control the maximum number of parallel query servers that can be started for the entire instance. The **PARALLEL_MIN_PERCENT** parameter determines the minimum number of parallel query slave processes that must be available for a query to be processed in parallel. The **PARALLEL_SERVER_IDLE_TIME** parameter sets the number of seconds a slave process can be idle before it is removed.

Oracle Instance Startup And Shutdown

An Oracle instance is started and stopped with the Server Manager program (usually named SVRMGR, SVRMGRl, SVRMGRG, or SVRMGRxx, where xx is the version level). On Windows-based systems, the Oracle Enterprise

Manager (OEM) interface can also be used to control instance startup and shutdown; however, we won't cover it here. The Server Manager is a command-line program and must be invoked before an instance can be started or shut down. The first step to any startup or shutdown is the invocation of the Server Manager.

Following the invocation of the Server Manager, the appropriate database control command is issued. Before an instance is created, the only option allowed is the **STARTUP NOMOUNT** command. This command starts a bare-bones instance process set but doesn't look at parameter or control files (indeed, the control files don't, as yet, exist).

The Creation Of A Database

Once a database instance has been initialized with the **STARTUP NOMOUNT** command, the **CREATE DATABASE** command is utilized to tell the Oracle kernel how you want the initial datafile (for the **SYSTEM** tablespace), the redo logs, and basic control files to be set up. In the **CREATE DATABASE** command, you specify the maximum values for many database structures, such as:

➤ MAXDATAFILES

➤ MAXLOGFILES

➤ MAXLOGMEMBERS

➤ MAXINSTANCES

➤ MAXLOGHISTORY

These **MAX** parameters determine the fixed size of the control file and may only be changed by rebuilding the control file. The **CREATE DATABASE** command is also used to set National Language System (NLS) parameters for the entire database.

The **CREATE DATABASE** command builds the initial datafile or datafiles for the **SYSTEM** tablespace, creates the redo logs, creates the alert log, and creates the control files, as well as starts any required service processes. Once the **CREATE DATABASE** command completes, you are left with a fully operational, though not very usable, database. Before any additional processing is done in the database, additional tablespaces, rollback segments, and, possibly, redo logs should be added, as well as additional users.

Startup Of A Database

Database startup consists of the following basic steps:

1. Invoke the SVRMGR program.

2. Connect to the instance using CONNECT INTERNAL.

3. Use the **STARTUP** command to mount and open the database.

Step 3 can also be replaced with the **STARTUP** command with options; the startup options are:

➤ **NOMOUNT** Used only for creation of a database and is performed automatically by all other options.

➤ **MOUNT** Used for certain maintenance operations and is performed automatically by using the following command options:

   ➤ **STARTUP**

   ➤ **STARTUP OPEN**

   ➤ **STARTUP FORCE**

   ➤ **STARTUP RESTRICT**

   ➤ **STARTUP RECOVER**

   Performs a startup of instance processes and mounts the database, leaving it accessible only to the Server Manager process.

➤ **OPEN** Used to **NOMOUNT, MOUNT,** and **OPEN** a database, the same as issuing a **STARTUP** command with no options.

➤ **FORCE** Used only in emergencies, it performs a **SHUTDOWN ABORT** followed by a **STARTUP OPEN**. This option is also used with certain undocumented initialization parameters to force open a corrupted database.

➤ **RECOVER** Used when it is known that a database will need recovery. (*Note:* Instance recovery will be performed automatically on instance startup). This option is only needed to force media recovery.

➤ **RESTRICT** Performs a **NOMOUNT, MOUNT,** and **OPEN,** leaving the database in restricted user mode. The restricted user mode allows only users (usually DBAs) with RESTRICTED SESSION privilege to log in to the instance.

➤ **PARALLEL** Used only when mounting the database for use in a parallel server configuration (one where multiple instances use the same set of database files).

   Once a database has been mounted and opened (in unrestricted mode, the default), users can log in and use the database.

Database Shutdown

To shut down a database, follow these basic steps:

1. Start the SVRMGR program.

2. Log on to the database as CONNECT INTERNAL or as a user with SYSDBA or SYSOPER roles.

3. Issue the **SHUTDOWN** command with the appropriate options.

The **SHUTDOWN** command has the following options:

➤ **NORMAL** This is the default if the **SHUTDOWN** command is issued with no options. It's the most polite of the shutdown options in that it waits patiently for all users to log off before shutting down the instance, whether they're actively engaged in transactions or just sitting idle. **NORMAL** is also the safest shutdown and is suggested as the only option to use prior to a cold backup. However, I've never experienced a problem recovering from a shutdown using the next option, **IMMEDI-ATE. SHUTDOWN NORMAL** is the slowest shutdown option. A startup from a **SHUTDOWN NORMAL** will be the fastest startup because no instance recovery is performed.

➤ **IMMEDIATE** This is the next most polite shutdown option; it waits until pending transactions are complete then logs users off and shuts down the instance. This is faster than using the **NORMAL** option. Instance recovery may be performed on startup from a **SHUTDOWN IMMEDIATE**. The **IMMEDIATE** option provides an alternative to killing user sessions then performing a **SHUTDOWN NORMAL**.

➤ **ABORT** This is the rude shutdown option; it immediately stops the Oracle processes and should only be used when all other options have failed to shut down the instance. It will leave the database in an inconsistent state from which it may not be able to be recovered if the only means of recovery is a cold backup taken after the **SHUTDOWN ABORT. SHUTDOWN ABORT** is the fastest of all the shutdown options but will always require instance recovery and, in some rare cases, may cause database corruption that isn't recoverable. Always follow a **SHUTDOWN ABORT** with a **STARTUP** and **SHUTDOWN NORMAL** if possible.

Shared Vs. Dedicated Server Configurations

A database is either a dedicated server or a shared server database. In a dedicated server environment, each user process gets its own connection service to the database. In a large user climate or one where the PQO is used, a dedicated server can require substantial overhead for system memory resources. In a shared server (known as multithreaded server or MTS), multiple user processes share an Oracle service, reducing system memory overhead. Where MTS should be used is a subject of debate with DBAs; some say an environment where you have more than 50 concurrent users, others say as high as 150 concurrent users. I say it's determined by the platform and other environmental factors such as memory and status of the PQO option. In fact, it may even benefit a situation in which the number of user processes is relatively small (such as less than 100 concurrent users) but each user's idle time is very high, thus a shared process preserves resources while not sacrificing performance.

Debates aside, Oracle says MTS should be used for more than 150 concurrent users.

Dedicated server systems do sorting inside the user's process global area or PGA. Individual servers are started for each user to connect to the database and read disk blocks. No additional files other than standard SQLNET files (tnsnames.ora, sqlnet.ora, and listener.ora) are required for setup of the dedicated server. The SQLNET listener process immediately starts a server process and hands the user connection to it for processing. However, it must be stressed that the user and server processes are separate processes. In a dedicated user environment, only discrete user/server process sets and combined user/server processes are allowed. The combined user/server process is also referred to as *single-tasked*.

Multithreaded servers do sorting inside the SGA in the UGA areas that are a part of the shared pool. For MTS environments, the shared pool size may be several times the size of a dedicated server shared pool. A pool of dispatcher and server processes is configured based on initialization parameters at startup (**MIN_SERVER** and **MIN_DISPATCHERS**) and more are added, if needed, up to predefined maximums (**MAX_SERVERS** and **MAX_DISPACTHERS**) to service users. The DBA is required to configure entries in the initialization file as well as the listener.ora file for MTS. Mistakes in the initialization file can lead to no connection, connection to the wrong database, or no startup of the effected instance. The SQLNET listener process assigns a user connection either as a dedicated connection or as a shared connection. If the SQLNET process determines that a user process should be made a part of a shared process, it is handed off to a dispatcher process that places it with one of the shared server processes. The MTS server will support shared servers, dedicated servers, and combined user/servers so they coexist in the same instance.

Exam Prep Questions

Question 1

> Which area do shared servers use for sorting?
>
> ○ a. PGA
>
> ○ b. SEP
>
> ○ c. UGA

The correct answer is c, the user global area (UGA). The UGA is actually a part of the shared pool in a shared environment because many users may need access to the same data. In a dedicated server (non-MTS), the PGA holds the sort areas. Therefore, answer a is wrong. The SEP tracks sort extents but doesn't actually do any sorting. Therefore, answer b is wrong. The key to this question is understanding the difference between how shared process (MTS) and dedicated (non-MTS) servers use sort areas.

Question 2

> Which component holds a user's session variables and arrays?
>
> ○ a. SGA
>
> ○ b. PGA
>
> ○ c. Shared Pool
>
> ○ d. Datafiles

The correct answer is b, the process global area (PGA). The PGA always contains the user's variables and arrays no matter if the database is being run as a single instance or a shared instance.

Question 3

> Which background process allows for recovery of committed data in the database buffer cache at the time of instance failure?
>
> ○ a. DBWR
>
> ○ b. GWR
>
> ○ c. ARCH
>
> ○ d. CKPT

The correct answer for this question is b, LGWR process. Answer a is incorrect because DBWR writes dirty blocks, but only at the request of the least recently used (LRU) algorithm, so it isn't going to help in a recovery situation. Answer c is incorrect because the ARCH process writes completed redo logs to the archive location; it's not used for recovery. The CKPT process helps write out SCN data to file headers, but doesn't help with recovery, so answer d is incorrect. This leaves LGWR, which writes committed data to the redo logs; in fact, a transaction isn't considered committed until it's recorded in the redo logs.

Question 4

Which structure contains the sort extent pool (SEP) ?

O a. SGA

O b. PGA

O c. UGA

The proper answer to this question is a, SGA. The pool tracks actual extents. The extents themselves may exist in either the shared pool area known as the UGA (for MTS instances), in the user's process area (PGA), or on disk. This is a trick question because you must realize that although the sort extents themselves are in several possible locations, the SEP is in one, the SGA. Therefore, answers b and c are incorrect choices.

Question 5

Which component stores the synchronization information needed for database recovery?

O a. Redo log files

O b. Control file

O c. Parameter file

O d. Trace file

The answer to this question is the control file, b. The control file tracks all SCN and timestamp information for all datafiles in the database. A backup copy can be used but only if the **USING BACKUP CONTROLFILE** clause is added to the **RECOVERY** command. The redo logs track all committed transactions, therefore, answer a is incorrect. The parameter file is a static file containing initialization parameters for an instance, so answer c is incorrect. And a trace file is generated by processes to allow tracking of operations and errors, making d an incorrect choice.

Question 6

> In which situation will the control file be accessed?
>
> ○ a. Only when starting an instance in **NOMOUNT** mode
>
> ○ b. Only when the database is being mounted
>
> ○ c. Only when the database is open
>
> ○ d. To mount and open the database

This question may be considered a trick question in that the answer isn't the only time the control file is accessed, just the only time in this list. The correct answer is d, to mount and open the database. Notice the wording in the other answers, they all contain the word "only." So although the control file is used in both answers b and c, it isn't used only in answers b and c, so they are incorrect choices. If the database is started in **NOMOUNT** mode, the control file is not accessed at all. Therefore, answer a is incorrect.

Question 7

> Which structure of the logical database must exist for the database to run?
>
> ○ a. **SYSTEM** tablespace
>
> ○ b. **DATA** tablespace
>
> ○ c. **INDEX** tablespace

Remember that there are physical files, such as datafiles, redo logs, control files, and logical structures, such as tablespaces, in an Oracle database. This question refers to the logical side of the database—the tablespaces. To run, a database must have a **SYSTEM** tablespace because this is where all data dictionary information is kept, as well as the required system rollback segment, so the proper answer is a, and answers b and c are, therefore, incorrect.

Question 8

> Which shutdown mode will require instance at the next startup?
>
> ○ a. **NORMAL**
>
> ○ b. **IMMEDIATE**
>
> ○ c. **ABORT**

This is another example of a trick question and really tests your understanding of shutdown options. In some cases, an immediate shutdown will require instance recovery, so you might think on a quick read that answer b is the correct choice. However, this would be wrong. Always read all of the answers available. With the **ABORT** option, instance recovery is always required. Thus, answer c is the most correct answer. No instance recovery is performed with the **NORMAL** startup option. Therefore, answer a is an incorrect option.

Question 9

> Which startup state is only used for starting up an instance prior to creating the database?
>
> ○ a. **NOMOUNT**
>
> ○ b. **MOUNT**
>
> ○ c. **OPEN**

Again, you must read the complete question as well as all the answers. If you miss the last part of this question—"prior to creating the database?"—you'll get it wrong. The only time **NOMOUNT** is used is before creating the database; however, **MOUNT** is used in virtually all other situations. If you just glance at the question and miss the part about database creation, you'll answer b and miss the question. The proper answer is, of course, a. **OPEN**, answer c, is incorrect because it requires the existence of a database.

Question 10

> When starting the database to make it available to all users, which step is first?
>
> ○ a. Open the database
>
> ○ b. Mount the database
>
> ○ c. Connect user AS sysdba
>
> ○ d. Invoke Server Manager
>
> ○ e. Start up the instance

The reason this is marked as a trick question is that not everyone uses Server Manager (SVRMGR) to start and stop a database. Also, people tend to think in steps rather than seeing the entire process. Logically, in starting the database, the process begins with invoking the Server Manager, so the correct answer is d. All of the other steps will logically follow the startup of the Server Manager program, so they are incorrect because they are not the *first* step. The next steps in order would be: c, b, a. The last answer, d, is actually almost synonymous with "start up the database" in a non-parallel server environment.

Question 11

> Which database object is a logical repository for physically grouped data?
>
> ○ a. Database
>
> ○ b. File
>
> ○ c. Tablespace
>
> ○ d. Segment
>
> ○ e. Extent
>
> ○ f. Block

The key to this question is the word "logical." This word, when combined with "repository," eliminates all answers but one. Though databases, files, segments, extents, and blocks are all repositories for physically grouped data, they are actual physical manifestations, not logical. The correct answer is c, a tablespace. Although a tablespace has logical existence in the database, it's the logical name for a collection (or repository) of physically grouped (located in the same files) data. The files in a tablespace are broken into blocks, extents, and segments, each of which has definable boundaries on the disk or disks they occupy.

Question 12

> Which tablespace will cause the database to shut down if it is taken offline?
>
> ○ a. **TEMP**
>
> ○ b. **RBS**
>
> ○ c. **SYSTEM**
>
> ○ d. **APPL1_DATA**
>
> ○ e. **APPL1_INDEX**

Actually, if you just stop and think about what you know about database creation, this question is an easy one. What is the only tablespace created by the **CREATE DATABASE** command? Although taking **TEMP**, **RBS**, **APPL1_DATA**, or **APPL1_INDEX** offline makes your users unhappy and prohibits certain activities, it won't cause the database to shut down. However, if you take the data dictionary, stored in **SYSTEM**, offline, the entire database comes crashing down. Therefore, answer c is the correct answer.

Question 13

> Which Oracle7 server configuration allows shared servers, dedicated servers, and combined user/servers to exist in the same instance?
>
> ○ a. Dedicated server process
>
> ○ b. Combined user/server process
>
> ○ c. Multithreaded server process
>
> ○ d. None

The correct answer is c. Only the multithreaded server allows all three types of connections. In an MTS environment, the SQLNET listener process determines if a user process should be shared or dedicated. A single-task linked utility or process can still connect with a combined user/server process as well as in an MTS environment, so MTS is the only one where all three connection methods can be used.

Need To Know More?

The first place you should go for much of your Oracle study is directly to the Oracle manuals. The Oracle concept, administration, and tuning guides provide answers to many of the OCP questions. However, the manuals also contain a great deal of fluff and verbosity.

In recent years, there has been a proliferation of third-party, after-market Oracle publications, many of high quality, but many are just good for holding up a crooked couch. Here are a few titles that I frequently reference:

 Ault, Mike: *Oracle 7.0 Administration & Management*. John Wiley & Sons. ISBN 0-47160-857-2. Although aged a bit, this still is a good resource. Some of the newer features (post-7.2.x) aren't covered. The revision, *ORACLE8 Administration and Management*, covers 7.3.x features as well as 8.0 features, and is another excellent source to use.

 Corey, Michael, Michael Abbey, and Dan J. Dechichio: *Tuning Oracle*. Oracle Press. ISBN 0-07881-181-3. This is a good general reference for tuning Oracle.

 Gurry, Mark and Peter Corrigan: *Oracle Performance Tuning, 2nd Edition*. O'Reilly & Associates. ISBN 1-056592-237-9. This is a must-have for tuning Oracle databases. This book covers all aspects of Oracle database tuning and any tuning related questions are covered inside this volume. A must-have for any DBA's bookshelf.

 Loney, Kevin: *Oracle DBA Handbook, 7.3 Edition*. Oracle Press, 1996. ISBN 0-07882-289-0. This is another excellent DBA reference. Loney tends to tread a more Oracle Corporation-based tuning and management path, but this is still another book that should be on your bookshelf.

I also suggest obtaining the latest *International Oracle Users Group (IOUG) Proceedings* and *Oracle Open World (OOW) Proceedings* because they have state-of-the-art tuning, architecture, and administration information.

Oracle Data Dictionary

Terms you'll need to understand:

√ Data dictionary

√ Virtual table

√ View

√ Packages

√ Procedures

√ Functions

√ SQL

Techniques you'll need to master:

√ Mining the data dictionary

√ Structuring the data dictionary

√ Using DBMS packages

√ Using SQL

In Chapter 2, we explored what makes up the physical and logical structure of the files and processes in an Oracle instance. In Chapter 3, we'll look at the guts of the Oracle system: the data dictionary and the Oracle-provided packages, procedures, and functions.

The Oracle Data Dictionary

The Oracle data dictionary stores the information required for the Oracle system to operate. All details about the structures that make up the items we think of as being in a database are stored in the data dictionary. The data dictionary is data about data, or, as it is more popularly called, *metadata*. Metadata details data types, lengths, precessions, and what data items are contained in which objects. All details of tables, indexes, synonyms, views, grants, roles, and so forth, are contained in the data dictionary. An expert with a few minutes' access to your data dictionary will know more about your database than you could have told him or her in the same amount of time. This is one reason why the SYS and SYSTEM user passwords should be instantly changed and jealously guarded after installation is complete.

 Oracle sets the SYSTEM and SYS passwords to MANAGER and CHANGE_ON_INSTALL. Always reset the passwords for SYSTEM and SYS.

Oracle also provides many packages of stored procedures for use by Oracle DBAs and developers. Collectively, these are known as the DBMS set of packages (even though some don't begin with DBMS anymore). You should study these Oracle-provided packages; we'll cover the ones important for you in this chapter. However, learn all you can about each of the DBMS packages provided, or you may find yourself reinventing already existing functionality.

Oracle C Structs And V$ Views

It may surprise some of you to realize Oracle is written in C. However, the main structures (called structs) are actually C struct blocks. These normally aren't visible to users; indeed you have to define a view against them to even be able to describe them. Listing 3.1 shows an example of a DPT. Until recently, these structs were only documented internally, and little documentation was available about them. Now, at least we can see their names (from a query against the SYS-owned virtual table, **V$FIXED_TABLE**) and get an idea of what each is used for by detective work in the virtual performance view structures documented in the virtual view **V$FIXED_VIEW_DEFINITION**.

Listing 3.1   Example V$ view and its definition.

```
VIEW_NAME               VIEW_DEFINITION
-------------------     ------------------------------------------
V$DATAFILE              select
                        fe.indx+1,decode(bitand(fe.festa,19),0,
                        'OFFLINE',1,'SYSOFF',
                        2,'ONLINE',3,'SYSTEM',16,'RECOVER',18,
                        'RECOVER','UNKNOWN'),
                        decode(bitand(fe.festa, 12),
                        0,'DISABLED',4,'READ ONLY',12,
                        'READ WRITE','UNKNOWN'),
                        to_number(fe.fecps),fh.fhfsz*fe.febsz,
                        fe.fecsz*fe.febsz,fn.fnnam from x$kccfe
                        fe,x$kccfn fn, x$kcvfh fh where
                        fe.fedup!=0 and fe.indx+1=fn.fnfno  and
                        fn.fntyp=3 and fh.hxfil=fn.fnfno and
                        fn.fnnam is not null
```

The DBA should be aware of two X$ tables used for SGA database block buffer tuning—the **X$KCBRBH** and **X$KCBCBH** tables. The **X$KCBRBH** table's **COUNT** column displays the number of additional cache hits gained by adding additional cache blocks (when summed over a contiguous interval of blocks). The **X$KCBCBH** table's **COUNT** column displays the number of lost cache hits gained by adding additional cache blocks (when summed over a contiguous interval of blocks).

You probably don't need to be concerned with the base C structs other than the **X$KCBRBH** and **X$KCBCBH** tables. However, you should study the virtual views (the **V$** views) that use them extensively, called dynamic performance tables or views (DPT or DPV). Listing 3.2 lists the major C structs, commonly called the X$ tables.

 I must stress the importance of knowing all you can about all of the **V$** views that you can; they make your life as an Oracle DBA much easier.

Listing 3.2   List of all X$ tables.

```
NAME
-------------------------------
X$KQFTA
X$KQFVI
X$KQFVT
X$KQFDT
X$KQFCO
X$KSPPI
```

```
X$KSLLT
X$KSLLD
X$KSLED
X$KSLES
X$KSLEI
X$KSUSE
X$KSUPR
X$KSUPRLAT
X$KSUSD
X$KSUSGSTA
X$KSUTM
X$KSUSESTA
X$KSUMYSTA
X$KSUSIO
X$KSUSECST
X$KSURU
X$KSUPL
X$KSUCF
X$KSUXSINST
X$KSULL
X$KSBDP
X$KSBDD
X$MESSAGES
X$KSMSD
X$KSMSS
X$KSMMEM
X$KSMFSV
X$KSMLRU
X$KGHLU
X$KSMSP
X$KSMSPR
X$KSMCX
X$KSQRS
X$KSQEQ
X$KSQDN
X$KSQST
X$TRACE
X$KSTEX
X$TRACES
X$NLS_PARAMETERS
X$KSULV
X$KSUSECON
X$KCCCF
X$KCCFN
X$KCCDI
X$KCCRT
X$KCCLE
```

```
X$KCCFE
X$KCCLH
X$KCBCBH
X$KCBRBH
X$BH
X$KCBWAIT
X$KCBFWAIT
X$KCKCE
X$KCKTY
X$KCKFM
X$KCFIO
X$KCLFH
X$KCLFI
X$LE
X$LE_STAT
X$KCVFH
X$KTADM
X$KTCXB
X$KTURD
X$KTTVS
X$KDNCE
X$KDNST
X$KDNSSC
X$KDNSSF
X$KDXST
X$KDXHS
X$KQRST
X$KQRPD
X$KQRSD
X$KQDPG
X$KGLOB
X$KGLLK
X$KGLPN
X$KGLST
X$KGLAU
X$KGLTR
X$KGLXS
X$KGLDP
X$KGLNA
X$KGLNA1
X$KKSBV
X$KGICC
X$KGICS
X$KGLLC
X$VERSION
X$KQFSZ
X$KZDOS
```

```
X$KZSRO
X$KZSPR
X$KZSRT
X$K2GTE2
X$K2GTE
X$KMMSI
X$KMMDI
X$KMMSG
X$KMMDP
X$KMMRD
X$KMCQS
X$KMCVC
X$UGANCO
X$OPTION
X$KXFPCST
X$KXFPCMS
X$KXFPSMS
X$KXFPCDS
X$KXFPSDS
X$KXFPDP
X$KXFPSST
X$KXFPYS
X$KLLCNT
X$KLLTAB
X$KVII
X$KVIS
X$KVIT
X$KCVFHONL
X$KCVFHMRR
X$KGLTABLE
X$KGLBODY
X$KGLTRIGGER
X$KGLINDEX
X$KGLCLUSTER
X$KGLCURSOR
```

Generally speaking, the **V$** tables are used to show transitory performance information based on the underlying C structs known as the **X$** tables. These DPTs are the only views in Oracle where the data will change almost every time you select from them. This dynamism is why they are called dynamic performance tables or views. Because they are based on C structs that are an integral part of the kernel of Oracle, they're also available in a mounted but not open database. The **V$** DPTs are created at database build by internalized procedures (except for a few special ones built by optional scripts as needed).

The only information about the data structures contained in the **X$** and **V$** objects is actual information that would be used in recovery, and the only information needed for recovery concerns the physical datafiles (**V$DBFILE**) and the redo logs (**V$LOGHIST** and **V$LOGFILE**). Other than these few views, the others concern performance statistics. The actual metadata is stored in database tables identical in structure to the tables and objects they document.

General database users usually don't need to access the **V$** DPTs. Some DPTs, like the **V$DATABASE** view, do contain useful information, such as the Oracle version and database name, for general users. I usually grant select permission to the public user for this view and verify that a public synonym is available.

You should know the following **V$** DPTs:

➤ **V$RECOVERY_STATUS** This view has been added to version 7.3 to allow the DBA to track the status of media recovery.

➤ **V$RECOVERY_FILE_STATUS** This view has been added to version 7.3 to allow the DBA to query the status of media recovery.

➤ **V$DB_OBJECT_CACHE** This view provides information on the amount of sharable memory used by a cached PL/SQL object.

➤ **V$SYSSTAT** This view has a plethora of system level statistics. Statistics such as sorts (memory) tell how many times a particular type of operation has been performed since startup. Sort location tracking is vital, generally speaking, for most applications, and sorts should be done in memory whenever possible, especially for online transaction processing (OLTP) applications. This view is also used to monitor client/server traffic statistics. When tuning the SGA, this view can be used in concert with the **X$KCBRBH** table to evaluate the effect of an increase or decrease in the size of the database buffer cache.

➤ **V$LATCH** This view contains information on latches and locks. The **SLEEPS** column indicates the number of times a process waited for a latch. For example, information on the requests for latches that were willing to wait (**WILLING_TO_WAIT** column) is contained in the **MISSES** and **GETS** columns of this view. If you suspect latch contention is happening, issue a query against this view's **SLEEPS** column to display the number of times a process has waited for a particular latch.

➤ **V$CACHE** This view is normally used only in parallel server installations. However, it's useful in more situations than that because you can use it to analyze the database buffer cache in both exclusive and shared server modes. The view shows only objects currently being cached.

➤ **V$SYSTEM_EVENT** This view contains information on systemwide events and is used by the utlbstat/utlestat scripts as a source of statistics. DBAs can query this view directly, if needed. System status, such as the need to increase the redo log buffer size (**LOG_BUFFER**), can be ascertained by looking at the system events (in this case, "log buffer space") listed in this view. Another system event DBAs should watch for is the "buffer busy waits" event, which indicates contention for the database buffer cache. The total number of event waits for each category is shown in this view.

➤ **V$TRANSACTION** This view contains information on all transactions in the database. Along with the **V$SESSION** view, **V$TRANSACTION** can be used to get details about a specific user transaction.

➤ **V$SESSION** This view documents all sessions currently attached to the database. It contains columns that indicate if the session is causing lock contention and, if so, in which row. The **SERIAL#** and **SID** columns are useful if you need to kill a user session because these values are required by the **ALTER SYSTEM KILL SESSION** command.

➤ **V$SESSION_EVENT** This view contains information on session-level events and is used by the utlbstat/utlestat scripts as a source of statistics. DBAs can query this view directly, if needed. It's also useful for determining whether there's I/O contention for the redo log files. Information such as systemwide waits per session are here as well.

➤ **V$LOGFILE** This view contains the list of all redo log files and their locations. When used with the **V$DBFILE** view, it provides input to the **CREATE CONTROLFILE** command.

➤ **V$DBFILE** This view contains the names and locations of all database datafiles. When used with the **V$LOGFILE** view, it provides input to the **CREATE CONTROLFILE** command. It also generates the commands used during a backup operation to back up the physical database datafiles. This information is also contained in the **DBA_DATA_FILES** view.

➤ **V$LIBRARYCACHE** This view documents activity in the shared pool library caches. The ratio of **RELOADS** to **PINS** for a specific type of cache must always be less than 1 percent in a properly tuned database. The **RELOADS** column represents the number of object definitions that have been aged out of the library cache for lack of space. The **PINS** column represents the executions of an item in the library cache. The

GETHITRATIO column should always show a value of greater than 0.9 in an ideally tuned database.

➤ **V$SESSION_WAIT** This view contains information on session waits and is used by the utlbstat/utlestat scripts as a source of statistics. DBAs can query this view directly, if needed. The wait times, indicated in the **WAIT TIME** column, record a session's last wait time.

➤ **V$SORT_SEGMENT** This view is a map to the sort extent pool (SEP); it contains such items as the total extents for the **TEMP** tablespace areas, and it's used to monitor sort segments in the **TEMP** tablespace. Each time an unused extent is found in the SEP, the column **EXTENT_HITS** is incremented by one.

➤ **V$WAITSTAT** This view contains information on wait statistics, such as high freelist contention. Entries in the **VALUE** column greater than zero indicate possible contention for that resource. For some perverse reason, Oracle likes to refer to rollback segments by the term *undo*, so any references to undo headers or blocks are referring to rollback segments.

The Oracle $ (Dollar) Tables

The final level of the Oracle internals (other than the views based upon them) are collectively known as the $ or *dollar tables*. They're called dollar tables because, initially, all of them ended with a dollar sign (for example, **COL$, TAB$, IND$**). But lately, Oracle has moved away from this standard, which can make identifying the actual data dictionary tables hard at times (a good reason not to place anything in the **SYSTEM** tablespace that isn't a part of the data dictionary or that doesn't belong to the SYS user). The dollar tables are built by the sql.bsq script, which, until recently, was a hands-off item. Oracle has finally allowed us to edit the sql.bsq script to improve storage parameters for the dollar tables and indexes (in early Oracle7 releases, this was done by experienced DBAs but not supported by Oracle itself). I suggest you look over the sql.bsq script because it has some interesting internal documentation that shines light into Oracle's data dictionary. Most of the tables created by the sql.bsq script contain comments on each of the table attributes (columns) detailing the column's purpose. Table 3.1 shows the names and descriptions of the dollar tables for a 7.3.x version Oracle database.

Generally speaking, access to dollar tables should be restricted to DBA personnel. Users, however, can use the next set of views we'll discuss: the **DBA_**, **USER_**, and **ALL_** set of data dictionary views.

Table 3.1 Dollar tables and their descriptions.

Table Name	Description
ACCESS$	Access table for database objects
ARGUMENT$	Procedure argument table, describes procedural arguments
AUD$	Audit trail table, contains entries for all audited actions
AUDIT$	Audit options table, tracks auditing actions activated
BOOTSTRAP$	Table used during instance startup
CCOL$	Table of all constraint columns for database
CDEF$	Table of all constraint definitions in database
CLU$	Table of all clusters in database
COL$	Table of descriptions for all columns used in database
COM$	Table of all object and column comments for the database
CON$	Table of all constraint names in the database
DEFROLE$	Table showing all default roles assigned to users in database
DEPENDENCY$	Table of all interobject dependencies in the database
DUAL	Single-column, single-value table used for nondirected selects
DUC$	Table for procedure tracking in database
ERROR$	Table showing current errors for all users in the database
EXPACT$	Table showing functions to run against tables during export
FET$	Table showing all free extents in database
FILE$	Table showing all files for the database tablespaces
HISTGRM$	Table showing specifications for histograms used in the database
HIST_HEAD$	Table of all database histogram header data
ICOL$	Table of all database index columns
IDL_CHAR$	IDL table for character pieces
IDL_SB4$	IDL table for SB4 pieces
IDL_UB1$	IDL table for UB1 pieces
IDL_UB2$	IDL table for UB2 pieces

(continued)

Table 3.1   Dollar tables and their descriptions (continued).

Table Name	Description
INCEXP	Incremental export support table
INCFIL	Table showing incremental export file names and users
INCVID	Table containing the identifier for last valid incremental export
IND$	Table showing all database indexes
JOB$	Table for all database defined jobs
LAB$	Table for all database defined labels
LINK$	Table showing all database links
MLOG$	Table showing all database snapshot local master tables
OBJ$	Table showing all database objects
OBJAUTH$	Table showing table authorizations
OBJPRIV$	Table showing privileges granted to objects in the database
PENDING_SESSIONS$	Child table for PENDING_TRANS$
PENDING_SUB_SESSIONS$	Child table for PENDING_SESSIONS$
PENDING_TRANS$	Table of pending or in-doubt transactions
PROCEDURE$	Table database procedures
PROFILE$	Table of database profile resource mappings
PROFNAME$	Table for database profile names
PROPS$	Table of database fixed properties
RESOURCE_COST$	Table of resource costs used with profiles
RESOURCE_MAP	Map of resource number to resource name
RGCHILD$	Table of all refresh group children
RGROUP$	Table of all refresh groups
SEG$	Table mapping all database segments
SEQ$	Table showing all database sequences
SLOG$	Table showing all snapshots on local masters
SNAP$	Table showing all local snapshots
SOURCE$	Table storing source code for all stored objects in database
STMT_AUDIT_OPTION_MAP	Table mapping audit actions to audit action names

(continued)

Table 3.1	Dollar tables and their descriptions *(continued)*.
Table Name	**Description**
SYN$	Table showing all synonyms in database
SYSAUTH$	Table showing all system privilege grants for database
SYSTEM_PRIVILEGE_MAP	Map of system privilege numbers to privilege names
TAB$	Table of all database tables
TABLE_PRIVILEGE_MAP	Map of table privilege numbers to table privilege names
TRIGGER$	Table of all trigger definitions for database
TRIGGERCOL$	Map of triggers to columns they work against
TS$	Table showing all tablespaces for database
TSQ$	Table showing all tablespace quota grants in database
UET$	Table showing all used extents in the database
UNDO$	Table showing all rollback segments for database
USER$	Table showing all user definitions for database
VIEW$	Table showing all view definitions for database
_default_auditing_options_	Map of all default auditing option numbers to names

The Data Dictionary User Views: DBA_, USER_, And ALL_

Usually, the view hierarchy flows from the C structs to the **V$** DPTs and from the dollar tables to the **DBA_**, **USER_**, and **ALL_** views. Sometimes short-cuts are taken and the C structs and dollar tables are both used, but rarely. Generally, the **DBA_** and other views of their type are based on the dollar tables.

The **DBA_** series of views are the DBA's windows into the data dictionary. The **DBA_** views contain the condensed versions of the dollar tables in readable format. The **USER_** views provide a window into the user/owner object details in the data dictionary, and the **ALL_** views contain information on every object the user has access to or the privilege of using. In most cases, the views in the different hierarchies are identical except that a nonmeaningful column (such as **OWNER** in the **USER_** views) may be excluded.

The **DBA_** views are usually kept from users by not declaring public synonyms against them. However, a knowledgeable user, if he or she wants or needs to, can get information from the views with a query, using the SYS schema prefix.

For the purpose of the exam, you can safely assume the views to be identical (unless the question is on how they differ!) and apply information gleaned about the **DBA_** views to the others.

In this section, we'll limit our discussion to the **DBA_** views. Table 3.2 lists these and their purposes.

For the most part, the names of the views are self-explanatory. For example, **DBA_TABLES** shows the details of all tables in the database. However, although some may have accurate names, they still may confuse inexperienced DBAs. As an example, views with the word "RESOURCE" in them apply to database profiles because resources are the part and parcel of profiles.

Table 3.2   DBA_ views and their descriptions.

View Name	Description
DBA_2PC_NEIGHBORS	Information about incoming and outgoing connections for pending transactions
DBA_2PC_PENDING	Information about distributed transactions awaiting recovery
DBA_ANALYZE_OBJECTS	Information about analyzed objects in the database
DBA_AUDIT_EXISTS	Lists audit trail entries produced by AUDIT NOT EXISTS and AUDIT EXISTS
DBA_AUDIT_OBJECT	Audit trail records for statements concerning objects, specifically: table, cluster, view, index, sequence, [public] database link, [public] synonym, procedure, trigger, rollback segment, tablespace, role, and user
DBA_AUDIT_SESSION	All audit trail records concerning CONNECT and DISCONNECT
DBA_AUDIT_STATEMENT	Audit trail records concerning GRANT, REVOKE, AUDIT, NO AUDIT, and ALTER SYSTEM
DBA_AUDIT_TRAIL	All audit trail entries
DBA_CATALOG	All database tables, views, synonyms, and sequences
DBA_CLUSTERS	Description of all clusters in the database
DBA_CLUSTER_HASH _EXPRESSIONS	Hash functions for all clusters
DBA_CLU_COLUMNS	Mapping of table columns to cluster columns
DBA_COL_DESCRIPTION	Description on columns of all tables and views
DBA_COL_PRIVS	All grants on columns in the database

(continued)

Table 3.2   DBA_ views and their descriptions (continued).

View Name	Description
DBA_CONSTRAINTS	Constraint definitions on all tables
DBA_CONS_COLUMNS	Information about accessible columns in constraint definitions
DBA_DATA_FILES	Information about database files
DBA_DB_LINKS	All database links in the database
DBA_DEPENDENCIES	Dependencies to and from objects
DBA_ERRORS	Current errors on all stored objects in the database
DBA_EXP_FILES	Description of export files
DBA_EXP_OBJECTS	Objects that have been incrementally exported
DBA_EXP_VERSION	Version number of the last export session
DBA_EXTENTS	Extents composing all segments in the database
DBA_FREE_SPACE	Free extents in all tablespaces
DBA_FREE_SPACE _COALESCED	Statistics on coalesced space in tablespaces
DBA_FREE_SPACE _COALESCED_TMP1	Coalesced free extents for all tablespaces
DBA_FREE_SPACE _COALESCED_TMP2	Free extents in tablespaces
DBA_HISTOGRAMS	Histograms on columns of all tables
DBA_INDEXES	Description for all indexes in the database
DBA_IND_COLUMNS	Columns composing indexes on all tables and clusters
DBA_JOBS	All jobs in the database
DBA_JOBS_RUNNING	All jobs in the database that are currently running, join V$LOCK and JOB$
DBA_KEEPSIZES	Used by the DBMS_SHARED_POOL package to temporarily store shared pool object sizes
DBA_OBJECTS	All objects in the database
DBA_OBJECT_SIZE	Sizes, in bytes, of various PL/SQL objects
DBA_OBJ_AUDIT_OPTS	Auditing options for all tables and views
DBA_PRIV_AUDIT_OPTS	Description of current system privileges being audited across the system and by user
DBA_PROFILES	Display of all profiles and their limits
DBA_RCHILD	All the children in any refresh group; this view is not a join

(continued)

Table 3.2   DBA_ views and their descriptions *(continued)*.

View Name	Description
DBA_REFRESH	All the refresh groups
DBA_REFRESH_CHILDREN	All the objects in refresh groups
DBA_REPAUDIT_ATTRIBUTE	Information about attributes automatically maintained for replication
DBA_REPAUDIT_COLUMN	Information about columns in all shadow tables for all replicated tables in the database
DBA_REPCAT	Information about replicated objects in the database
DBA_REPCATLOG	Information about asynchronous administration requests
DBA_REPCOLUMN_GROUP	All column groups of replicated tables in the database
DBA_REPCONFLICT	All conflicts for which users have specified resolutions in the database
DBA_REPDDL	Arguments that do not fit in a single replicated log record
DBA_REPGENERATED	Objects generated to support replication
DBA_REPGROUP	Information about all replicated object groups
DBA_REPGROUPED_COLUMN	Columns in the all column groups of replicated tables in the database
DBA_REPKEY_COLUMNS	Primary columns for a table using column-level replication
DBA_REPOBJECT	Information about replicated objects
DBA_REPPARAMETER _COLUMN	All columns used for resolving conflicts in the database
DBA_REPPRIORITY	Values and their corresponding priorities in all priority groups in the database
DBA_REPPRIORITY_GROUP	Information about all priority groups in the database
DBA_REPPROP	Propagation information about replicated objects
DBA_REPRESOLUTION	Description of all conflict resolutions in the database
DBA_REPRESOLUTION _METHOD	All conflict resolution methods in the database
DBA_REPRESOLUTION _STATISTICS	Statistics for conflict resolutions for all replicated tables in the database
DBA_REPRESOL_STATS _CONTROL	Information about statistics collection for conflict resolutions for all replicated tables in the database
DBA_REPSCHEMA	*N*-way replication information

(continued)

Table 3.2   DBA_ views and their descriptions (continued).

View Name	Description
DBA_REPSITES	N-way replication information
DBA_RGROUP	All refresh groups; this view is not a join.
DBA_ROLES	All roles that exist in the database
DBA_ROLE_PRIVS	Roles granted to users and roles
DBA_ROLLBACK_SEGS	Description of rollback segments
DBA_SEGMENTS	Storage allocated for all database segments
DBA_SEQUENCES	Description of all sequences in the database
DBA_SNAPSHOTS	All snapshots in the database
DBA_SNAPSHOT_LOGS	All snapshot logs in the database
DBA_SOURCE	Source of all stored objects in the database
DBA_STMT_AUDIT_OPTS	Description of current system auditing options across the system and by user
DBA_SYNONYMS	All synonyms in the database
DBA_SYS_PRIVS	System privileges granted to users and roles
DBA_TABLES	Description of all tables in the database
DBA_TABLESPACES	Description of all tablespaces
DBA_TAB_COLUMNS	Columns of user's tables, views, and clusters
DBA_TAB_DESCRIPTION	Description of all tables and views in the database
DBA_TAB_PRIVS	All grants on objects in the database
DBA_TRIGGERS	All triggers in the database
DBA_TRIGGER_COLS	Column usage in all triggers
DBA_TS_QUOTAS	Tablespace quotas for all users
DBA_UPDATABLE_COLUMNS	Description of database updatable columns
DBA_USERS	Information about all users of the database
DBA_VIEWS	Text of all views in the database

Oracle Add-On Tables And Utility Scripts

Numerous scripts are housed in the $ORACLE_HOME/rdbms/admin directory on Unix and in the Orawin95 or orant\rdbms\Admin directories on Windows 95 and Windows NT. Many are automatically run by the catalog.sql and catproc.sql scripts during automated database builds or must be run manually during a manual build; others are optional. The optional scripts provide help in tuning the database, checking lock problems and adding useful tables that a DBA should know about.

The catalog.sql script creates all of the commonly used data dictionary views. Scripts, such as cataudit.sql (which creates the audit tables and is run by catproc.sql), have their antiscript, for example catnoaud.sql. Generally, an antiscript will have "no" embedded in its name.

The catproc.sql script also runs virtually all of the dbms*.sql and prvt*.sql scripts, such as dbmsutil.sql, which builds the **DBMS_APPLICATION_INFO** package and other useful utilities. The scripts that are considered extra but that are extremely useful are:

➤ **utlchain.sql** This creates the default table for storing the output of the **ANALYZE LIST CHAINED ROWS** command.

➤ **utldidxs.sql** This procedure has two parameters to allow DBAs to specify which statistics are desired out of **INDEX$INDEX_STATS** and **INDEX$BADNESS_STATS**.

➤ **utldtree.sql** This procedure, view, and temporary table will allow you to see all objects that are (recursively) dependent on the given object. Note that you'll only see objects for which you have permission.

➤ **utlbstat.sql and utlestat.sql** These are companion scripts. The utlestat.sql script generates the delta statistics based on the initial statistics loaded using utlbstat.sql. These scripts are used to generate the report.txt output file of statistics used for tuning.

➤ **utlexcpt.sql** This script creates the **EXCEPTIONS** table used to hold table entry information that causes conflicts when creating constraints. The rowid, table name, owner, and violated constraints are listed.

➤ **utllockt.sql** This script generates a simple lock wait-for graph. This script prints the sessions in the system that are waiting for locks and the locks that they are waiting for. The printout is tree structured. If a sessionid is printed immediately below and to the right of another session, it's waiting for that session. The sessionids printed on the left-hand side of the page are the ones everyone is waiting for.

➤ **dbmspool.sql and prvtpool.sql** These scripts build the **DBMS_SHARED_POOL** package of procedures for managing the shared pool. This package contains procedures for monitoring and pinning objects such as large packages or procedures in the shared pool.

➤ **utloidxs.sql** This procedure is used to find information about the selectivity of columns. Use it to:

- ➤ Identify prospective columns for new indexes.

- ➤ Determine how selective a current index is.

- ➤ Determine whether or not a current index is useful.

➤ **utlsidxs.sql** This script uses the utloidxs.sql script to analyze all indexes in a schema for usefulness.

➤ **utltkprf.sql** This script grants public access to all views used by TKPROF with **verbose=y** option, and it creates the TKPROFER role.

➤ **utlxplan.sql** This script creates the table (**PLAN_TABLE**) that is used by the **EXPLAIN PLAN** statement. The **EXPLAIN** statement used in the **SET AUTOTRACE ON** command in SQL*Plus requires the presence of this table to store the descriptions of the row sources. The data in the **PLAN_TABLE** is used to query and evaluate SQL statements using the **EXPLAIN** clause with the **AUTOTRACE** command, without using tracing and TKPROF.

➤ **catblock.sql** This script creates many useful views about database locks. These views are:

- ➤ **DBA_KGLLOCK**

- ➤ **DBA_LOCK** (with synonym **DBA_LOCKS**)

- ➤ **DBA_LOCK_INTERNAL**

- ➤ **DBA_DML_LOCKS**

- ➤ **DBA_DDL_LOCKS**

- ➤ **DBA_WAITERS**

- ➤ **DBA_BLOCKERS**

The creation of a database is not complete until several scripts have been run. These scripts create the data dictionary views and install the procedure options and utilities. The catalog.sql script creates the most commonly used data dictionary views and catproc.sql creates the procedural options and utilities (**DBMS_** packages). In addition to these "must have" scripts, you should also run the catblock.sql, the dbmspool.sql, and the prvtpool.sql scripts. I also suggest that the catparr.sql script, which installs the parallel server views, be run because some of these views are useful for tuning purposes.

The questions about the data dictionary and Oracle internals will mostly be in the realm of tuning and monitoring. The questions will generally be of the form "To find out X, what table/view/ structure do I query?" Your biggest problem will be that you'll tend to outsmart yourself. You'll say, "Naw, the answer can't be that, that's too easy." Remember, the data dictionary was designed to be easy to use (at least at the higher levels), so objects are named for the items they contain.

An example of what I'm talking about is the use of the **DBA_** views. If you review the listing showing the views and their uses, you should have noticed a trend: **DBA_TABLES** monitors all tables, **USER_TABLES** monitors a single user's tables, and **ALL_TABLES** monitors all tables a user has access to. Likewise, the **V$** views are named for the functions they perform: the **V$DBFILES** view shows database datafiles, **V$INSTANCE** gives instance-specific values, **V$SESSION** monitors sessions, and so forth. With a little experience, and by keeping your head, most of the answers can be derived from the questions.

Exam Prep Questions

Question 1

> If you query the **X$KCBRHB** virtual table, which value will the **COUNT** column display?
>
> ○ a. The number of blocks in the database buffer cache
> ○ b. The number of additional cache hits gained by adding additional cache blocks
> ○ c. The number of reads in the database buffer cache
> ○ d. The number of buffers added to the database buffer cache

Answer b is the correct choice. The **COUNT** column corresponds to the number of cache hits either gained or lost from the addition or removal of buffers. One row exists for each block monitored as determined by the least recently used (LRU) block statistics initialization parameters. If you remember that the "R" in **X$KCBRHB** stands for *raise* and the second "C" in **X$KCBCHB** stands for *chop*, it'll help you keep track of which table tracks raises (increases) and which table tracks chops (decreases) in the database block buffers.

Question 2

> Which data dictionary view would you query to display information related to profiles?
>
> ○ a. **RESOURCE_COST**
> ○ b. **USER_USERS**
> ○ c. **DBA_CONSTRAINTS**
> ○ d. **USER_CONSTRAINTS**

This is a trick question because it involves one of the few tables that doesn't reflect its true purpose, even though its name is accurate. To answer this question, you need to know what a profile is and that it uses values called resources. Once you know that a profile has resources assigned to it, there's only one possible answer and that's a, **RESOURCE_COST**.

Question 3

Which view could you query to display users with **CREATE PRO-CEDURE** privileges?

- ○ a. **DBA_USER_PRIVS**
- ○ b. **DBA_SYS_PRIVS**
- ○ c. **DBA_COL_PRIVS**
- ○ d. **USER_TAB_PRIVS_RECEIVED**

If you know that **CREATE PROCEDURE** is a **SYSTEM**-level privilege, you should know that will query the **DBA_SYS_PRIVS** view. Therefore, answer b is correct. This question could also be considered a trick question. A quick glance and a general knowledge of how Oracle names work might lead you to choose answer a, **DBA_USER_PRIVS**. However, this view doesn't exist. Once you eliminate a, you can also quickly eliminate answers c and d because they deal with column (**COL**) and table (**TAB**) privileges.

Question 4

Which category of data dictionary views does not have an **OWNER** column?

- ○ a. **USER_**
- ○ b. **DBA_**
- ○ c. **ALL_**
- ○ d. All categories of data dictionary views have an **OWNER** column

You should be able to quickly answer this one. You know that **DBA_** views show all objects for which they where created, and an **OWNER** column would be mandatory. Therefore, answer b is incorrect. Likewise, because the **ALL_** views show all objects for which a user has access, an **OWNER** column is required in this type of view as well. Therefore, answer c is incorrect. You should know answer d is incorrect. This leaves answer a, **USER_**. Because the **USER_** views are for objects in which the user is the owner, there's no need for an **OWNER** column.

Question 5

> Which data dictionary view could a user query to display the number of bytes charged to their username?
>
> ○ a. **ALL_USERS**
>
> ○ b. **USER_USERS**
>
> ○ c. **DBA_TS_QUOTAS**
>
> ○ d. **USER_TS_QUOTAS**
>
> ○ e. Only the DBA can display the number of bytes charged to a user

This question refers to a quota. Once you understand this, you can apply the naming convention rules. The question asks what data dictionary view can a *user* query. This means we're looking for a **USER_** view. Quotas are placed on tablespaces, so we're looking for a view for tablespaces (**TS_**) and one about quotas. The only view named that meets the above criteria is answer d, **USER_TS_QUOTAS**.

Notice that each time we have an answer like "only the DBA can do this," it's usually incorrect. In most cases, this will be true; beware of easy answers, they're almost always wrong!

Question 6

> Which view would you query to display the users who have been granted SYSDBA and SYSOPER system privileges?
>
> ○ a. **USER_USERS**
>
> ○ b. **ALL_USERS**
>
> ○ c. **V$PWFILE_USERS**
>
> ○ d. **DBA_USERS**

If you know the **DBA_USERS** view, you know that although it contains a username, default and **TEMP** tablespaces, profile assignment, and other user-related data, it contains no privilege information or grant information of any kind. Therefore, any views based on the **DBA_** view (USER_USERS or ALL_USERS) won't have any privilege or grant information. With these two tidbits, we've eliminated three of four answers. In this case, we are left with answer c, **V$PWFILE_USERS**. This view is new and is only used to identify users who've been granted SYSDBA and SYSOPER.

Question 7

Which script file creates the base data dictionary tables?

○ a. utlmontr.sql

○ b. catexp.sql

○ c. sql.bsq

○ d. cataud.sql

○ e. catproc.sql

Again, if we don't know the answer right off, with a little name sleuthing, we can eliminate what the answer is not. We should realize the utlmontr.sql is probably for utilities and concerns monitoring, obviously not data dictionary base tables. The catexp.sql script is probably about catalogs (that is, views or tables) and exports. Again, not a data dictionary base table-type item. The cataud.sql deals with a catalog and probably auditing. Finally, catproc.sql, I would venture an educated guess, concerns catalogs and procedures, not a base-level item. This leaves the sql.bsq script, answer c, which is, indeed, the answer. One way to remember that sql.bsq is about data dictionary base tables is to equate the "b" in bsq with base.

Question 8

Which package can you use to pin large objects in the library cache?

○ a. **STANDARD**

○ b. **DBMS_STANDARD**

○ c. **DIUTL**

○ d. **DBMS_SHARED_POOL**

This question requires you to remember that the library cache is another name for the shared pool. The only answer that concerns the shared pool is d, **DBMS_SHARED_POOL**.

Question 9

Which new Oracle version 7.3 fixed view can you query to get the status of media recovery?

○ a. **V$CONTROLFILE**

○ b. **V$RECOVERY_FILE_STATUS**

○ c. **V$DATAFILE**

○ d. **V$RECOVERY_STATUS**

In this question, you have to answer the question exactly. Both **V$RECOVERY_FILE_STATUS** and **V$RECOVERY_STATUS** show recovery status; we can eliminate the other **V$** DPTs shown by using name conventions. However, **V$RECOVERY_FILE_STATUS** shows the status of the database's datafiles during recovery. The **V$RECOVERY_STATUS** view shows the status of media recovery, so d is the correct answer.

Need To Know More?

 Ault, Michael R.: *Oracle8 Administration and Management.* John Wiley & Sons, 1998. ISBN 0-47119-234-1. For a comprehensive look at Oracle8 and Oracle7.x management, this book is great. Use it for the definitions of all **DBA_-**, **V$-**, and data dictionary-related topics.

 Corrigan, Peter and Mark Gurry: *Oracle Performance Tuning.* O'Reilly & Associates, Inc., December 1993. ISBN 1-56592-048-1. This book is an excellent tuning reference and also a source of information on the use of the **V$** tables.

 Oracle7 Server Reference Manual. Oracle Corporation, January 1996. Part Number A32589-1. This Oracle manual provides information about the **V$** views, **DBA_** views, and the **X$** tables and their uses.

Data Definition Language

4

Terms you'll need to understand:

√ Storage

√ DDL

√ INITIAL

√ NEXT

√ PCTINCREASE

√ PCTFREE

√ PCTUSED

√ INITRANS

√ MAXTRANS

√ Initial extents

√ MAXEXTENTS

√ CREATE

Techniques you'll need to master:

√ Using all storage parameters

√ Using CREATE command for all objects

The OCP exam covers the storage parameters and their various uses in great detail. A DBA must know all of the ins and outs of the storage parameters, particularly those dealing with the prevention of chaining and fragmentation.

Data Definition Language (DDL) includes all commands used to create, alter, and drop database objects. These include tables, indexes, clusters, sequences, triggers, procedures, functions, and packages (including package bodies). The **CREATE** command is used to create all of these objects (with differing modifiers and options). Likewise for those objects that can be modified. The **ALTER** command is used to alter database objects, and the **DROP** command is used to drop them. This first DDL chapter is dedicated to the most complex of these command sets, the **CREATE** commands.

The CREATE Command

The **CREATE** command is used to make all database objects. It and its optional **STORAGE** clause will be the subject of most of the DDL-related questions on the examination. The following shows the syntax of the generic **CREATE** command:

```
CREATE <modifier> object_type object_name
create options,
        STORAGE (storage parameters)
```

The CREATE Command For Databases

All things in an Oracle database reside in the database. Therefore, the first **CREATE** command we'll discuss is the **CREATE DATABASE** command. To use the command, some systems require the user to have the OSDBA or SYSDBA role. Figure 4.1 shows the format for this command.

The parameters have the following definitions:

➤ **database_name** Name of the database comprised of a maximum of eight characters.

➤ **AUTOEXTEND** Used to allow your datafiles to automatically extend as needed. Be very careful with this command because it can use up a great deal of disk space rather rapidly if a mistake is made during table builds or inserts.

Note: File specifications for log files depend on the operating system.

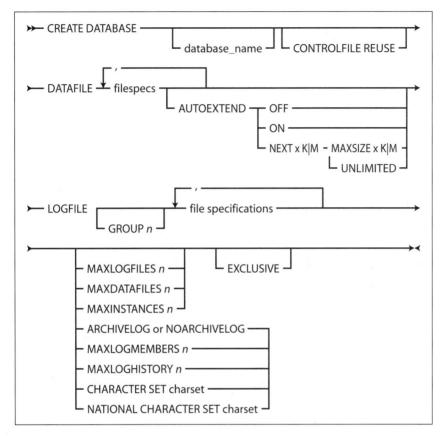

Figure 4.1   The Syntax for the **CREATE DATABASE** command.

➤ **MAXLOGFILES, MAXDATAFILES, and MAXINSTANCES** Sets hard limits for the database and should be set to the maximum you ever expect.

➤ **MAXLOGMEMBERS and MAXLOGHISTORY** Hard limits.

➤ **CHARACTER SET** Determines the character set that data will be stored in. This value is operating system-dependent.

➤ **ARCHIVELOG** Used to set archive logging.

➤ **NOARCHIVELOG** Used if you don't need to set archive logging.

➤ **EXCLUSIVE or PARALLEL** Databases are either **EXCLUSIVE** or **PARALLEL** mode. A database must be altered into **PARALLEL** mode after creation. **EXCLUSIVE** mode sets the database so that only one instance of Oracle at a time has access. **PARALLEL** mode allows one or more instances to have access to the same database but requires an additional license purchase from Oracle.

➤ **NATIONAL CHARACTER SET** Specifies the national character set used to store data in columns specifically defined as **NCHAR** or **NVARCHAR2**. You can't change the national character set after creating the database. If not specified, the national character set defaults to the database character set.

The **CREATE DATABASE** command allows initial specification of database maximum values, such as the maximum allowed number of database datafiles, log files, and log file groups. It also allows for specification of the initial database datafile for the **SYSTEM** tablespace.

The CREATE Command For Tablespaces

All objects in an Oracle database are stored in *tablespaces*, which are the unit of logical storage for an Oracle database. The **CREATE TABLESPACE** command allows you to create a tablespace and one or more initial datafiles. It also permits specification of default storage parameters. Figure 4.2 shows the **CREATE TABLESPACE** syntax.

The following are the keywords and parameters of the **CREATE TABLESPACE** command:

➤ **tablespace_name** Name of the tablespace to be created.

➤ **DATAFILE** Specifies the datafile or files to compose the tablespace.

➤ **MINEXTENTS** Integer that controls free space fragmentation in the tablespace by ensuring that every used and/or free extent size in a tablespace is at least as large as and is a multiple of the integer. (**MINEXTENTS** is located in the **storage_clause** parameter.)

➤ **AUTOEXTEND** Enables or disables the automatic extension of the datafile.

➤ **OFF** Disables **AUTOEXTEND** if it's turned on. **NEXT** and **MAXSIZE** are set to zero. After **AUTOEXTEND** is disabled, to re-enable the feature, values for **NEXT** and **MAXSIZE** must be specified again in further **ALTER TABLESPACE AUTOEXTEND** commands.

➤ **ON** Enables **AUTOEXTEND**.

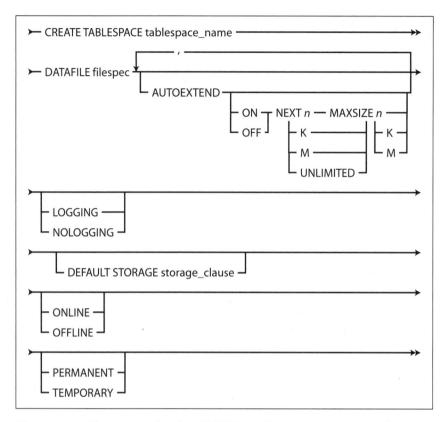

Figure 4.2   The syntax for the **CREATE TABLESPACE** command.

➤ **NEXT** Specifies disk space to allocate to the datafile when more extents are required.

➤ **MAXSIZE** Specifies the maximum disk space allowed for allocation to the datafile.

➤ **UNLIMITED** Tells Oracle to set no limit on allocating disk space to the datafile.

➤ **LOGGING/NOLOGGING** Specifies the default logging attributes of all tables, indexes, and partitions within the tablespace. **LOGGING** is the default. If **NOLOGGING** is specified, no undo and redo logs are generated for operations that support the **NOLOGGING** option on the tables, indexes, and partitions within the tablespace. The tablespace-level logging attribute can be overridden by logging specifications at the table, index, and partition levels.

➤ **DEFAULT STORAGE** Specifies the default storage parameters for all objects created in the tablespace.

➤ **ONLINE** Makes the tablespace available immediately after creation to users who have been granted access to the tablespace.

➤ **OFFLINE** Makes the tablespace unavailable immediately after creation.

*Note: If you omit both the **ONLINE** and **OFFLINE** options, Oracle creates the tablespace online by default. The data dictionary view **DBA_TABLESPACES** indicates whether each tablespace is online or offline.*

➤ **PERMANENT** Specifies that the tablespace will be used to hold permanent objects. This is the default.

➤ **TEMPORARY** Specifies that the tablespace will only be used to hold temporary objects, for example, segments used by implicit sorts to handle **ORDER BY** clauses.

The major decisions in the **CREATE TABLESPACE** command are the placement of the datafiles and the specification of the default storage options. You should be familiar with file placement and what happens to objects created using the default storage options. The **STORAGE** clause and its options are shown in Figure 4.3.

The following are the definitions for the parameters shown in Figure 4.3:

➤ **INITIAL** Size in bytes of the initial extent of the object segment. The default is 10,240 bytes. The minimum is 4,096 bytes, the maximum 4,095 megabytes. All values are rounded to the nearest Oracle block size.

➤ **NEXT** Size for the next extent after **INITIAL** is used. The default is 5 blocks, the minimum is 1 block, the maximum is 4,095 megabytes. This is the value that will be used for each new extent if **PCTINCREASE** is set to 0.

➤ **MINEXTENTS** Number of initial extents for the object. Generally, except for rollback segments, it's set to 1. If a large amount of space is required and if there's not enough contiguous space for the table setting, a smaller extent size and specifying several extents may solve the problem.

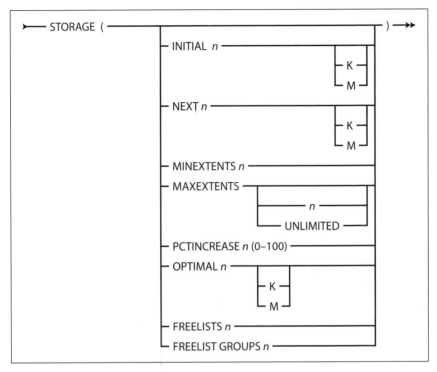

Figure 4.3   The syntax for the **STORAGE** clause.

➤ **MAXEXTENTS** Largest number of extents allowed for the object. This defaults to the maximum allowed for your block size.

➤ **PCTINCREASE** Parameter that tells Oracle how much to grow each extent after the **INITIAL** and **NEXT** extents are used. A specification of 50 will grow each extent after **NEXT** by 50 percent for each subsequent extent. This means that for a table created with one initial and a next extent, any further extents will increase in size by 50 percent over their predecessor. In Oracle7.2 and later versions, this parameter is only applied against the size of the previous extent. Increase this value if you don't know how much the table will grow, only that it will grow significantly. The value of **PCTINCREASE** indicates a growth *rate* for subsequent extents. A tablespace with a default storage setting for **PCTINCREASE** of zero will not be automatically coalesced.

➤ **OPTIMAL** Used only for rollback segments and specifies the value to which a rollback segment will shrink after extending.

➤ **FREELIST GROUPS** Parameter that specifies the number of freelist groups to maintain for a table or index.

➤ **FREELISTS** For objects other than tablespaces, specifies the number of freelists for each of the freelist groups for the table, index, or cluster. The minimum value is 1 and the maximum is block-size dependent. This parameter is generally only meaningful for parallel server databases.

Tablespaces are subject to fragmentation as their chief space-related problem. As tables are created and dropped, rollback segments grow and are shrunk back to optimal or indexes are reorganized and rebuilt, and all of these result in extents being allocated or dropped. This frequent deallocation of extents results in fragmented tablespaces. We'll discuss the **ALTER TABLESPACE** command in the **ALTER** command section that will allow coalescence of contiguous free space areas (deallocated extents that lie next to each other).

The CREATE Command For Tables

Tables are structures in an Oracle database that contain header and data sections. The segment header contains freelist information, the block header contains transaction entries, and the row header contains row length (1 byte if less than 256 bytes, otherwise 3 bytes if longer than 256 bytes) and datatype indicators. The data, or row sections, contain the actual data values. The header grows from the bottom up while the data area grows from the top down.

Table placement in relation to other database objects is important for optimal database performance. You should attempt to minimize contention by placing tables away from their associated indexes and away from other I/O-intensive database objects such as redo logs and rollback segments.

For some large tables, you may want to consider manual striping against several disks. However, this is a labor-intensive operation, and before considering its use, you must thoroughly understand how your data is used. This manual striping of tables involves manually striping tablespace datafiles across several disks, then sizing the table extents such that they just fill a single tablespace datafile.

Because all other database objects either depend completely on tables for existence (such as indexes) or operate against tables (functions, procedures, packages) or provide data for tables (sequences), it makes sense to discuss the **CREATE** command in relation to tables next. Figure 4.4 shows the **CREATE TABLE** command syntax.

The following are the definitions for the specified parameters:

➤ **table_name** Formatted as either user.name or just the name, defaulting to the current user. This must be a unique user name. This unique name applies to tables, views, synonyms, clusters, and indexes. For uniqueness,

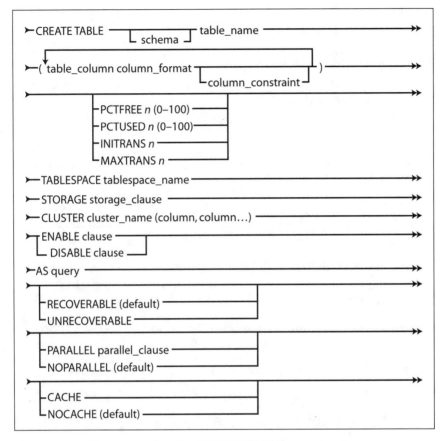

Figure 4.4 The syntax for the **CREATE TABLE** command.

the user portion counts. The name must begin with a letter (unless surrounded by quotes) and must not contain the characters "%", "*", ";", ":", or "@" because these are used in Oracle commands; the pound sign "#", underscore "_" or dollar sign "$" can be used in Oracle table names.

➤ **table_column** A unique name by table. The column name can be up to 30 characters long and can't contain a quotation, slash, or character other than A to Z, 0 to 9, _, $, and #. A column name must not duplicate an Oracle reserved word (see the SQL manual for a list of these words). To use mixed case, include the mixed-case portion in quotation marks. Here are some example of column names:

➤ EMP

➤ CATS

➤ AUTHOR.EXPENSES

➤ **"SELECT"** (Even though **SELECT** is a reserved word, if it's enclosed in quotes it's okay to use.)

➤ **"OPEN AND CLOSE"** (Even spaces are allowed with quotes.)

Names should be meaningful, not a bunch of symbols like A, B, C, and so forth. The Oracle CASE and Designer products always make the names of tables plural; if you'll be using CASE or Designer, you'll want to follow this convention.

➤ **column_format** One of the allowed SQL datatypes. They're listed in the SQL manual. A brief list is:

➤ **CHAR(size)** Character-type data; max size 255 bytes. Under Oracle7, **CHAR** will be right-side padded to specified length. It defaults to 1 byte if the value for size is not specified.

➤ **VARCHAR2(size)** Variable-length character up to 2,000 bytes. It must have length specification when declared because it has no default size.

➤ **DATE** Date format from 1/1/4712 B.C. to 12/31/4712 A.D. Standard Oracle format is (10-APR-99).

➤ **LONG** Character up to 65,535 bytes long. Only one **LONG** per table.

➤ **RAW(size)** Raw binary data, max of 2,000 bytes under Oracle7.

➤ **LONG RAW** Raw binary data in hexadecimal format, two gigabytes maximum.

➤ **ROWID** Internal data type, not user definable. Used to uniquely identify table rows.

➤ **NUMBER(p,s)** Numeric data with p being precision and s being scale. Defaults to 38 p, null s.

➤ **DECIMAL(p,s)** Same as numeric.

➤ **INTEGER** Defaults to **NUMBER(38)**, no scale.

➤ **SMALLINT** Same as **INTEGER**.

➤ **FLOAT** Same as **NUMBER(38)**.

➤ **FLOAT(b)** **NUMBER** with precision of 1 to 126.

➤ **REAL** Same as **NUMBER(63)**.

➤ **DOUBLE PRECISION** Same as **NUMBER(38)**. If no scale is specified for numeric datatypes where it's allowed, then the value is treated as a floating point.

➤ **column_constraint** Used to specify *constraints*. Constraints are limits placed either on a table or column.

➤ **CONSTRAINT** Name constraint type. Constraints also may be of the form:

   ➤ **NULL CONSTRAINT** constraint_name

   ➤ **NOT NULL CONSTRAINT** constraint_name

   ➤ **PRIMARY KEY CONSTRAINT** constraint_name

   ➤ **UNIQUE CONSTRAINT** constraint_name

   ➤ **CHECK** condition **CONSTRAINT** constraint_name

   ➤ **REFERENCES** table_name (column_name) **CONSTRAINT** constraint_name

   ➤ **DEFAULT** default_value_clause

In these formats, the **CONSTRAINT constraint_name** is optional. There can be unlimited **CHECK**-type constraints per column and a **NOT NULL** is converted internally into a **CHECK** constraint by Oracle. A **CHECK** constraint requires that a condition be true or unknown for each value in the column it affects. They're the only constraints allowed to call system functions such as **USER** or **SYSDATE**. **NOT NULL** constraints can only be defined at the column level. Constraints can be added, enabled, disabled, or dropped.

Tables may also have the additional constraints, as seen here:

```
FOREIGN KEY (column, column)
     REFERENCES table_name (column, column)
     CONSTRAINT constraint_name
   PRIMARY KEY (column, column)
     USING INDEX TABLEPACE tablespace_name
     STORAGE (storage_clause)
     CONSTRAINT constraint_name
```

The foreign key constraint is enforced such that its values must match its corresponding primary or unique key values. However, no index is automatically generated. It's suggested that indexes be maintained on foreign keys or excessive full table scans may result. A primary key will automatically have an index-generated named for the constraint. A primary key automatically forces its column or columns to be not null and if a single column—unique, and for a composite set of columns—

the resulting set must be unique. Foreign and primary key constraints are referred to as referential constraints. Referential integrity violations occur when a parent record is deleted and children records still exist: Orphan records are not permitted in the child table of a parent-child relationship where primary and foreign key constraints are in place.

User-defined constraints are used to enforce business rules. Constraints that enforce typing (such as inserts of number-into-number columns) are column constraints and are generally enforced with no action on the part of the DBA or designer.

Declarative constraints, though they provide instant feedback to the users, can make it difficult to get an overview of what declarative constraints are in effect on the database.

➤ **PCTFREE** Parameter that tells Oracle how much space to leave in each Oracle block for future updates and the addition of new rows. This defaults to 10 percent. If a table will have a large number of updates, a larger value is needed; if the table will be static, a small value can be used. This is very table- and table-usage-specific. Improper specification can result in chaining (if set too low) or improper space usage (the table will require more blocks if this is set too high), and both result in performance degradation. If a table is updated frequently, set this value high; if it's updated infrequently, set this value low. If a block's free space drops below **PCTFREE**, it's removed from the freelist.

You must understand row chaining (row migration). Row chaining is caused when a row is updated and there is insufficient space available to insert the new data. Row migration usually happens with **VARCHAR2** and **NUMBER** types that can vary in size but more so with **VARCHAR2**. Other datatypes that may vary in length (such as **RAW**, **LONG**, and **LONG RAW**) can also cause row chaining. Row chaining causes Oracle to have to perform multiple disk reads to get a single row, most times forcing the read head for the disk to jump from a smooth read to reading all over the disk. This increase in disk I/O can cause extreme performance degradation. A large value for **PCTFREE** can reduce or eliminate row chaining, but can also reduce increased storage requirements. Remember that unless the **PCTUSED** and **PCTFREE** are set so their sum exactly equals 100, an increase or decrease in one may have no affect on the other.

➤ **PCTUSED** Parameter that tells Oracle the minimum level of space to maintain in a block. **PCTUSED** defaults to 40. A block becomes a candidate for updates if its storage falls below **PCTUSED**. This parameter only applies for **DELETE** DML activity because a block is not placed on the updatable list until **PCTUSED** is reached from deletion activity. If a table has frequent inserts and updates, then **PCTUSED** should be set low. If the value for **PCTFREE** is left at 10 percent and **PCTUSED** is set high, there may be an increase in processing costs due to freelist maintenance.

The sum of **PCTFREE** and **PCTUSED** may not exceed 100. A high **PCTUSED** value can result in more efficient space utilization but higher overhead as Oracle must work harder to maintain the free block list. Also, having a big **PCTFREE** and low **PCTUSED** will result in more unused space in a block and inefficient storage. Unfortunately, once improperly specified, the only solution to correct the resulting problems in existing blocks is to rebuild the affected table or cluster.

➤ **INITRANS** Specifies the initial number of active transactions that are allocated within each block. A large value will reduce the amount of space available for data in a block. A change to this parameter only affects blocks added after the change.

➤ **MAXTRANS** Specifies the maximum number of active transactions that can update a block concurrently.

*Note: Together **INITRANS** and **MAXTRANS** determine the number of active transactions that can access a single block concurrently.*

➤ **TABLESPACE** Specifies the tablespace if other than the user's default.

➤ **STORAGE** Specifies the storage options for the objects in a tablespace if this is a default storage specification. These values determine how extents will be allocated for tables, clusters, and indexes.

➤ **CLUSTER** Specifies the table is to be part of the specified cluster through the specified columns. **PCTFREE, PCTUSED,** and **TABLESPACE** options will produce errors when used with the **CLUSTER** clause.

➤ **ENABLE/DISABLE** Enable or disable constraints or triggers for a table.

➤ **RECOVERABLE/UNRECOVERABLE** Determines if the operation that creates the table should generate redo/rollback data or simply fail in the event of a problem.

➤ **PARALLEL parallel_clause/NOPARALLEL** Sets the default parallelism of the table (for a parallel query situation, sets how many processes will be used).

➤ **CACHE/NOCACHE** Tells Oracle whether or not to cache the table in the SGA.

As you can see, there are myriad modifiers and options added to the basic **CREATE** command.

The **CREATE** Command For Indexes

Indexes can be created implicitly, such as with specification of unique or primary key constraints, or explicitly with the **CREATE INDEX** command. Only normal, B-tree-type indexes are created by default. Normally (except in the case of **BITMAPPED** indexes), you should only index a column or set of columns that contain a wide range of values. If a table is small, an index may decrease the speed of a query against it because small tables may be cached in memory or may better be searched with a full table scan. The format for the **CREATE INDEX** command is shown in Figure 4.5.

The definitions for the specified parameters are:

➤ **index_name** User unique index name.

➤ **table_name** Name of the table to be indexed. The table must exist.

➤ **column_name** Name of the column to include in the index, up to a maximum of 16 columns. If more than one column is used, the index is said to be a composite or concatenated index. Concatenated indexes are

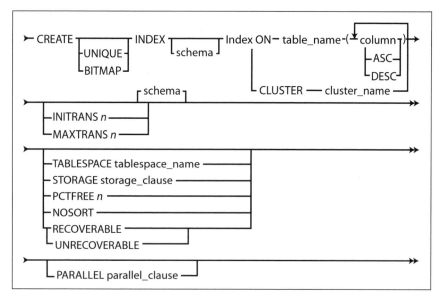

Figure 4.5 The syntax for the **CREATE INDEX** command.

generally used to increase performance of a specific query. The order of a concatenated key is important. Only queries that access columns in this order will use the index. For example, table **EXAMPLE** has 16 columns. The first three are used as the concatenated index. Only queries that contain columns 1,2,3 or 1,2 or 1 will use the index.

➤ **tablespace_name** Name of the tablespace in which to store the index.

➤ **storage_clause** Standard storage clause (except **FREELIST GROUPS** is not allowed).

➤ **NOSORT** Tells Oracle not to sort the index. It should only be used if the table is already loaded into Oracle in ascending order.

➤ **RECOVERABLE/UNRECOVERABLE** Used to tell Oracle whether to generate redo/rollback information. For large index creates, it's suggested that the **UNRECOVERABLE** option be used to speed index creation. However, any index can be created as unrecoverable if desired.

➤ **UNIQUE** Causes Oracle to enforce uniqueness of the entire key. If **UNIQUE** is left out, the index is nonunique. In Oracle7, the primary key and unique key constraints automatically generate the required indexes.

➤ **BITMAP** Causes the index to be stored as a bitmap and should only be used for low cardinality data such as sex, race, and so forth. A **BITMAP** index has a substantial reduction of space usage compared to other types of indexes. The option is only available as beta in pre-7.3.2.2 releases (7.3 only) and is bundled with the parallel query option. Several initialization parameters are required to use the option in earlier versions of 7.3, including the following parameters to turn on bitmapped indexes (which must be set regardless of version):

➤ **COMPATIBLE** set to 7.3.2 or higher

➤ **V733_PLANS_ENABLED** set to **TRUE**

In addition, specific events (commands that turn on specific pieces of code in the Oracle kernel) must be set for bitmapped indexes to work, as seen here:

```
event = "10111 trace name context forever"
    event = "10112 trace name context forever"
    event = "10114 trace name context forever"
```

➤ **PCTFREE** Parameter that specifies the amount of space reserved for insertion of additional index entries into an existing block.

When the **CREATE INDEX** command is used to create a cluster index, an additional type of index known as a *cluster index* can be created. The cluster index is created against the cluster key that can have a maximum of 16 columns assigned to it. We'll discuss more about clusters and their peculiarities in the next section.

The CREATE Command For Clusters

A cluster can be used when several tables store a row that's of the same datatype and size in the same location. This reduces storage requirements and, in some cases, can speed access to data. The major drawback is that, in operations involving updates, inserts, and deletes, performance degradation can occur. The DBA should look at the expected mix of transaction types on the tables to be clustered and only cluster those that are frequently joined and those that don't have numerous updates, inserts, and deletes.

Clusters store shared data values in the same physical blocks (the cluster key values). For tables that are frequently joined, this can speed access; for tables frequently accessed separately, joining is not the answer. An exception is when a single table is clustered. A single table cluster forces the key values for that table into a single set of blocks, thus, accesses of that table can be sped up. Usually this single table clustering also uses a hash structure to further improve access times.

Oracle7 added an additional cluster feature: the ability to specify a hash cluster. A hash cluster uses a hash form of storage and no index. Hash structures should only be used for static tables. *Hashing* is the process in which a value, either of a unique or nonunique row, is used to generate a hash value. This hash value is used to place the row into the hashed table. To retrieve the row, the value is simply recalculated. Hashes can only by used for equality operations. The syntax of the **CREATE CLUSTER** command is shown in Figure 4.6.

The specified parameters are as follows:

➤ **cluster_name** Name for the cluster. If the user has DBA privileges, a user name may be specified (user.cluster).

➤ **(column datatype, column datatype...)** List of columns and their datatypes called the cluster key. The names for the columns do not have to match the table column names, but the datatypes, lengths, and precisions do have to match.

➤ *n* An integer (not all of the *n*'s are the same value, *n* is just used for convenience).

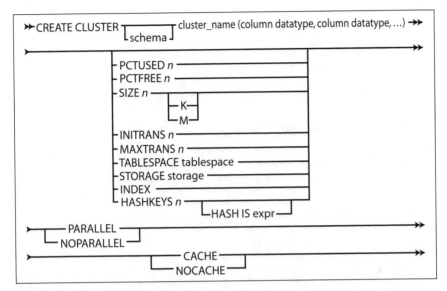

Figure 4.6 The syntax for the **CREATE CLUSTER** command.

➤ **SIZE** Expected size of the average cluster. This is calculated by 19 + (sum of column lengths) + (1 × number of columns).

SIZE should be rounded up to the nearest equal divisor of your block size. For example, if your block size is 2,048 and the cluster length is 223, round up to 256. This, along with **HASHKEYS**, will limit the number of cluster keys stored in a single data block. If **SIZE** is small, then the number of keys that can be assigned to a single block will increase, allowing many keys to be assigned to a single block. If you have very few rows for a cluster key, set **SIZE** to a small value to minimize wasted space in the data block.

➤ **STORAGE** Used as the default for the tables in the cluster.

➤ **INDEX** Specifies to create an indexed cluster (default).

➤ **HASH IS** Specifies to create a hash cluster. The specified column must be a zero-precision number.

➤ **HASHKEYS** Creates a hash cluster and specifies the number (n) of keys. The value is rounded up to the nearest prime number. This value, along with **SIZE**, will limit the number of keys stored in a single data block. The number of hash values generated will be **HASHKEYS+1**.

➤ **PCTFREE** Parameter for clusters that applies only to the cluster and not to the individual tables in the cluster.

The other parameters are the same as for the **CREATE TABLE** command.

To create a cluster, follow these steps:

1. First, create the cluster.

2. Create the cluster index by using the following snippet:

```
CREATE INDEX index_name ON CLUSTER cluster_name
```

*Note: You don't specify the columns. This is taken from the **CREATE CLUSTER** command that was used to create the named cluster.*

3. Create the tables that will be in the cluster by using the following:

```
CREATE TABLE cluster_table
(column_list)
CLUSTER cluster_name (cluster column(s))
```

In this instance, *cluster table* is a table name for a table that will be a part of the cluster, and *column list* is a list of columns for the table, specified identically to the **CREATE TABLE** command's normal format.

Remember, the cluster columns don't have to have the same name but must be the same datatype, size, and precision and must be specified in the same order as the columns in the **CREATE CLUSTER** command.

The CREATE Command For Sequences

Sequences allow for automatic generation of sequential nonrepeating or, if you desire, repeating integer values for use in keys or wherever numbers of this type should be used. Sequences can be either positive or negative in value and can range from 10e-27 to (10e27)-1 in value. The way in which a sequence increments can be controlled, as can the number of values cached for performance reasons in the SGA of an instance. The syntax of the **CREATE SEQUENCE** command is shown in Figure 4.7.

The specified parameters are defined as follows:

➤ **sequence_name** The name you want the sequence to have. This may include the user name if created from an account with DBA privileges.

➤ *n* An integer, positive or negative.

➤ **INCREMENT BY** Tells the system how to increment the sequence. If it's positive, the values are ascending; if it's negative, values are descending.

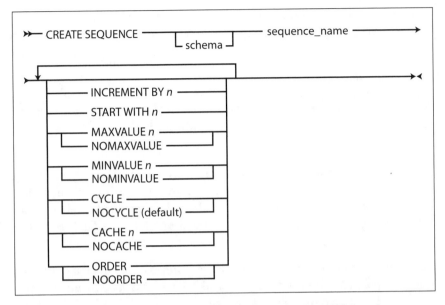

Figure 4.7 The syntax for the **CREATE SEQUENCE** command.

➤ **START WITH** Tells the system what integer to start with.

➤ **MINVALUE** Tells the system how low the sequence can go. For ascending sequences, it defaults to 1; for descending sequences, the default value is 10e27-1.

➤ **MAXVALUE** Tells the system the highest value that will be allowed. For descending sequences, the default is 1; for ascending sequences, the default is 10e27-1.

➤ **CYCLE** Causes the sequence to automatically recycle to **MINVALUE** when **MAXVAULE** is reached for ascending sequences; for descending sequences, it will cause recycle from **MINVALUE** back to **MAXVALUE**.

➤ **CACHE** Will cache the specified number of sequence values into the buffers in the SGA. This speeds access, but all cached numbers are lost when the database is shut down. Default value is 20, maximum value is **MAXVALUE - MINVALUE**.

➤ **ORDER** Forces sequence numbers to be output in order of request. In cases where they are used for time stamping, this may be required. In most cases, the sequence numbers will be in order anyway, and **ORDER** is not required.

Sequences avoid the performance problems associated with sequencing numbers generated by application triggers of the form, as seen here:

```
DECLARE
    TEMP_NO NUMBER;
BEGIN
    LOCK TABLE PO_NUM IN EXCLUSIVE MODE NOWAIT;
    SELECT MAX(PO_NUM)+1 INTO TEMP_NO FROM SALES;
END;
```

If the application requires numbers that are exactly in sequence (that is, 1,2,3, and so on), this trigger may be your only recourse, because if a statement that references a sequence is rolled back (canceled), that sequence number is lost. Likewise, any cached sequence numbers are lost each time a database is shut down.

Sequences can't be accessed directly; they can only have their values retrieved using the pseudocolumns **CURRVAL** and **NEXTVAL**. The pseudocolumns can either be selected from **DUAL** into a holding variable in PL/SQL or from the table being inserted (via the **VALUES** clause) into or updated (in the **SET** clause). A value must first be accessed via the **NEXTVAL** pseudocolumn before the **CURRVAL** pseudocolumn can be accessed.

Uses And Restrictions Of **CURRVAL** And **NEXTVAL**

Sequence **CURRVAL** and **NEXTVAL** are used:

➤ With the **VALUES** clause on an **INSERT** command.

➤ With the **SELECT** subclause of a **SELECT** command.

➤ In the **SET** clause of an **UPDATE** command.

CURRVAL and **NEXTVAL** cannot be used:

➤ In a subquery.

➤ In a view or snapshot query.

➤ With a **DISTINCT** clause.

➤ With **GROUP BY** or **ORDER BY**.

➤ In a **SELECT** command in combination with another.

➤ In the **WHERE** clause.

➤ In the **DEFAULT** column value in a **CREATE TABLE** or **ALTER TABLE** command.

➤ In a **CHECK** in a constraint.

The **CREATE** Command For Views

Views are stored queries in Oracle that can be treated as tables. Until fairly recently, views were essentially read only. Now, with certain caveats, views can be updatable. They're used to hide or to enhance data structures, make complex queries easier to manage, and enforce security requirements. Figure 4.8 shows the syntax for the **CREATE VIEW** command.

The specified parameters are defined as follows:

➤ **view_name** Name for the view.

➤ **alias** Valid column name. It isn't required to be the same as the column it's based on. If aliases aren't used, the names of the columns are used. If a column is modified by an expression, it must be aliased. If four columns are in the query, there must be four aliases.

➤ **subquery** Any valid **SELECT** statement that doesn't include an **ORDER BY** or **FOR UPDATE** clause. A view can only be based on one or more tables and/or views.

➤ **WITH CHECK OPTION** Specifies that inserts and updates through the view must be selectable from the view. This can be used in a view based on a view.

➤ **READ ONLY** Specifies that the view is read only and can't be changed by using the **INSERT, UPDATE,** and **DELETE** operations.

➤ **CONSTRAINT** Specifies the name associated with the **CHECK OPTION** constraint.

➤ **FORCE** Specifies that the view be created even if all permissions or objects it specifies as part of the view aren't available. Before the view can be used, the permissions or objects must be in the database and accessible. **NO FORCE** is the default option.

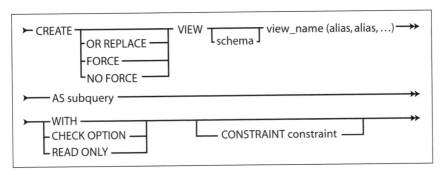

Figure 4.8   The syntax for the **CREATE VIEW** command.

➤ **NO FORCE (default)** Means all objects and permissions must be in place before the view can be created.

A view can usually be used in the following commands:

➤ **COMMENT**

➤ **DELETE**

➤ **INSERT**

➤ **LOCK TABLE**

➤ **UPDATE**

➤ **SELECT**

A view's **SELECT** statement in the subquery can't select a **CURRVAL** or **NEXTVAL** from a sequence or directly access **ROWID, ROWNUM,** or **LEVEL** pseudocolumns. To use the pseudocolumns for a table, a view select must alias them.

A view is just a window to data; it can't store data itself. Views can be used in a SQL statement just like a table.

You can't update a view if it does one of the following:

➤ Contains a join

➤ Contains a **GROUP BY, CONNECT BY,** or **START WITH** clause

➤ Contains a **DISTINCT** clause or expressions like AMOUNT+10 in the column list

➤ Doesn't reference all **NOT NULL** columns in the table (all **NOT NULLs** must be in the view and assigned a value by the update)

You can update a view that contains pseudocolumns or columns modified by expressions if the update doesn't affect these columns.

You can query the view, **USER_UPDATABLE_COLUMNS,** to find out if the columns in a join view are updatable. Generally speaking, as long as all of the **NOT NULLs** and key columns are included in a join view for a table, then that table may be updatable through the view.

A join view can have the commands **INSERT, UPDATE,** and **DELETE** used against it if:

➤ The DML affects only one of the tables in the join.

➤ For **UPDATE,** all of the columns updated are extracted from a key preserved table. In addition, if the view has a **CHECK OPTION**

constraint, join columns and columns taken from tables that are referenced more than once in the view are shielded from update.

➤ For **DELETE**, there is one and only one key-preserved table in the join,
and that table can be present more than once if there is no **CHECK
OPTION** constraint on the view.

➤ For **INSERT**, all of the columns are from a key-preserved table, and the
views don't have a **CHECK OPTION** constraint.

As with all stored objects, to create a view, the user must have direct grants on
all objects that are a part of the view, including those objects that may be used
in views that are used in the new view. The grants used to create a view can't be
from a role; they must be direct grants.

Partition Views

Oracle7.3 provides a new type of view called the *partition view*. The partition
view joins several tables with identical structure into a single entity that can be
queried as if all of the component parts were actually in one table. The purpose
for a partition view is to allow physical partitioning of data into several table
partitions. These table partitions are hand built by the DBA to spread data
across several disk volumes and to separate data by a preset algorithm that is
application-controlled. An example would be an application that breaks sales
data down by month and stores it in independent monthly sales tables. A par-
titioned view could be created to join all of the monthly sales tables in quarterly,
yearly, or whatever views of all sales for that period.

To create a partition view, follow these steps:

1. Create the tables that will compose the view or alter existing tables.

2. Give each table a constraint that limits the values that may be stored in
   the table.

3. Create an index on the constrained columns of each table.

4. Create the partition view as a series of **SELECT** statements that are
   combined using the **UNION ALL** join. The view should select all
   underlying columns from all tables (that is, there should be identical
   columns in all of the tables making up the view).

5. If parallel query is available, specify that the view is parallel so all tables
   in the view are scanned in parallel rather than serially. This is accomplished by one or more of the following:

   ➤ Specify parallel for all underlying tables.

   ➤ Give a "parallel" hint in the select statement for the view.

There is no special syntax or partition clause for the **CREATE VIEW**. To create a partition view, Oracle7 interprets a **UNION ALL** of several tables, each of which have identical local indexes on the same columns as a partition view.

CREATE Command For Synonyms

Synonyms are a database shorthand that allow long, complex combinations of schema, object name, and connection strings to be reduced to a simple alias. They remove the requirement to prefix a table, view, or sequence with a schema name, thus performing a simple type of data hiding by allowing tables from one or more schemas to appear to be located in the user's schema. The **CREATE SYNONYM** command syntax is shown in Figure 4.9.

The specified parameters are defined as follows:

➤ **PUBLIC** Creates a public synonym that can be used by all users. Usually only DBAs create public synonyms.

➤ **synonym_name** Name or alias you want the object to assume.

➤ **schema** Schema in which the object resides.

➤ **object_name** Actual name of the object on which the synonym is being created.

➤ **@dl** Database link that's only used if the object resides in another database.

Views can cause poor performance if nested too deeply. This can easily occur when they're created against the **DBA_**, **USER_**, or **ALL_** views.

CREATE Command For Rollback Segments

Rollback segments store system undo data, allowing noncommitted transactions to be rolled back. They can be likened to before-image logs or journals in other database systems. Rollback segments store the before images of changed data. Large transaction failures can usually be attributed to the following rollback-related problems:

➤ Inadequate space in the rollback segment (usually named RBS) tablespace for rollback segment expansion.

➤ Improper storage specifications for the rollback segment being used, resulting in that segment exceeding its **MAXEXTENTS** value.

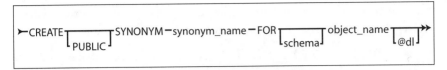

Figure 4.9   The syntax for the **CREATE SYNONYM** command.

➤ Improper scheduling, allowing other transactions to cause Snapshot Too Old errors to occur in the transaction (which can also be caused by improper **INITRANS** setting).

In addition to the **SYSTEM** rollback segment created when the database is built for use strictly by the **SYSTEM** tablespace, there must be at least one additional rollback segment created. Usually, the number of private rollback segments is calculated by determining how many concurrent users will access the database and deciding how many users should be assigned to each rollback segment (by specifying the **MINEXTENTS** value). For example, if you have 100 concurrent users and you want (on the average) 20 users per rollback segment, then the **MINEXTENTS** would be set to 20 for each of 5 rollback segments. For private rollback segments, the calculated ratio of the initialization parameters—**TRANSACTIONS** divided by **TRANSACTIONS_PER_ROLLBACK_SEGMENT**—rounded up to the nearest integer should be used to determine the number of rollback segments created. The syntax of the **CREATE ROLLBACK SEGMENT** command is shown in Figure 4.10.

The specified parameters are defined as follows:

➤ **rollback_name**   Name for the rollback segment, which must be unique.

➤ **tablespace_name**   Name of the tablespace in which the segment is to be created. If not specified, the rollback segment is created in the user's default tablespace.

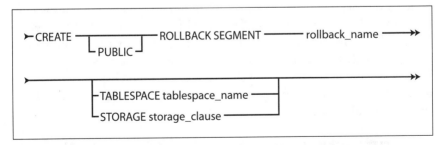

Figure 4.10   The syntax for the **CREATE ROLLBACK SEGMENT** command.

➤ **storage_clause** Specifies the required storage parameters for the rollback segment. It's strongly suggested that the following guidelines be used:

➤ **INITIAL = NEXT INITIAL** sets the size of the initial segment in a rollback segment. **NEXT** sets the size for the next extent in the rollback segment and subsequent extents assuming **PCTINCREASE** is set to zero. (**NEXT** can be modified after rollback segment creation.)

➤ **MINEXTENTS = 20 (or your calculated value; 2 is the default on CREATE ROLLBACK) MINEXTENTS** sets the minimum number of extents that are initially allocated when the rollback segment is created.

➤ **MAXEXTENTS** = A calculated maximum based on size of the rollback segment tablespace, size of rollback segment extents, and number of rollback segments. If set to **UNLIMITED**, the **MAXEXTENTS** parameter could allow the rollback segment to use up all available rollback tablespace free area (disk space allocated to rollback segments). **MAXEXTENTS** can be modified after rollback segment creation.

➤ **OPTIMAL** Reflects the size that the system will restore the rollback segment to by deallocating extents after the rollback segment has been increased by a large transaction. **OPTIMAL** should be set to allow your average-sized transaction to complete without wrapping or causing shrinks. **OPTIMAL** and **MINEXTENTS** could be used by the Oracle server to determine the optimal number of extents for rollback segments. **OPTIMAL** can be modified after rollback segment creation.

PCTINCREASE can no longer be set in Oracle7.3 for rollback segments; in earlier versions, it should always be set to zero.

When a rollback segment is created, it's not online. To be used, it must be brought online using the **ALTER ROLLBACK SEGMENT** name **ONLINE;** command, or the database must be shut down, the init.ora parameter **ROLLBACK_SEGMENTS** modified, and the database restarted. In any case, the init.ora file parameter should be altered if the rollback segment is to be used permanently, or it won't be acquired when the database is shut down and restarted.

The **CREATE** Command For Control Files

The control file is one of the more important files for the Oracle database system. The control file is a storage location for the names and places of all physical datafiles for the system, as well as acting as a database of the SCN and timestamp information that apply to those data files. Without one functional control file (the first one in the list in the **CONTROL_FILES** parameter), the database won't start up.

Sometimes it may be necessary for a DBA to re-create a control file. This option can be used when a control file has become damaged and no viable copy is available or when a database name must be changed or when a fixed limit such as **MAX_DATA_FILES** has to be altered for a database. If the DBA has good documentation for his database, the **CREATE CONTROLFILE** command can be issued manually, however, it's usually easier to periodically use the **ALTER DATABASE** command to automatically create a control file rebuild script.

Exam Prep Questions

Question 1

Evaluate this command:

```
CREATE TABLE sales_items
SELECT id_number, description
FROM inventory
WHERE quantity > 500;
```

Why will this statement cause an error?

- ○ a. A keyword is missing.
- ○ b. A clause is missing.
- ○ c. The **WHERE** clause can't be used when creating a table.
- ○ d. All of the columns in the inventory table must be included in the subquery.
- ○ e. The datatypes in the new table were not defined.

The correct answer is a because the keyword **AS** is missing right before the subquery. Note that **AS** is a keyword and not a clause. Any valid subquery can be used in a **CREATE TABLE** command, including **WHERE** clauses. A table created with a subquery takes on the datatypes of the selected columns. Any portion of a table or set of tables can be selected for use in a new table. You don't have to select all columns.

Question 2

What is increased when the database contains migrated rows?

- ○ a. **PCTUSED**
- ○ b. I/O
- ○ c. Shared pool size
- ○ d. **PCTFREE**

At first glance, you might be tempted to answer d for this question, but look again. It's not asking how to correct migrated rows (by increasing **PCTFREE** in the affected table) but what's increased in the database when you have migrated rows. Obviously the answer is b—I/O—because multiple reads are required for each migrated row. Migrated rows have nothing whatsoever to do with the shared pool, and even if the question was asking how to correct migrated rows, you'd never increase **PCTUSED** to correct migrated rows.

Question 3

> The inventory application has tables that undergo numerous deletes. To which value should you set **PCTUSED** for tables of this nature?
>
> ○ a. 20
>
> ○ b. 10
>
> ○ c. 50
>
> ○ d. 0

This is actually a trick question. Furthermore, it's a bit ambiguous and is asking for an opinion, not a fact. However, if you remember that the exam developers look for opportunities to plant exaggerations following the axiom that if a little is good, a lot must be great. Using this axiom, the answer is c, which is the highest value.

Question 4

> What is the size of the first extent if the storage parameters are **INITIAL 50K, NEXT 20K**, and **PCTINCREASE 30**?
>
> ○ a. 20K
>
> ○ b. 30K
>
> ○ c. 50K
>
> ○ d. 70K

Again, this is a trick question. Exam developers try to confuse you here with too much information. The question asks what is the size of the first extent, the answer is c, because the **INITIAL** value is set to 50K. The **INITIAL** storage parameter sets the size of the first extent.

Question 5

Which parameter value would you use if your tables will have frequent inserts and deletes?

- ○ a. Lower **PCTFREE**
- ○ b. Higher **PCTFREE**
- ○ c. Lower **PCTUSED**
- ○ d. Higher **PCTUSED**

This is another trick question. Just from quickly looking at the question, you would probably choose b assuming an answer dealing with migrated or chained rows was sought. You'd be incorrect because the keyword in the question is *deletes*. The parameter that deals directly with deletes is **PCTUSED**, and to allow for inserts and deletes, the value needs to be lowered. The correct answer is c.

Question 6

Which two constraints are implicitly defined on a primary key column?

- ❑ a. **UNIQUE**
- ❑ b. **CHECK**
- ❑ c. Foreign key
- ❑ d. **NOT NULL**

This question's proper answers are a and d. A little reasoning and recall about what the definition of a primary key is will give you the answers. A primary key is a **UNIQUE, NOT NULL** identifier for a table's row. Given that definition of a primary key, it logically follows that if any two constraints will be defined they'll be a, a **UNIQUE** constraint and d, a **NOT NULL** constraint.

Question 7

> Which parameter value setting will reserve more room for future updates?
>
> ○ a. Lower **PCTFREE**
>
> ○ b. Higher **PCTFREE**
>
> ○ c. Lower **PCTUSED**
>
> ○ d. Higher **PCTUSED**

Given Question 5, you may be tempted to answer c, lower **PCTUSED**, but you'd be wrong. The key to this question are the words *future updates*. The only parameter that provides for future updates is **PCTFREE**, so if you want to reserve room for future updates, you'd need to increase **PCTFREE**. Therefore, the proper answer is b.

Question 8

> In which two statements would you typically use the **CURRVAL** pseudocolumn?
>
> ❏ a. **SET** clause of an **UPDATE** command
>
> ❏ b. **SELECT** list of a view.
>
> ❏ c. **SELECT** statement with the **HAVING** clause
>
> ❏ d. Subquery in an **UPDATE** statement
>
> ❏ e. **VALUES** clause of an **INSERT** statement

The correct answers are a and e. The pseudocolumns, **CURRVAL** and **NEXTVAL**, of a sequence can only be used in the **SET** clause of an **UP-DATE** command, in the **VALUES** clause of an **INSERT** statement, and in the target of an **INSERT INTO** statement. The pseudocolumns can't be used in a view, in a snapshot definition, or in a subquery.

Question 9

> Which SQL statement creates the **parts_456874_vu** view that contains the ID number, description, and quantity for **manufacturer_id 456874** from the inventory table and does not allow the manufacturer values to be changed through the view?
>
> ○ a.
> ```
> CREATE VIEW parts_456874_vu
>     AS SELECT id_number, description, quantity
>     FROM inventory
>     WHERE manufacturer_id = 456874
>     WITH READ ONLY;
> ```
>
> ○ b.
> ```
> CREATE VIEW parts_456874_vu
>     AS SELECT id_number, description, quantity
>     FROM inventory
>     HAVING manufacturer_id = 456874
>     WITH READ ONLY;
> ```
>
> ○ c.
> ```
> CREATE VIEW parts_456874_vu
>     AS SELECT id_number, description, quantity
>     FROM inventory
>     WHERE manufacturer_id = 456874
>     WITH CHECK OPTION;
> ```
>
> ○ d.
> ```
> CREATE VIEW parts_456874_vu
>     AS SELECT id_number, description, quantity
>     FROM inventory
>     WITH CHECK CONSTRAINT;
> ```

The correct answer is a because it has complete clauses, restricts the view to the proper range of values (those belonging to the **manufacturer_id 456874**), and specifies the proper format **READ ONLY** clause. Answer b won't even compile; c doesn't restrict to **READ ONLY**; and d won't compile.

Question 10

What is the size of the third extent if the storage parameters are **INITIAL 50K**, **NEXT 20K**, and **PCTINCREASE 30**?

○ a. 20K

○ b. 26K

○ c. 30K

○ d. 36K

○ e. 40K

○ f. 100K

The correct answer is b. This is a straightforward calculation. Remember that **NEXT** sets the size for the **NEXT** extent, and **PCTINCREASE** is applied after the **INITIAL** and **NEXT** have been utilized against the value of **NEXT**, so the third extent will be **NEXT** + (**NEXT** * **PCTINCREASE**/100) or, in this case, 20 + (20 * 30/100) = 20 + 6 = 26.

Question 11

The size of the **INITIAL** storage parameter for your rollback segments is 1MB. To which value should you set the **NEXT** storage parameter?

○ a. 2MB

○ b. 4MB

○ c. 256KB

○ d. 1MB

The correct answer is d. For rollback segments the **INITIAL** should equal the **NEXT** extent.

Question 12

When attempting to control the space allocation and usage of a cluster's data segment, which storage parameter applies to the cluster and not to the individual tables?

  ○ a. **PCTFREE**

  ○ b. **MAXTRANS**

  ○ c. **INITRANS**

  ○ d. **SIZE**

  ○ e. **INITIAL**

The correct answer is a. In **CREATE CLUSTER** statements, the **PCTFREE** only applies to the cluster itself, not the individual tables. The cluster stores the cluster key values.

Question 13

Which length will be assigned to a **VARCHAR2** column if it's not specified when a table is created?

  ○ a. 1

  ○ b. 25

  ○ c. 255

  ○ d. 38

  ○ e. A column length must be specified for a **VARCHAR2** column.

The correct answer is e. Unlike a **CHAR** column that has a default value of 1, if a length is not specified, the **VARCHAR2** has no default and must have a length specified.

Question 14

If a character column will store 266 bytes, how many bytes will the column length be?

○ a. 0

○ b. 1

○ c. 2

○ d. 3

○ e. 250

○ f. 266

The correct answer is f. For character data, the data storage is one byte per character, so a column that stores 266 bytes will have a length of 266.

Question 15

What is the maximum number of columns in a cluster key?

○ a. 1

○ b. 2

○ c. 4

○ d. 8

○ e. 16

○ f. 32

The correct answer is e. A cluster key can have up to 16 columns.

Need To Know More?

 Ault, Michael R.: *Oracle8 Administration and Management.* John Wiley & Sons, 1998. ISBN 0-471-19234-1. For a comprehensive look at Oracle8 and Oracle7.x management, this book is great. Use it for command syntax definitions for all **CREATE** commands.

 DBA Pipeline at http://www.revealnet.com/ is a great place to ask those last-minute questions and to peruse for up-to-the-minute questions, problems, and solutions.

 Oracle7 Server SQL Reference Manual, Release 7.3. Oracle Corporation, February 1996. Part No. A32538-1. This is the source book for all Oracle SQL for version 7.3. It can be found on the Web in several locations. A quick Alta Vista search found copies at http://www.nw.mdx.ac.uk/oracle.htm, http://is.dal.c/~oracle/, and http://www.techiesinc.com/oracledocs/DOC/products.htm; however, these sites come and go so I suggest doing your own search. I found these using search string "oracle+online+documentation".

 RevealNet Oracle Administrator from RevealNet, Inc. This online reference provides diagrams with hot links to definitions and examples of all DDL commands. It's one of the fastest online searchable references I've come across (even though I might be a bit prejudiced because I'm its principal author). It's a bit more expensive than a book, at around $300 to $400; however, you'll use it long after the books have been put away. It can be downloaded from http://www.revealnet.com/.

ALTER, DROP, And Other Commands

Terms you'll need to understand:

√ ALTER command

√ DROP command

√ TRUNCATE command

√ COMMENT command

Techniques you'll need to master:

√ Using the ALTER command

√ Using the DROP command

√ Using the TRUNCATE command

√ Using the COMMENT command

This chapter is devoted to the other major DDL commands: **ALTER, DROP, TRUNCATE,** and **COMMENT.** Like **CREATE,** the **ALTER** command has numerous incarnations. Because it is the most complex of the remaining DDL commands, I will cover it first. The **ALTER** command allows for the various things DBAs and designers overlook when first creating objects, as well as allowing additions and removals from existing objects. The **DROP** command allows obsolete objects to be removed and **TRUNCATE** provides a rapid method to remove a table's data. **COMMENT** allows for documentation of database objects. All of these commands are important, and DBAs must be familiar with their various aspects.

The ALTER Command

The **ALTER** command is used to alter the characteristics of database objects that can be changed. (For the purpose of this chapter, a *change* is defined as an alteration of structure or characteristics, not simply a recompile.) The **ALTER** command is used against databases, systems, tablespaces, tables, indexes, clusters, and sequences. Procedures, functions, packages, package bodies, triggers, and views can only be compiled through use of the **ALTER** command, as seen in this code snippet:

```
ALTER object_type schema.object_name COMPILE;
```

One thing to remember about any DDL command, such as **ALTER, DROP,** or **CREATE,** is that it results in an implicit **COMMIT** command. An implicit **COMMIT** command causes any uncommitted changes to be committed to the database, so if you perform **INSERT, UPDATE,** or **DELETE** commands then do a **CREATE, ALTER,** or **DROP,** the previous commands will be committed.

The ALTER Command For Databases

Even the best designed database eventually has to be changed. New log group member files may need to be added, datafiles may need to be renamed or moved, archive logging status changed, and so forth. These all are accomplished through the use of the **ALTER DATABASE** command. The syntax for this command is shown in Figure 5.1.

The command options and variables for the **ALTER DATABASE** command are defined as follows:

➤ **database_name** The database name. It can only be eight characters long. If the name is not specified, the value in the init.ora file will be used.

➤ **filespec** A file specification in the format of

```
'file_name' SIZE n K or M REUSE
```

where:

- ➤ file_name is an operating system-specific full path name.

- ➤ **SIZE** sets the size in bytes, kilobytes, or megabytes. If **SIZE** isn't specified, 500K will be used.

- ➤ K or M is an integer as expressed in kilobytes or megabytes.

- ➤ **REUSE** specifies to reuse existing file if it exists. **REUSE** is optional and is used if the file specified already exists and is of the proper size. If the file is incorrect in size, an error will result.

➤ **file_name** A full path file name.

➤ **MOUNT** Indicates the database is available for some DBA functions but not normal functions. **MOUNT** has two modes: either exclusive (which is default) or **PARALLEL** if the database is part of a shared server. A mounted database can have the **CREATE CONTROL FILE** command issued against it. To use the **RENAME FILE** option in this command, the database must be mounted.

➤ **STANDBY DATABASE** With version 7.3 and newer, the command operates against a hot-standby database. A *hot-standby database* is one that is left in recovery mode and archive logs are automatically applied against it to keep it current. It usually is located on a second, remote server and acts as an automatic failover instance for the current one.

➤ **OPEN** Database is mounted and opened for general use, either with **RESET LOGS** if an incomplete recovery was performed or with **NORESET LOGS** (the default).

➤ **ACTIVATE STANDBY DATABASE** Used to activate a standby database.

➤ **ADD LOGFILE THREAD** Adds a thread or redo log to a **PARALLEL** instance.

➤ **ADD LOGFILE MEMBER** Adds a logfile member to an existing group.

➤ **CLEAR LOGFILE** Reinitializes a specified online redo log and, optionally, not archive the cleared redo log. **CLEAR LOGFILE** is

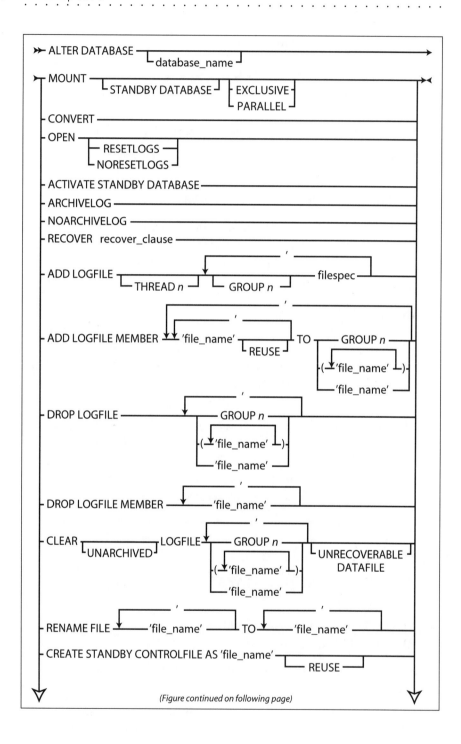

(Figure continued on following page)

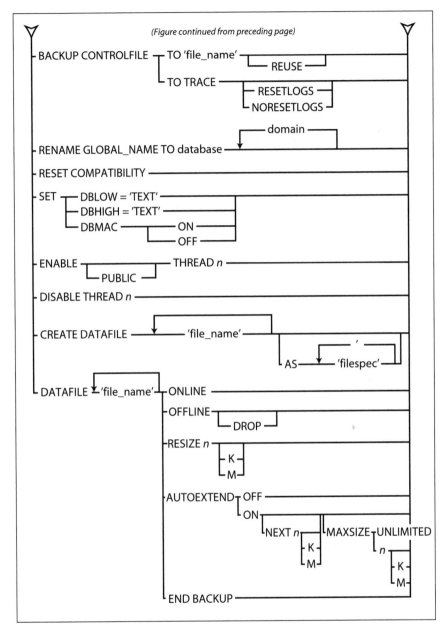

Figure 5.1   The **ALTER DATABASE** command syntax.

similar to adding and dropping a redo log except that the command may be issued even if there are only two logs for the thread and also may be issued for the current redo log of a closed thread. **CLEAR LOGFILE** can't be used to clear a log needed for media recovery. If it's necessary to clear a log containing redo after the database checkpoint, then incomplete media recovery will be necessary. The current redo log of an open thread can never be cleared. The current log of a closed thread can be cleared by switching logs in the closed thread.

*Note: If the **CLEAR LOGFILE** command is interrupted by a system or instance failure, the database may hang. If so, the command must be reissued once the database is restarted. If the failure occurred because of I/O errors accessing one member of a log group, that member can be dropped and other members added.*

UNARCHIVED must be specified if you want to reuse a redo log that was not archived. Note that specifying **UNARCHIVED** will make backups unusable if the redo log is needed for recovery.

UNRECOVERABLE DATAFILE must be specified if the tablespace has a datafile offline and the unarchived log must be cleared to bring the tablespace online. If this is the case, then the datafile and the entire tablespace must be dropped once the **CLEAR LOGFILE** command completes.

➤ **DROP LOGFILE** Drops an existing log group.

➤ **DROP LOGFILE MEMBER** Drops an existing log member.

➤ **RENAME** Renames the specified database file. This command is also used when a file must be moved from one location to another because of media failure.

➤ **ARCHIVELOG/NOARCHIVELOG** Turns archive logging on or off.

➤ **RECOVER** Puts the database into recovery mode. The form of recovery is specified in the recovery clause.

➤ **BACKUP CONTROLFILE** This can be used in two ways: first, to make a recoverable backup copy of the control file (**TO** 'file_name') and second, to make a script to rebuild the control file (**TO TRACE**). The **TO TRACE** option can also be used to create a database rename script and to show the procedures needed to recover if you have read-only tablespaces in the database.

➤ **CREATE DATAFILE** Creates a new datafile in place of an old one. You can use this option to re-create a datafile that was lost with no backup. The 'file_name' must identify a file that was once a part of the database. The 'filespec' specifies the name and size of the new datafile. If you omit the **AS** clause, Oracle creates the new file with the same name and size as the file specified by 'file_name'.

➤ **CREATE STANDBY CONTROLFILE** Creates a control file for use with the standby database.

➤ **DATAFILE** Allows you to perform manipulations, such as resizing, turning autoextend on or off, and setting backup status against the datafiles in the instance.

➤ **ENABLE THREAD/DISABLE THREAD** Allows the enabling and disabling of redo log threads (only used for parallel databases).

➤ **RESET COMPATIBILITY** Marks the database to be reset to an earlier version of Oracle7 when the database is next restarted. This will render archived redo logs unusable for recovery.

Note: This option will not work unless you have successfully disabled Oracle7 features that affect backward compatibility.

➤ **SET DBLOW/DBHIGH/DBMAC** Used with Secure Oracle.

➤ **RENAME GLOBAL_NAME TO** Changes the global name of the database. A rename will automatically flush the shared pool. It doesn't change data concerning your global name in remote instances, connect strings, or database links.

 The **ALTER DATABASE** command option that you should be most aware of is the **ALTER DATABASE BACKUP CONTROLFILE** command. Study the difference between when a control file is backed up to trace and when it's physically backed up.

When a control file is backed up to trace, a script file is created that allows re-creation of the control file. The script created by a **BACKUP TO TRACE** can also be used to rename an existing database or to document the steps required to recover the database, especially if read-only tablespaces are used.

You also need to understand when the **RESETLOGS** option is used with the **ALTER DATABASE OPEN** command. **RESETLOGS** is only used after an incomplete media recovery is performed.

The **ALTER SYSTEM** Command

A special DDL command, **ALTER SYSTEM**, is used to alter the characteristics of the actual database environment.

> *Note: Although not actually used to modify data structures, this seemed the logical place to cover the ALTER SYSTEM command because it is a derivation of the ALTER command.*

The syntax for the **ALTER SYSTEM** command is shown in Figure 5.2.

The clauses and options of the **ALTER SYSTEM** command are defined as follows:

➤ **RESOURCE_LIMIT** Either enables (**TRUE**) or disables (**FALSE**) the use of resource limits.

➤ **GLOBAL_NAMES** Either enables (**TRUE**) or disables (**FALSE**) the use of global names in database links.

➤ **MTS_SERVERS** The *n* specifies the number of shared server processes to enable, up to the value of the **MAX_SERVERS** parameter.

➤ **MTS_DISPATCHERS** The *protocol* specifies the network protocol for the dispatcher(s) and the *n* specifies the number of dispatchers for the specified protocols up to the value of **MAX_DISPATCHERS** (as a sum of all dispatchers under all protocols).

➤ **SWITCH LOGFILE** Switches the active logfile groups.

➤ **CHECKPOINT** Performs either a **GLOBAL** (all open instances on the database) or **LOCAL** (current instance) checkpoint.

➤ **CHECK DATAFILES** Verifies access to datafiles. If **GLOBAL** is specified, all datafiles in all instances accessing the database are verified accessible. If **LOCAL** is specified, only the current instance's datafiles are verified.

➤ **ENABLE RESTRICTED SESSION** Only allows users with a **RESTRICTED SESSION** privilege to log into the database.

➤ **DISABLE RESTRICTED SESSION** Allows any user to log on to the instance.

➤ **ENABLE DISTRIBUTED RECOVERY** Enables distributed recovery.

➤ **DISABLE DISTRIBUTED RECOVERY** Disables distributed recovery.

➤ **ARCHIVE LOG** Manually archives redo logfiles or enables or disables automatic archiving, depending on the clause specified.

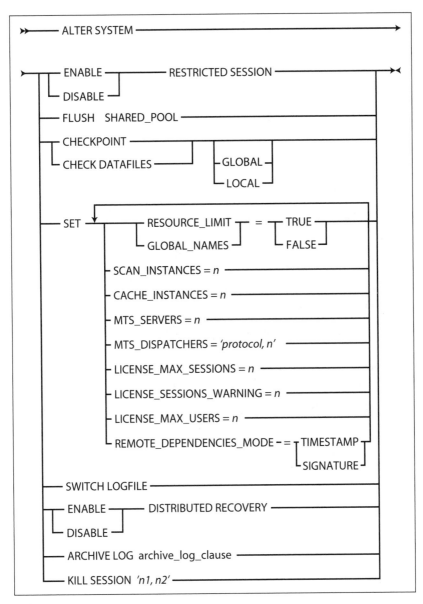

Figure 5.2   The **ALTER SYSTEM** command syntax.

A Detailed Look At *ARCHIVE LOG* Clauses

For Oracle7, the archive log command is removed from SQLDBA and SVRMGR (except for the pull-down display) and is placed under the **ALTER SYSTEM** command. The new command has additional clauses to handle the more complex archive log scheme under Oracle7. The new syntax handles the threads and groups associated with the new archive logs. The new syntax follows:

```
ALTER SYSTEM ARCHIVE LOG clause;
ARCHIVE LOG clauses:
    THREAD n
    [SEQ n] [TO 'location']
    [CHANGE n] [TO 'location']
    [CURRENT] [TO 'location']
    [GROUP n] [TO 'location']
    [LOGFILE 'file_name'] [TO 'location']
    [NEXT] [TO 'location']
    [ALL] [TO 'location']
    [START] [TO 'location']
    [STOP]
```

The ARCHIVE LOG clauses are defined as:

➤ **THREAD** Specifies the specific redo log thread to affect. If this isn't specified, then the current instance redo log thread is affected.

➤ **SEQ** Archives the redo log group that corresponds to the integer specified by the integer given as the argument.

➤ **CHANGE** Corresponds to the System Change Number (SCN) for the transaction you want to archive. It will force archiving of the log containing the transaction with the SCN that matches the integer given as the argument to the **CHANGE** argument.

➤ **CURRENT** Causes all nonarchived redo log members of the current group to be archived.

➤ **GROUP** Manually archives the redo logs in the specified group. If both **THREAD** and **GROUP** are specified, the group must belong to the specified thread.

➤ **LOGFILE** Manually archives the group that contains the file specified by 'file_name'. If a thread is specified, the file must be in a group contained in the thread specified.

➤ **NEXT** Forces manual archiving of the oldest online redo log that requires it. If no thread is specified, Oracle archives the oldest available unarchived redo log file group.

➤ **ALL** Archives all online archive logs that are part of the current thread that haven't yet been archived. If no thread is specified, then all unarchived logs from all threads are archived.

➤ **START** Starts automatic archiving of redo log file groups. This only applies to the thread assigned to the current instance. This command also modifies the control file so that the archive status is recorded and used the next time the database is started.

➤ **TO** Specifies where to archive the logs. This must be a full path specification.

➤ **STOP** Disables automatic archiving of redo file log groups. This applies to your current instance.

 You should be familiar with the **ALTER SYSTEM** command and its effects on archive logging, so these command options are very important to learn backwards and forwards.

The ALTER Command For Tablespaces

Tablespaces can be altered to add datafiles, change online status, change recoverability, change backup status, and change the default storage characteristics for the tablespace. The command to perform these tablespace changes is the **ALTER TABLESPACE** command and its syntax is shown in Figure 5.3.

The keywords and parameters for the **ALTER TABLESPACE** command are as follows:

➤ **tablespace_name** Name of the tablespace to be altered.

➤ **ADD DATAFILE** Adds the datafile specified by 'filespec' to the tablespace. You can add a datafile while the tablespace is online or offline, but be sure that the datafile is not already in use by another database. Adding a datafile using svrmgrl will result in an automatic prompting to back up the control file. You should back up the control file after any change to the database's physical structure.

➤ **AUTOEXTEND** Enables or disables the autoextending of the size of the datafile in the tablespace. The two options for **AUTOEXTEND** are as follows:

   ➤ **OFF** Disables autoextend if it's turned on. **NEXT** and **MAXSIZE** are set to zero. Values for **NEXT** and **MAXSIZE** must be respecified in further **ALTER TABLESPACE AUTOEXTEND** commands.

   ➤ **ON** Enables autoextend.

➤ **NEXT** Size (in bytes) of the next increment of disk space to be automatically allocated to the datafile when more extents are required. You can also use K or M to specify this size in kilobytes or megabytes. The default is one data block.

➤ **MAXSIZE** Maximum disk space allowed for automatic extension of the datafile.

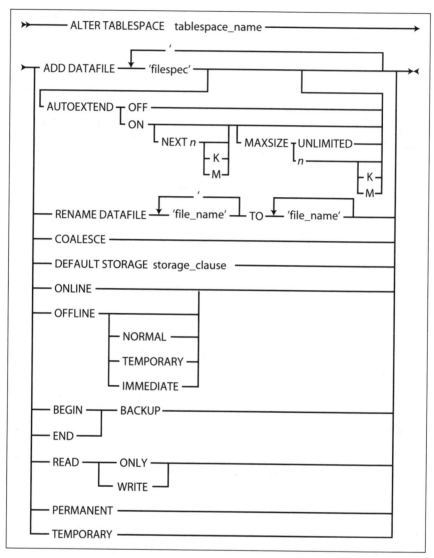

Figure 5.3 Syntax for the **ALTER TABLESPACE** command.

➤ **UNLIMITED** Sets no limit on allocating disk space to the datafile.

➤ **RENAME DATAFILE** Renames one or more of the tablespace's datafiles. Take the tablespace offline before renaming the datafile. Each 'file_name' must fully specify a datafile using the conventions for file names on your operating system. This clause only associates the tablespace with the new file rather than the old one. It doesn't actually change the name of the operating system file; you must change the name of the file through your operating system.

➤ **COALESCE** Coalesces all contiguous free extents into larger contiguous extents for each datafile in the tablespace. The space transaction for a **COALESCE** will not be committed until eight **ALTER TABLESPACE** commands have been executed. If **PCTINCREASE** is set to a nonzero value, the **SMON** process will perform this operation automatically.

Note: COALESCE can't be specified with any other command option.

➤ **DEFAULT STORAGE** Specifies the new default storage parameters for objects subsequently created in the tablespace. (See the **STORAGE** clause for more details of this option.)

➤ **ONLINE** Brings the tablespace online.

➤ **OFFLINE** Takes the tablespace offline and prevents further access to its segments. The options for **OFFLINE** are as follows:

➤ **NORMAL** Performs a checkpoint for all datafiles in the tablespace. All of these datafiles must be online. You don't need to perform media recovery on this tablespace before bringing it back online, but you must use this option if the database is in **NOARCHIVELOG** mode.

➤ **TEMPORARY** Performs a checkpoint for all online datafiles in the tablespace but does not ensure that all files can be written. Any offline files may require media recovery before you bring the tablespace back online.

➤ **IMMEDIATE** Does not ensure that tablespace files are available and does not perform a checkpoint. You must perform recovery on the tablespace before bringing it back online.

The default is **NORMAL**. If you're taking a tablespace offline for a long time, you may want to alter any users who have been assigned the tablespace as either a default or temporary tablespace to use some other tablespace for these purposes. When the tablespace is offline, these users can't allocate space for objects or sort areas in the tablespaces that are offline. You can reassign users new default and temporary tablespaces with the **ALTER USER** command.

➤ **BEGIN BACKUP** Signifies that an online backup is to be performed on the datafiles that compose this tablespace. This option doesn't prevent users from accessing the tablespace. You must use this option before beginning an online backup. You can't use this option on a read-only tablespace. **BEGIN BACKUP** can only be used in **ARCHIVELOG** mode. This command suspends updates to the header block of the datafiles for the referenced tablespace and places the redo logs into block mode where entire changed blocks are recorded instead of just transactions.

While the backup is in progress, you can't:

➤ Take the tablespace offline normally.

➤ Shut down the instance.

➤ Begin another backup of the tablespace.

➤ **END BACKUP** Signifies that an online backup of the tablespace is complete. Use this option as soon as possible after completing an online backup. If a tablespace is left in **BACKUP** mode, the database will think it needs recovery the next time the database is shut down and started, and you may not be able to recover. You can't use this option on a read-only tablespace, and this option can't be specified unless the database is in **ARCHIVELOG** mode.

➤ **READ ONLY** Signifies that no further write operations are allowed on the tablespace. The benefits of using read-only tablespaces is that after the initial data backup, the data no longer has to be backed up, and no redo or rollback is generated in the use of read-only tablespaces.

➤ **READ WRITE** Signifies that write operations are allowed on a previously read-only tablespace.

➤ **PERMANENT** Specifies that the tablespace is to be converted from a temporary one to a permanent one. A permanent tablespace is one in which permanent database objects are stored. This is the default when a tablespace is created.

➤ **TEMPORARY** Specifies that the tablespace is to be converted from a permanent to a temporary one. A temporary tablespace is one in which no permanent database objects can be stored.

At least one of the lines following the **ALTER TABLESPACE** command must be supplied. The definitions for most of the arguments are the same as those for the **CREATE** command. The addition of the **COALESCE** clause is very welcome in that for those tablespaces in which SMON doesn't choose to clean up free space (that is, any with a default storage option **PCTINCREASE** of zero), the command option forces a scavenge of free segments. There are now three options for the **OFFLINE** clause:

➤ **NORMAL** This means wait for users to finish.

➤ **TEMPORARY** This means do a checkpoint of all of its datafiles.

➤ **IMMEDIATE** This means do it immediately.

The **ALTER** Command For Tables

Tables can be altered to add columns; change column types and lengths; or add, change, or drop column or table constraints. Tables can't be altered to rename or drop a column. A table's storage characteristics can also be altered (for subsequent extents or data blocks only). The syntax for the **ALTER TABLE** command is shown in Figure 5.4.

The **ENABLE** constraint clause has the following syntax:

```
>-- UNIQUE -- ( column list )----------------------------------->
|-PRIMARY KEY ||-USING INDEX-index clause-| |-EXCEPTIONS INTO x|
|- CONSTRAINT constraint----|
```

The **INDEX** clause syntax is:

```
>------------------------------------------------------------->
      |-- INITRANS n ----------------------|
      |-- MAXTRANS n----------------------|
      |-- TABLESPACE tablespace_name --------|
      |-- STORAGE storage cause-------------|
      |-- PCTFREE n ----------------------|
```

The **DISABLE** constraint clause has the syntax:

```
>--UNIQUE ---- (column list)------------------------------->
  |-PRIMARY KEY ---------------|          |-CASCADE-|
  |-CONSTRAINT constraint ------|
```

Specifying the **CASCADE** option with either **DISABLE** or **DROP** allows Oracle to cascade the operation to all dependent integrity constraints. **DISABLE** turns a constraint off (note that for **UNIQUE** and **PRIMARY KEY** constraints, this also drops the related indexes). **ENABLE** or **ADD** turns a constraint on or creates it. For **UNIQUE** or **PRIMARY KEY** constraints, an index will be created. If the index clause is not specified, the index is created in the default tablespace of the creator with the default storage characteristics of that tablespace.

ALTER TABLE Specifics

The following are things you can do with the **ALTER TABLE** command:

➤ Add columns that can have null values to any table using the **ADD** clause.

➤ Modify columns to a larger size or numeric columns to different precision using the **MODIFY** clause.

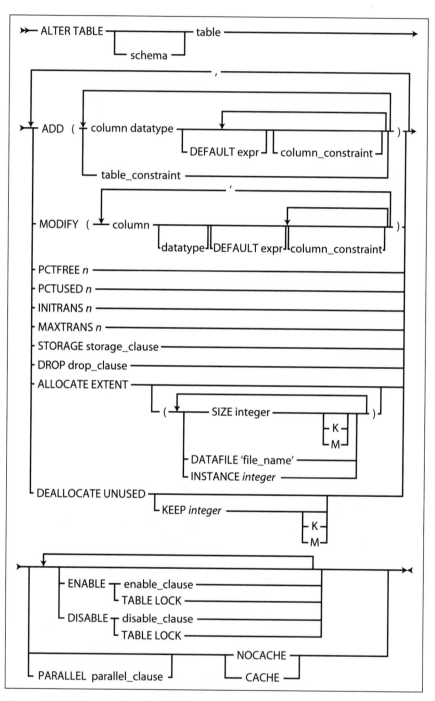

Figure 5.4 Syntax for the **ALTER TABLE** command.

➤ Modify columns that have all null values to be shorter or to a different datatype using the **MODIFY** clause.

➤ Alter the **PCTFREE, PCTUSED, INITRANS,** or **MAXTRANS** for any table.

➤ Alter the storage parameters for any table with the **STORAGE** clause.

➤ Change or remove the parallelism of a table using the **PARALLEL** clause.

➤ Specify if a table is to be cached or not with **CACHE** or **NOCACHE**.

➤ Remove a constraint using the **DROP** clause.

➤ Add a default value to any column using the **DEFAULT** value clause.

➤ Disable a constraint using the **DISABLE** clause. (This is the only way to disable a constraint.) When the **CASCADE** option is specified with the **DISABLE**, it also disables all dependent integrity constraints.

➤ Deallocate space that is not being used with the **DEALLOCATE UNUSED** clause. (You can specify a safety margin above the high-water mark using the **KEEP** option.)

➤ Enable a constraint that was created as disabled using the **ENABLE** clause. (The **ENABLE** clause can only be used in **CREATE** and **ALTER TABLE** commands.)

➤ Add a **PRIMARY, NOT NULL, CHECK,** or **FOREIGN KEY** constraint to an existing table using the **ADD CONSTRAINT** clause.

Following are the things you can't do with the **ALTER TABLE** command:

1. Modify a column that has values to be shorter or to be a different datatype than it already is.

2. Add a **NOT NULL** column to a table that has rows.

3. Alter a column to **NOT NULL** if it has rows with null values in that column.

4. Drop a column from a table.

5. Rename a column.

6. Change a column's datatype to a noncompatible datatype.

The **ALTER TABLE** command also allows for allocation of new extents with specification of size and placement (in different tablespaces, if desired) and deallocation of unused extents. When deallocating unused extents, the bytes reserved for future inserts above the high-water mark are set using the **KEEP** clause of the **DEALLOCATE** clause.

If a table will grow at a rate that makes calculation of exact sizing difficult, increase the value of the **PCTINCREASE** parameter. Usually, I suggest doing space calculations as accurately as possible and then applying a 50 percent fudge factor to allocate enough space and setting **PCTINCREASE** at zero. However, in some situations, the only way to handle extreme table growth is through use of a high **PCTINCREASE**.

ALTER Command For Clusters

Clusters are altered via the **ALTER CLUSTER** command. Only the sizing and storage parameters may be altered. No additional columns may be added to the cluster or removed using the **ALTER CLUSTER** command. The syntax of the command is shown in Figure 5.5.

The definitions for the **ALTER CLUSTER** parameters are the same as for the **CREATE TABLE**, **CREATE CLUSTER**, and storage clause definitions.

You only need to know how these parameters relate to tables.

ALTER Command For Indexes

Indexes are altered using the **ALTER INDEX** command. Indexes can have their physical storage clauses altered, and they can also be rebuilt. You can't add, modify, or remove columns from an existing index using the **ALTER INDEX** command. To change an index's columns, the index must be dropped and re-created. The syntax for the **ALTER INDEX** command is shown in Figure 5.6.

The parameters for the physical_attri_clause are zero, one, or more of the following:

➤ PCTFREE *n*

➤ INITRANS *n*

➤ MAXTRANS *n*

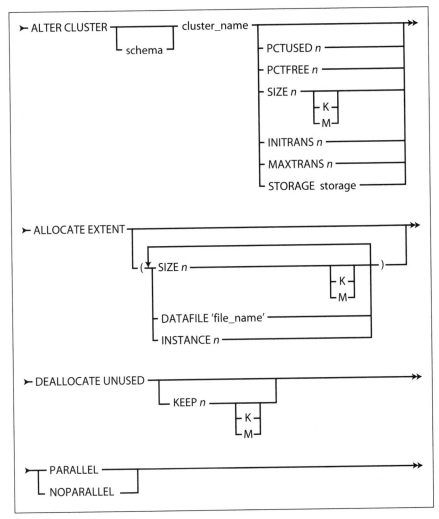

Figure 5.5   Syntax for the **ALTER CLUSTER** command.

➤   STORAGE storage_clause

For the **ALTER INDEX** command, the parameters are same in the **CRE-
ATE TABLE** command with the exception of the **REBUILD** clause. The
REBUILD clause allows the specified index to be rebuilt on the fly in versions
7.3.x and newer databases.

The major use of the **ALTER INDEX** command is to deallocate oversized
index space, change the storage characteristics of an existing index, or rebuild
existing indexes. Notice that you can move an index using the **TABLESPACE**
clause from its existing location to a new location.

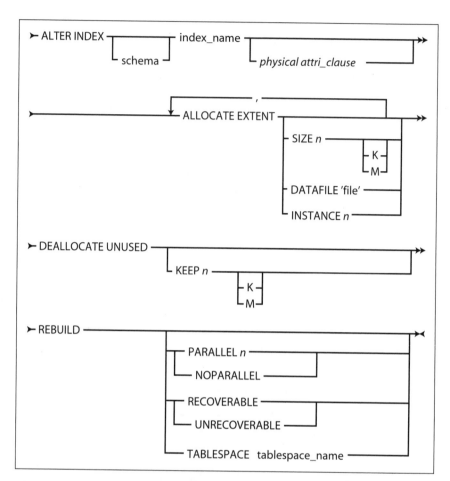

Figure 5.6 Syntax for the **ALTER INDEX** command.

ALTER Command For Sequences

Sequences can be altered to change minimum, maximum, caching, and increment. The syntax for the **ALTER SEQUENCE** command is shown in Figure 5.7.

Only future sequence numbers are Affected by the **ALTER SEQUENCE** command. To alter the **START WITH** clause, the sequence must be dropped and re-created. For ascending sequences, the **MAXVALUE** can't be less than the current sequence value. For descending sequences, the **MINVALUE** can't be greater than the current sequence value.

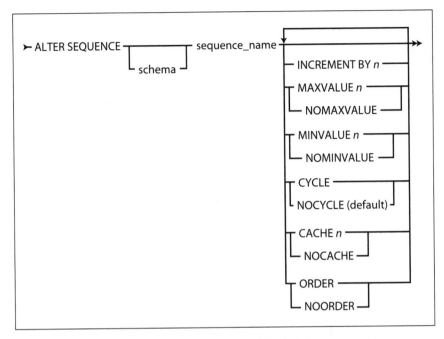

Figure 5.7   The syntax for the **ALTER SEQUENCE** command.

ALTER Command For Rollback Segments

Like other database objects, rollback segments may need to be altered. The only items that can be altered on a rollback segment are the items that deal with storage characteristics or rollback segment status and size. Rollback segments can be altered to affect the **NEXT, OPTIMAL**, and **MAXEXTENTS** storage parameters. Rollback segments can be taken offline or placed online. Rollback segments may be shrunk using the **SHRINK** clause either to a specified size or to the value of **OPTIMAL** if the size isn't specified. The syntax for the **ALTER ROLLBACK SEGMENT** command is shown in Figure 5.8.

Although a view can't be changed using an **ALTER** command, it can be re-created without loss of privilege grants by using the **CREATE OR REPLACE** command. So, to alter a view, you must re-define the entire specification for the view using the **CREATE OR REPLACE**. Use of the **CREATE OR REPLACE** command removes the need to first drop the view then re-create it and regrant privileges.

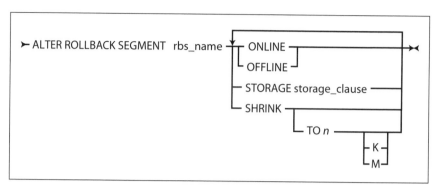

Figure 5.8 The **ALTER ROLLBACK SEGMENT** command syntax.

COMMENT Command

Although the **COMMENT** command may not be a true DDL command, it fits in with the **ALTER**-type commands, so I'll cover it here. The **COMMENT** command adds comments either at the **TABLE, VIEW,** or **COLUMN** level to the data dictionary. The comments entered by the **COMMENT** command can be seen by using the **DBA_TAB_COMMENTS** and **DBA_COL_COMMENTS** views or their related **USER_** and **ALL_** series of views. The syntax of the **COMMENT** command is shown in Figure 5.9.

The **COMMENT** command is an excellent way of documenting your application tables, views, snapshots, and columns internally, so a simple query using the **DBA_, USER_,** or **ALL_** views will produce documentation concerning a table, view, snapshot, or individual column's purpose.

DROP Command

The only way to drop an object is to use the **DROP** command. The **DROP** is used for tables, indexes, clusters, tablespaces, sequences, stored objects, and synonyms. Any command, such as an **ALTER** with a **DEALLOCATE,** a **DROP,** or a **TRUNCATE** can result in tablespace fragmentation. The general syntax for a **DROP** command is shown in Figure 5.10.

The **DROP** command options are defined as follows:

➤ **object_type** Type of object to drop. Accepted object types are:

  ➤ TABLE (can use CASCADE CONSTRAINTS)

  ➤ TABLESPACE (can use INCLUDING CONTENTS)

  ➤ USER (can use CASCADE)

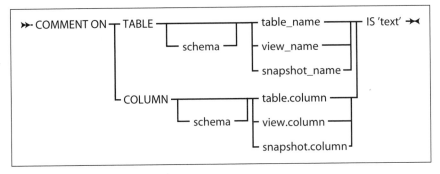

Figure 5.9 **COMMENT** command syntax.

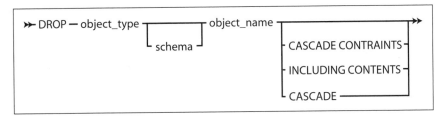

Figure 5.10 The **DROP** command general syntax.

> ➤ PROCEDURE

> ➤ PACKAGE (only standalone, you can't drop individual package items)

> ➤ FUNCTION (only standalone, you can't drop individual package items)

> ➤ TRIGGER

> ➤ SYNONYM

> ➤ DATABASE LINK

> ➤ VIEW

➤ **schema** Owner of the object to be dropped (usually only required if you are not the owner, then you must have adequate **DROP** privileges against the object or have been granted the privilege databasewide with the **DROP ANY...**-type privilege).

➤ **object_name** Name of the object to be dropped.

➤ **CASCADE CONSTRAINTS** Tells Oracle to drop any related foreign key constraint for a parent table. If **ON DELETE CASCADE** is in effect, all related rows will also be dropped from child tables.

➤ **INCLUDING CONTENTS** Forces a drop for tablespaces, even if the tablespaces still contain objects.

➤ **CASCADE** Allows users who still have objects in the database to be dropped. This drops the users' objects along with the users.

A **DROP** command is a DDL command and can't be rolled back. Any dropped object must be re-created if the **DROP** command was issued in error. If you find yourself frequently dropping and creating the same table, consider making the table permanent and just issuing **TRUNCATE** commands. If a table that is frequently created and dropped is shared among several users, add a trigger to populate a session identifier (**SESSIONID**) column and then just delete the rows from that user when the user is finished.

Exam Prep Questions

Question 1

> Which SQL command syntax would you use to remove the view
> **parts_vu**?
>
> ○ a. **DELETE VIEW parts_vu;**
>
> ○ b. **DELETE parts_vu;**
>
> ○ c. **DROP parts_vu;**
>
> ○ d. **DROP VIEW parts_vu;**

The correct answer is d; it's the only one of the listed commands that uses the correct syntax. Answer a has incorrect syntax. Answer b will delete the data contained in the underlying tables for view **parts_vu** if the criteria allowing deletion are fulfilled. Answer c doesn't supply the **object_type** required by the command syntax for a **DROP** command.

Question 2

> Evaluate this SQL command:
>
> ```
> ALTER TABLESPACE users COALESCE;
> ```
>
> Which background process performs the same task?
>
> ○ a. PMON
>
> ○ b. SMON
>
> ○ c. DBWR
>
> ○ d. LGWR

The proper answer is b, SMON. SMON performs space management under its system monitoring tasks. Answer a is incorrect: PMON cleans up process-related areas and does no space management at the system level. Answer c, DBWR, is incorrect because DBWR performs dirty buffer writes and does no space management functions at all. Answer d, LGWR, is incorrect because log writer writes out the log buffer and checkpoint data but performs no space management functions.

Question 3

Which two parameters are storage parameters for rollback segments and can be altered?

☐ a. **NEXT**

☐ b. **PCTINCREASE**

☐ c. **OPTIMAL**

☐ d. **FREELISTS**

☐ e. **ROLLBACK_SEGMENTS**

The correct answers are a, **NEXT**, and c, **OPTIMAL**. Answer b is incorrect
because for Oracle7.3 **PCTINCREASE** is no longer a modifiable parameter
for rollback segments; it's set to zero and can't be changed. Answer d is incorrect because **FREELISTS** aren't set for rollback segments, and answer e is
incorrect because **ROLLBACK_SEGMENTS** is an initialization parameter
for the instance and not a storage parameter for rollback segments.

Question 4

When altering a table, which parameter indicates the number of
bytes above the high-water mark that the table will have after
deallocation?

○ a. **ENABLE**

○ b. **DEALLOCATE UNUSED**

○ c. **KEEP**

○ d. **ALLOCATE EXTENT SIZE**

The correct answer is c, **KEEP**. Answer a is incorrect because **ENABLE** is
used to enable constraints or triggers and has nothing to do with space management. Answer b, although dealing with space management, has nothing to
do with the amount of space retained above the high-water mark. Answer d
concerns extent allocation not deallocation, so it, too, is incorrect.

Question 5

A change to which storage parameters will affect only subsequently added data blocks?

○ a. **INITRANS**

○ b. **MAXTRANS**

○ c. **INITIAL**

○ d. **MINEXTENTS**

The correct answer is a, **INITRANS**. Answer b, **MAXTRANS**, will apply to all extents, not just subsequently added ones. **INITIAL**, answer c, is set when the object is created and can't be changed unless the object is dropped and re-created. Answer d is the same as for c; it's set at creation and can't be reset unless the object is re-created.

Question 6

Which clause would you use in an **ALTER TABLE** command to drop a column from a table?

○ a. **REMOVE**

○ b. **DROP**

○ c. **DELETE**

○ d. **ALTER**

○ e. A column can't be dropped from a table

This is a trick question that is actually testing whether you know what can and can't be done to a table. The proper answer is e: You can't drop a column from a table. Answer a is wrong because first, you can't do it, and second, there's no **REMOVE** clause in an **ALTER TABLE** command. Answer b is incorrect because first, you can't do it, and second, **DROP** is only used to drop a constraint. Answer c is incorrect because first, you can't do it, and second, there's no **DELETE** option for the **ALTER TABLE** command. Answer d is incorrect because first, you can't do it, and second, there's no **ALTER** clause for the **ALTER TABLE** command.

Question 7

You alter the database with this command:

```
ALTER TABLE inventory
MODIFY (price NUMBER(8,2) DEFAULT 0);
```

Which task was accomplished? (Choose the best answer.)

○ a. A new column was added to the table.

○ b. A column constraint was added to the table.

○ c. A column was altered.

○ d. A default value was added to a column.

This is also a trick question because from common understandings (or perhaps I should say misunderstandings) there are several correct answers. However, only one is the right answer. The correct answer is d. Answer a is incorrect because we used a **MODIFY** clause, which only works on existing columns. Answer b may be considered correct in some circles because the default value is considered a constraint in some references and is viewed using the same views as the other constraints. However, for the purposes of the exam, this answer is not correct (or at least, the least correct). Answer c might also be correct, but because we don't have an exhibit to compare the **NUMBER(8,2)** with, we can't be sure, so we must assume this answer is also incorrect. The only answer that is 100 percent correct is d.

Question 8

Which **ALTER** statement would you use to add a primary key constraint on the **manufacturer_id** column of the inventory table?

○ a.
```
ALTER TABLE INVENTORY
MODIFY manufacturer_id CONSTRAINT PRIMARY KEY;
```

○ b.
```
ALTER TABLE inventory
MODIFY CONSTRAINT PRIMARY KEY manufacturer_id;
```

○ c.
```
ALTER TABLE inventory
ADD CONSTRAINT PRIMARY KEY (manufacturer_id);
```

○ d.
```
ALTER TABLE inventory
ADD CONSTRAINT manufacturer_id PRIMARY KEY;
```

The proper answer for this question is c. Answer a is incorrect because it uses the incorrect syntax. Only a **NOT NULL** constraint can be added or removed using a column constraint syntax in an **ALTER TABLE** command. Answer b is incorrect because you can't modify a constraint. Besides, looking at the question, it says to *add* a primary key. Answer d is incorrect because it doesn't specify the column with **PRIMARY KEY**. If a column would have been specified with d, a primary key constraint named **manufacturer_id** would have been created.

Question 9

You logged onto the database to update the inventory table. After your session began, you issued three **UPDATE** commands then you issued an **ALTER TABLE** command to add a column constraint. You were just about to issue a **COMMIT** command when the system crashed. Which changes were made to the inventory table?

- ○ a. Only the **UPDATE** commands
- ○ b. Only the **ALTER TABLE** command
- ○ c. Both the **UPDATE** commands and the **ALTER TABLE** command
- ○ d. None

The correct answer is c. This is almost a trick question because the question is checking whether or not you understand that an implicit commit is issued after each DDL command. Answer a is incorrect because we know that the **UPDATE** preceded the **ALTER TABLE** and the **ALTER TABLE** does an implicit commit, committing both sets of operations. Answer b is incorrect because we know that the **UPDATE** commands that preceded the **ALTER TABLE** command were covered by its implicit commit. Answer d is incorrect because we know a DDL command always does an implicit commit, thus both sets of operations are committed.

Question 10

You issue this command:

```
ALTER TABLESPACE ADD DATAFILE ...
```

What is the result of this command on the database?

- ○ a. There is none.
- ○ b. A tablespace is added.
- ○ c. The physical database configuration is altered.
- ○ d. The logical database configuration is altered.

The correct answer is c. Answer a is incorrect because the database is affected. Answer b is incorrect because we are altering, not adding. Answer d is incorrect because we are altering an existing tablespace, not adding a new one.

Question 11

What does the **COMMENT ON TABLE** command do?

- ○ a. Assigns a table alias.
- ○ b. Adds a comment column to a table.
- ○ c. Adds a comment about a column to the data dictionary.
- ○ d. Adds a comment about a table to the data dictionary.

The proper answer is d. Answer a is incorrect because alias assignment is only done in DML, not DDL statements. Answer b is incorrect because a column can only be added to a table using the **ALTER TABLE** command. Answer c is incorrect because the **COMMENT ON COLUMN** command is used to insert column comments into the database data dictionary, not the **COMMENT ON TABLE** command.

Need To Know More?

 Ault, Michael R.: *Oracle8 Administration and Management.* John Wiley & Sons, 1998. ISBN 0-471-19234-1. For a comprehensive look at Oracle8 and Oracle7.x management, this book is great. Use it for command syntax definitions for all **CREATE** commands.

 Oracle7 Server SQL Reference Manual, Release 7.3. Oracle Corporation, February 1996. Part No. A32538-1. This is the source book for all Oracle SQL for version 7.3. In a quick search, I found several copies on the Web at http://www.nw.mdx.ac.uk/oracle.htm, http://is.dal.c/~oracle/, and http://www.techiesinc.com/oracledocs/DOC/products.htm. I found these using the Alta Vista search engine with a search of "oracle+online+documentation".

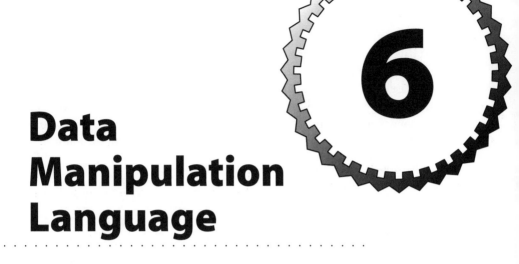

Data Manipulation Language

Terms you'll need to understand:

- √ SELECT
- √ INSERT
- √ UPDATE
- √ DELETE
- √ TRUNCATE

- √ COMMIT
- √ ROLLBACK
- √ Equijoin
- √ Outside join
- √ Function

Techniques you'll need to master:

- √ Using INSERT
- √ Using UPDATE
- √ Using DELETE
- √ Using SELECT
- √ Using TRUNCATE
- √ Using equijoins
- √ Using outside joins

- √ Using WHERE clauses
- √ Using ORDER BY clauses
- √ Using GROUP BY clauses
- √ Using intrinsic SQL functions
- √ Using and applying COMMIT and ROLLBACK commands in Oracle

All of the database structures, objects, and files would do you no good if you didn't have a means of putting data into the database, retrieving that data when needed, and removing that data when it's no longer needed. This manipulation of database data is handled with Data Manipulation Language (DML) statements. In this chapter, I'll cover the Oracle DML elements. In this series of exams, one focuses entirely on SQL (which consists of DDL and DML) and PL/SQL (the subject of Chapter 7). You should be familiar with the following:

➤ Identification of improper command syntax.

➤ Analysis of tables to determine the SQL to be used to generate appropriate result sets.

➤ Use of Oracle intrinsic SQL functions.

➤ Understanding of how basic SQL statements operate against a database.

It's vital for the DBA to have a complete understanding of SQL, DDL, DML, and PL/SQL.

DML Elements

The actual command elements that form the DML portion of SQL are few in number; they are: **INSERT, UPDATE, DELETE, SELECT,** and **TRUNCATE.** Oracle also contains operators (unary and binary) and functions. I'll discuss operators and functions first because they're used to construct parts of the DML commands.

Oracle Operators

Oracle has two types of operators, unary and binary. Unary operators operate on only one operand and are shown in the format:

```
Operator operand
```

A binary operator operates on two operands and generally is shown in the format:

```
Operator operand, operand
```

Special operators also exist that can operate on more than two operands.

If an operator is given a **NULL** argument, and if it's any operator other than the concatenation operator (a double pipe ||), its results are **NULL**.

Precedence governs the order in which operands are evaluated. Those with high precedence are evaluated before those with low precedence, and equal precedence operators are evaluated left to right.

Precedence of operators are as follows:

➤ **(+) and (-)** Addition and subtraction and the **PRIOR** operators.

➤ **(*) and (/)** Multiplication and division operators.

➤ **Binary (=)** Arithmetic operators and the (||) concatenation operator.

➤ **All comparison operators** This includes the **NOT, AND,** and **OR** logical operators.

 Parentheses always override precedence. Operators inside parentheses are always evaluated first.

Set operators are also supported in Oracle SQL. The set operators are:

➤ **UNION** Shows all nonduplicate results from queries A and B.

➤ **UNION ALL** Shows all results from queries A and B.

➤ **INTERSECT** Shows common results from queries A and B.

➤ **MINUS** Shows only noncommon results from queries A and B.

 All set operators have equal precedence.

Comparison operators allow the comparison of two values. The comparison operators are:

➤ **(=)** Does A equal B?

➤ **(!=)** Does A not equal B?

➤ **(~=)** Does A not equal B?

➤ **(<>)** Does A not equal B?

➤ **(>)** Is A greater than B?

➤ **(<)** Is A less than B?

➤ **(>=)** Is A greater than or equal to B?

➤ **(<=)** Is A less than or equal to B?

➤ **IN** Is A in this set?

➤ **NOT IN** Is A not in this set?

➤ **ANY SOME** Combines with (=, !=, <, >, <=, >=) and compares a value to each value in a list returned from a query. Evaluates to **FALSE** if no rows are returned.

➤ **ALL** Combines with (=, !=, <, >, <=, >=) and says a value must relate to the entire list or to the subquery as indicated.

➤ **[NOT] BETWEEN** x **AND** y Checks for inclusion between x and y values inclusive of the values x and y.

➤ **EXISTS** **TRUE** if a subquery returns at least one row.

➤ x**[NOT] LIKE** y **[ESCAPE 'z'] TRUE** if x does not match the pattern y. The y value can contain the wildcard characters ('%' and '_'). Any character except '%' and '_' can follow the **ESCAPE** clause to allow comparison against restricted characters such as the wildcards. A wildcard can be used if preceded by the **ESCAPE** character.

➤ **IS [NOT] NULL** Tests for **NULL** values and is the only valid method to test for nulls. **NULL** values cannot be tested for using equality or nonequality operators because by definition a **NULL** is undefined.

 The logical operator most used in SQL is probably the **AND** operator because it is used to add additional conditional clauses to a **WHERE** clause. The logical operator used to search a list of values is the **IN** operator. The operator most used in single-row subqueries is the equal operator.

SQL Functions

SQL functions allow the manipulation of values, and they return a result. Functions can have multiple arguments yet always return a single value. Functions have the general format:

```
Function(arg1, arg2, ...)
```

Functions will do implicit conversion, if possible, of datatypes if other than the one needed is specified to them. Calling most functions with a **NULL** will return a **NULL**. The only functions that don't return a **NULL** are:

➤ **CONCAT** Concatenates strings.

➤ **DECODE** Performs explicit conversions.

➤ **DUMP** Dumps a value.

➤ **NVL** Allows for **NULL**-value substitution.

➤ **REPLACE** Allows for string replacement.

Functions are either scalar (single row) or aggregate (group) in nature. A single-row function returns a single value for each row queried, whereas an aggregate function returns a single value for a group of rows.

A single-value function can appear in a **SELECT** if the **SELECT** doesn't contain a **GROUP BY** clause. Single value functions can also appear in **WHERE, START WITH,** and **CONNECT BY** clauses. Single-row functions can also be nested.

Group functions can be used in select lists and **HAVING** clauses. If used in a **SELECT** with a **GROUP BY** clause, the **GROUP BY** must include all columns not affected by the function.

Functions are divided into **NUMBER, CHARACTER,** and **DATE** functions.

The SQL Numeric Functions

The **NUMBER** functions are:

➤ **ABS(n)** Returns the absolute value of n.

➤ **CEIL(n)** Rounds n up.

➤ **COS(n)** Returns the cosine of n.

➤ **COSH(n)** Returns the hyperbolic cosine of n.

➤ **EXP(n)** Returns e raised to the nth power (natural log).

➤ **FLOOR(n)** Rounds n down.

➤ **LN(n)** Returns the natural log of n where n is greater than zero.

➤ **LOG(m,n)** Returns the logarithm, base m, of n. The base can be any positive number other than 0 or 1 and n can be any positive number.

➤ **MOD(m,n)** Returns the remainder of m divided by n. Returns m if n is 0.

➤ **POWER(m,n)** Returns m raised to the nth power.

➤ **ROUND(n [,m])** Returns n rounded to m decimal places. M can be positive or negative, depending on which side of the decimal you wish to round.

➤ **SIGN(n)** Returns (-1) if n is less than 0, 0 if n equals 0, and 1 if n more than 0.

➤ **SIN(n)** Returns the sine of n.

➤ **SINH(n)** Returns the hyperbolic sine of n.

➤ SQRT(n) Returns the square root of n.

➤ TAN(n) Returns the tangent of n.

➤ TANH(n) Returns the hyperbolic tangent of n.

➤ TRUNC(n [,m]) Returns n truncated to m decimal places. If m is omitted, it truncates to zero decimal places.

Numeric function provides great calculational ability within Oracle. You can perform almost any arithmetic operation with the proper combination of the above functions and operators.

Character Functions That Return Character Values

Oracle also provides a rich function set for character data. Character data, such as **CHAR** and **VARCHAR2** values, can be altered, translated, truncated, or appended to using functions. The character functions included in Oracle are:

➤ CHR(n) Returns the character having the ASCII code equivalent to n in the current character set for the database.

➤ CONCAT(*char*1, *char*2) Returns *char*1 concatenated to *char*2.

➤ INITCAP(*char*) Returns *char* with the first letter of each word in uppercase.

➤ LOWER(*char*) Returns *char* with all characters lowercased.

➤ LPAD(*char*1, n [,*char*2]) Returns *char*1 left padded with either blanks or the value of *char*2.

➤ LTRIM(*char*1 [,*set*]) Returns *char*1 left trimmed of either blanks if *set* isn't specified or trimmed of *set* characters if it is.

➤ NLS_INITCAP(*char* [, '*nlsparams*']) Returns *char* with all initial letters capped. The *nlsparams* entry determines the **NLS_SORT** setting or is set to **BINARY**.

➤ NLS_LOWER(*char* [, '*nlsparams*']) Returns *char* all lowercase. The *nlsparams* values are the same as for **NLS_INITCAP**.

➤ NLS_UPPER (*char* [, '*nlsparams*']) Returns *char* all uppercase. The *nlsparams* values are the same as for **NLS_INITCAP**.

➤ REPLACE(*char*, *search_string* [,*replacement_string*]) Replaces all instances of *search_string* in *char* with the value of *replacement_string*, or remove them if no *replacement_string* is specified.

➤ RPAD(*char*1, *n* [,*char*2]) Right-place pads *char*1 with the value of *char*2, or blank if *char*2 isn't specified, to a length of *n*.

➤ RTRIM(*char* [,*set*]) Returns *char* with the rightmost characters in *set* removed. If *set* isn't specified, all rightmost blanks are removed.

➤ SOUNDEX(*char*) Returns the soundex equivalent of the value of *char*. This is useful in searching for words that sound alike but are spelled differently.

➤ SUBSTR(*char m* [,*n*]) Returns the substring located in *char*, starting at *m* and ending at *n*. If *n* isn't specified, it returns the value, starting at *m* to the end of the *char* value. The value for *m* can be positive to search forward or negative to search backwards.

➤ SUBSTRB(*char m* [,*n*]) Returns the byte substring located in *char*, starting at *m* bytes and ending at *n*. If *n* is unspecified, it returns the value, starting at *m* bytes to the end of the *char* value. The value for *m* can be positive to search forward or negative to search backwards. Single-byte character sets are the same as **SUBSTR**.

➤ TRANSLATE(*char*, *from*, *to*) Returns *char* with the values in *from* translated to the values in *to*.

➤ UPPER(*char*) Returns *char* in all uppercase.

Character Functions That Return Numeric Values

The following functions return numeric values from character inputs. Outputs, such as length or position, are generated by these functions:

➤ ASCII(*char*) Returns the ASCII equivalent of the first byte of *char*. This is the inverse of the **CHR()** function. If you need to know the value to insert into a **CHR()** for a specific character, use a **SELECT ASCII(*char*) FROM DUAL** to get it.

➤ INSTR(*char*1, *char*2 [, *n* [, *m*]]) Returns the numeric position of the *m*th occurrence of *char*2 in *char*1, starting at the *n*th character. The value of *m* must be positive if specified. The value of *n*, if negative, says to search backwards. If this returns zero, the search was not successful.

➤ INSTRB(*char*1, *char*2 [, *n* [, *m*]]) Returns the numeric byte position of the *m*th occurrence of *char*2 in *char*1 starting at the *n*th byte. The value of *m* must be positive if specified. The value of *n*, if negative, says to search backwards. If this returns zero, the search wasn't successful. This is the same as **INSTR()** for single-byte character sets.

➤ LENGTH(*char*) Returns the length in characters of *char*. If *char* is a CHAR, it includes trailing blanks. If *char* is null, it returns a NULL.

➤ LENGTHB(*char*) Returns the length in bytes of *char*. If *char* is a CHAR, it includes trailing blanks. If *char* is null, it returns a NULL. It's the same as LENGTH for single-byte character sets.

➤ NLSSORT(*char* [, '*nlsparams*']) Returns the string of bytes used to sort *char*.

Date And Time Functions

Almost all databases deal with dates and time. Humans are time-based creatures who want to know "when" as well as "what, who, and how." This requires the ability to deal with date and time values. Oracle provides numerous date and time functions, which are discussed in the following:

➤ ADD_MONTHS(*d,n*) Adds *n* months to date *d*. Returns a DATE value.

➤ LAST_DAY(*d*) Returns the last day of the month that contains date *d*. Returns a DATE value.

➤ MONTHS_BETWEEN(*d*1, *d*2) Returns either the positive or negative difference between date *d*1 and date *d*2. This value is returned as a numeric value.

➤ NEW_TIME(*d*, *z*1, *z*2) Returns the date and time in time zone *z*2 when date *d* is in time zone *z*1.

➤ NEXT_DAY(*d*, *char*) Returns the first weekday named by *char* that is later than date *d*. The returned value is a DATE.

➤ ROUND(*d* [,*fmt*]) Returns date *d* rounded to the unit specified by the *fmt* string. For example, a *fmt* of 'YEAR' will return only the year portion of the specified date value.

➤ SYSDATE Has no arguments and returns the current system date and time. It can't be used in a CHECK constraint.

➤ TRUNC(*d* [,*fmt*]) Returns date *d* with the time truncated to the unit specified by the format string *fmt*. If *fmt* is left off, the entire time portion of *d* is removed.

Subtraction of two date values (when converted using the TO_DATE function) results in the difference in days between the two dates.

Conversion Functions

Oracle provides conversion routines for standard datatype conversions. In many cases, Oracle will do implicit conversions for compatible datatypes; however, it's suggested that explicit conversions be done to prevent performance problems inherent in some implicit conversions. The conversion functions are:

➤ CHARTOROWID(*char*) Converts *char* to Oracle's internal **ROWID** format. The value of *char* must follow **ROWID** datatype guidelines.

➤ CONVERT(*char*, *dest_char_set* [,*source_char_set*]) Converts *char* to the character set specified in *dest_char_set*. If *char* is in a different character set than the database default, *source_char_set* must be included to specify the character set of the *char* value.

➤ HEXTORAW(*char*) Converts the hexadecimal value in *char* to its equivalent **RAW** value.

➤ RAWTOHEX(*raw*) Converts the raw data value in *raw* to its hexadecimal equivalent.

➤ ROWIDTOCHAR(*rowid*) Converts the row ID value in *rowid* to its character equivalent.

➤ TO_CHAR(*d*, [,*fmt* [, '*nlsparams*']]), TO_CHAR(*label* [,*fmt*]) or TO_CHAR(*number*) Converts from a date value, *d*, to a character value in the format specified by *fmt*, using any guidelines in the *nlsparams* variable. It can also convert the label specified in *label* to the specified character format in *fmt* or convert the number value in *number* to a character value. It also formats using date, number, or label format strings to specify the proper output form.

➤ TO_DATE(*char* [,*fmt* [, '*nlsparams*']]) Converts the specified character value in *char* to the internal Oracle **DATE** value as translated via the *fmt* and, if specified, the *nlsparams* value.

➤ TO_LABEL(*char* [,*fmt*]) Converts the specified character value in *char* to a **LABEL** datatype using the default format if no *fmt* is specified.

➤ TO_MULTI_BYTE(*char*) Converts the character value *char* to its equivalent multibyte representation.

➤ TO_NUMBER(*char* [,*fmt* [, '*nlsparams*']]) Converts the number represented in the character value *char* to a number based on translation in the format string *fmt* (if specified) and the *nlsparams* value.

➤ TO_SINGLE_BYTE(*char*) Converts the multibyte value in *char* to its single-byte equivalent.

Other Functions

Other functions in Oracle don't quite fit in any category. These functions are described here:

➤ DUMP(*expr* [, *return_format* [,*start_position* [, *length*]]]) Returns a VARCHAR2 value containing the datatype code, length in bytes, and internal representation of *expr*. The *return_format* tells Oracle to return the value as octal (8), decimal (10), hexadecimal (16), or single characters (17). The *start_position* and *length* values determine which portion representation to return.

➤ GREATEST(*expr* [,*expr*] ...) Returns the greatest of the specified values.

➤ LEAST(*expr* [,*expr*] ...) Returns the least of the specified values.

➤ NVL(*expr1*, *expr2*) Returns *expr1* if *expr1* isn't null; *expr2* if *expr1* is null. Be careful with any conversion routines or substitution functions when used in mathematical formulas, especially in division. Don't substitute a zero for a **NULL** in division $Y / (NVL(X, 0))$ or a divide-by-zero exception will result.

➤ UID Has no arguments and returns the user ID of the current user.

➤ USER Has no arguments, returns the username of the current user.

➤ USERENV(*option*) Returns the specified setting for the current environment. Possible values of *option* are:

  ➤ OSDBA Returns **TRUE** if the OSDBA role is enabled for this user.

  ➤ LABEL Returns the current session label.

  ➤ LANGUAGE Returns the language and territory used by this session.

  ➤ TERMINAL Returns the operating system ID of this session's terminal.

  ➤ SESSIONID Returns your auditing session ID.

  ➤ ENTRYID Returns the available auditing entry identifier.

  ➤ CLIENT_INFO Returns the setting from **V$SESSION** of CLIENT_INFO for this session.

  ➤ LANG Returns the ISO language setting for this session.

➤ VSIZE(*expr*) Returns the number of bytes in the internal representation of *expr*.

Oracle Group Functions

Oracle also provides group functions to act on groups of values, rather than individual items. You should know how to use these in conjunction with SELECT, INSERT, UPDATE, or DELETE:

➤ **DISTINCT** Returns only unique values for the specified data set grouping.

➤ **ALL** Returns all values, including duplicates, for the specified data set grouping.

➤ **AVG([DISTINCT|ALL]** *n*) Returns the average value for the specified set of numbers. You can exclude duplicates by use of **DISTINCT** or include them with **ALL**, which is the default.

➤ **COUNT({* | [DISTINCT|ALL]** *expr*}) Returns the count of rows (*), distinct values using **DISTINCT**, all values (the default) using **ALL**, or all values that satisfy the values generated from the expression in *expr*.

➤ **MAX([DISTINCT|ALL]** *expr*) Returns the maximum value generated from the expression in *expr*.

➤ **MIN([DISTINCT|ALL]** *expr*) Returns the minimum value generated from the expression in *expr*. The expression can be numeric or character data. If the value is a character, the sum of the ASCII values for the letters is used to determine what value is minimum.

➤ **STDDEV([DISTINCT|ALL]** *expr*) Returns the standard deviation of the values generated from the expression in *expr*.

➤ **SUM([DISTINCT|ALL]** *expr*) Returns the sum of the values generated from the expression in *expr*.

➤ **VARIANCE([DISTINCT|ALL]** *expr*) Returns the variance of the values generated from the expression in *expr*.

The *expr* Clause

In many of the commands, function definitions, and statement definitions, you may see the term *expr*. This clause represents several possible expressions that can be placed in commands, functions, and statements, but not all commands will accept all forms of the *expr* formats. Lists can contain up to 254 expressions. Figures 6.1 through 6.5 show the various forms of the *expr* clause.

The form of the *expr* clause shown in Figure 6.1 is used when the expression represents a pseudocolumn in a table such as **LEVEL**, **ROWID** or **ROWNUM**, a constant, a sequence number, or a **NULL** value.

The form of the *expr* clause shown in Figure 6.2 is used as a host variable with an optional indicator variable. This form can only be used in embedded SQL or through the Oracle Call Interface (OCI).

The form of the *expr* clause shown in Figure 6.3 is used when calling an implicit SQL function.

The form of the *expr* clause shown in Figure 6.4 is used when called a user-defined function.

The form of the *expr* clause shown in Figure 6.5 is used when a combination of other expressions is required. Some combinations are inappropriate, such as

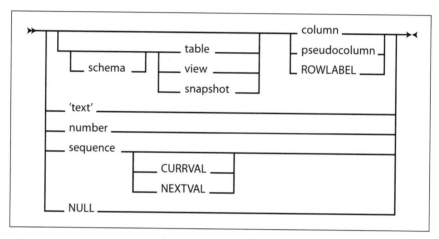

Figure 6.1 Form 1 of the *expr* clause.

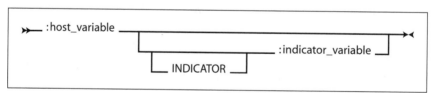

Figure 6.2 Form 2 of the *expr* clause.

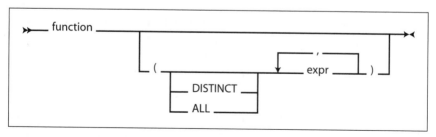

Figure 6.3 Form 3 of the *expr* clause.

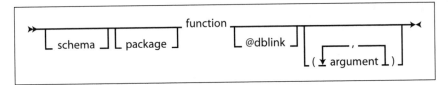

Figure 6.4 Form 4 of the *expr* clause.

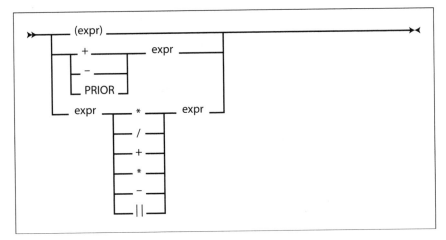

Figure 6.5 Form 5 of the *expr* clause.

use of a **LENGTH** expression in a **GROUP BY**. In the case of an inappropriate expression combination, the expression will be rejected.

When an expression contains a numeric value or a character value enclosed in single quotes, these values are known as *literals*. Literals can be concatenated to other literals or to column values. The simplest literal would be a blank space enclosed with single quotes. Special characters, such as the forward slash (/) and percent sign (%), can be used in a literal if they're preceded by the escape character. An escape character is either the backslash or the character designated with the **ESCAPE** clause in a **LIKE** operator statement.

Expressions can be used in:

➤ The select list of the **SELECT** command.

➤ A condition in the **WHERE** and **HAVING** clauses.

➤ The **CONNECT BY, START WITH,** or **ORDER BY** clauses.

➤ The **VALUES** clause of the **INSERT** command.

➤ The **SET** clause of the **UPDATE** command.

DECODE Function

The **DECODE** function is important in that it can be used to perform quasi-if...then processing inside SQL statements. Figure 6.6 shows the format to use for the **DECODE** function.

When the **DECODE** function is invoked, Oracle compares *expr* to each *search* value one by one. If the values of *expr* and *search* match, *result* is substituted. If *default* is not specified, the null value is returned; otherwise, *default* is returned.

Condition Clauses

The entire purpose of SQL is to allow insert, update, delete, and retrieval of data. Limiting retrieval of data to just what we want requires some means of limiting the return set of data. The condition clauses allow for the weeding out the data that's not wanted or needed. Just like the *expr* clause, the condition clause has several forms. Figures 6.6 through 6.9 show the various condition clauses.

The condition clause in Figure 6.7 shows a comparison with expressions or subquery results.

The condition clause in Figure 6.8 shows a comparison with any or all members in a list or subquery.

The condition clause in Figure 6.9 shows a comparison to test for membership in a group or subquery.

DML Commands

I'll cover **INSERT** first because the other commands do you little good if there's no data in the database to manipulate. Insertions can't override constraints, such as **NOT NULL** or **UNIQUE,** or specify nonconverted values that can't be implicitly converted to the datatype in the destination table.

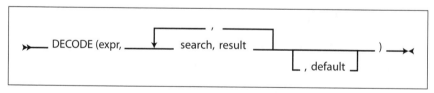

Figure 6.6   Form 1 of the condition clause.

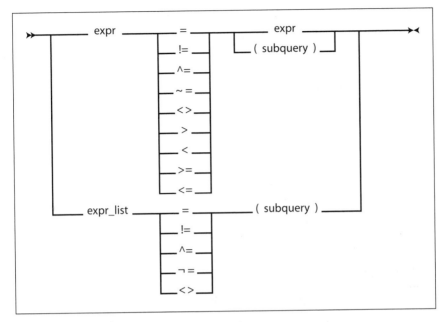

Figure 6.7   Form 2 of the condition clause.

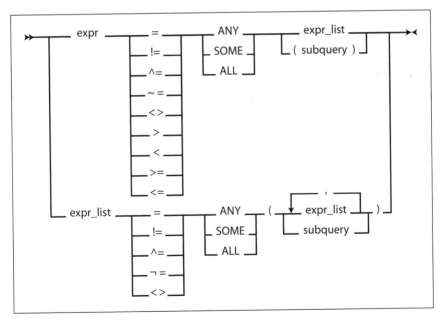

Figure 6.8   Form 3 of the condition clause.

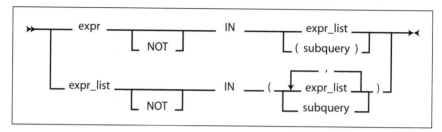

Figure 6.9 Form 4 of the condition clause.

The INSERT Command

The **INSERT** command is used to add new data into existing database tables from SQL. The syntax of the **INSERT** command is shown in Figure 6.10.

The parameters have the following definitions:

➤ **schema** The owner of the table or view.

➤ **table_name, view_name** Name of the table or updatable view.

➤ **@dbl** The database link for a remote table or view.

➤ **subquery1** A subquery that is identical to a view query.

➤ **subquery2** A subquery that returns rows or values to be inserted.

➤ **column** The column name(s) to be inserted into. If they're omitted, all the table or view columns must have a matching value or **subquery2** item.

➤ **expr** An expression or list of values corresponding to the inserted values.

An **INSERT** that uses a **VALUES** clause can only insert a single row of data into a table. On the other hand, a query with a subselect instead of a **VALUES** clause can insert multiple rows.

The **INSERT** command is used to add table values, and it can also be used to insert data into an updatable view's base table. If a view is to be inserted into, and if that view has a **WITH CHECK OPTION** clause with its definition, then the inserted rows must meet the criteria in the views defining query.

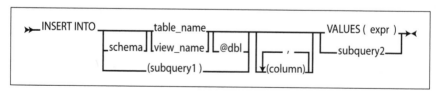

Figure 6.10 The syntax for the **INSERT** command.

A view can't be inserted into if:

➤ It has a join.

➤ It uses a set operator.

➤ It contains a **GROUP BY** clause.

➤ It uses any group function.

➤ It uses a **DISTINCT** operator.

The **INSERT** command causes any triggers on the table or underlying tables acted on by the **INSERT** to fire. It can't be used to force insert of data of incorrect or a nonimplicitly convertible datatype into a noncompatible row or to violate a **NOT NULL, UNIQUE,** or **CHECK** constraint limitation, and it can't be used to violate foreign or primary key constraints.

The UPDATE Command

The **UPDATE** DML command is used to alter or change the contents of an existing table row column or columns or the base columns for an updatable view. The syntax for an **UPDATE** command is shown in Figure 6.11.

The parameters have the following definitions:

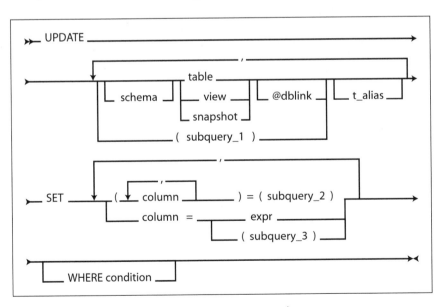

Figure 6.11   Syntax of the **UPDATE** command.

➤ **schema** Owner of table, view, or snapshot.

➤ **table_name, view_name, snapshot** Table or base table of the specified view or snapshot to be updated.

➤ **@dbl** A database link to the update item's remote location (if needed).

➤ **t_alias** Alias for object name to be used in subqueries and in **WHERE** clauses to make them more readable or more logical.

➤ **subquery_1** A subquery that's in the same format as a view definition.

➤ **subquery_2** A subquery that returns values to be used to update the object.

➤ **subquery_3** A subquery that returns a single value.

➤ **column** A column or list of columns to be updated. Lists must be in parentheses. If not mentioned in the clause, a column's value is not updated.

➤ **expr** New value or values assigned to the subquery or column list of columns.

➤ **WHERE** A clause used to limit what rows are updated by the **UPDATE** command. If a **WHERE** clause is not specified, then all rows are updated.

The **UPDATE** command is used to change table values, and it can be used to update an updatable view's base table. If a view is to be updated and that view has a **WITH CHECK OPTION** clause with its definition, the updated rows must meet the criteria in the views defining query.

A view can't be updated if:

➤ It has a join.

➤ It uses a set operator.

➤ It contains a **GROUP BY** clause.

➤ It uses any group function.

➤ It uses a **DISTINCT** operator.

The **UPDATE** command causes any **UPDATE** triggers on the table or underlying tables of the **UPDATE** to fire.

The DELETE Command

Once a table has been loaded with data, it may be necessary periodically to remove rows from the data set that results. This removal of data is accomplished with one of two commands. The **DELETE** command is used to remove some or all rows from a table allowing **ROLLBACK** of the command if no **COMMIT** is executed. The **TRUNCATE** command is used to remove all rows from a table, and no **ROLLBACK** is allowed. The syntax of the **DE-LETE** command is shown in Figure 6.12.

The parameters have the following definitions:

➤ **schema** Name of object owner.

➤ **table_name, view_name** Name of table or view whose base table is to be deleted from.

➤ **@dblink** Database link to remote instance if object is not local.

➤ **alias** Shorthand for table, view, or subquery for use in the **WHERE** clause.

➤ **subquery** A subquery that selects data to be deleted. This subquery is executed, and the resulting rows are deleted. The subquery can't query a table that appears in the same **FROM** clause as the subquery.

➤ **WHERE condition** Allows deletion of rows that meet the specified condition only.

The **DELETE** command is used to remove table values, and it can be used to remove rows from an updatable view's base table. A view can't be deleted from if:

➤ It has a join.

➤ It uses a set operator.

➤ It contains a **GROUP BY** clause.

➤ It uses any group function.

➤ It uses a **DISTINCT** operator.

A **DELETE** will fire any **DELETE** triggers specified on the tables or underlying tables of the **DELETE** command.

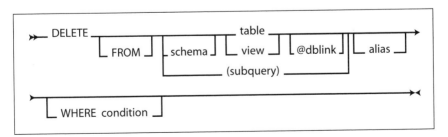

Figure 6.12   Syntax of the **DELETE** command.

The SELECT Command

The **SELECT** command is used to retrieve values that have been stored in a table or set of tables based on some selection criteria. An unrestricted **SELECT** retrieves all values from the specified table, view, or snapshot. The **SELECT** command is also the basis for all subqueries in all other commands.

Unless forced by the **DESC** qualifier into descending order, all **SELECT** query results are returned in ascending order.

At the absolute minimum, a **SELECT** command consists of a **SELECT** with an expression and a **FROM**, which specifies from where the data is to be selected. This is why the **DUAL** table is required when doing nondirected **SELECT** statements, such as from sequences or non-table-related, single-row functions. Figure 6.13 shows the complete syntax for the **SELECT** command.

The parameters have the following definitions:

➤ **DISTINCT** Returns only one copy of any duplicate rows or of specific columns determined by the position of the **DISTINCT** and returned by the **SELECT**. If the **DISTINCT** is placed immediately following the **SELECT**, all combinations of the columns that follow will be distinct.

➤ **ALL** Returns all rows with duplicates (default value).

➤ ***** Used to return all columns from the specified table, view, or snapshot.

➤ **expr** Selects an expression.

➤ **c_alias** Column alias used in subsequent statements in the **SELECT** command to refer to its column.

➤ **schema** Owner of the table, view, or snapshot.

➤ **table_name, table, view_name, view, snapshot** Name of the object from which values are selected.

➤ **@dblink** The database link to the remote instance where the object of the **SELECT** command is located. If not specified, the object must be local.

➤ **subquery** Subquery that's specified identically to a view query definition.

➤ **WITH READ ONLY** Specifies that the subquery can't be updated.

➤ **t_alias** Table alias to be used in subsequent subqueries or in **WHERE** conditions. Once a table alias is specified, the table name can no longer be used, or an error will be generated.

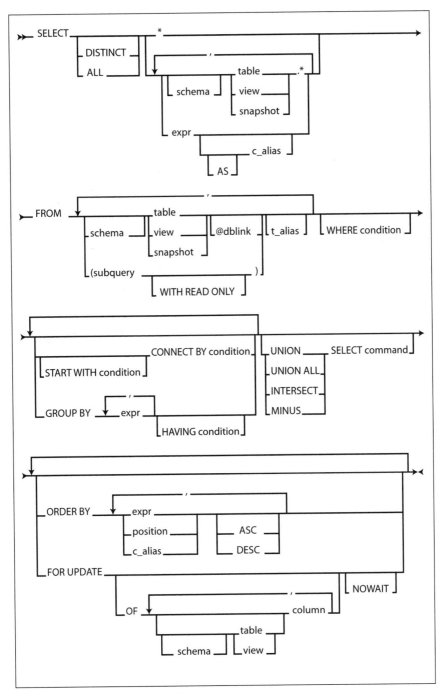

Figure 6.13 Syntax of the **SELECT** command.

➤ **WHERE** Used to restrict the returned rows to a designated subset. Only **WHERE** clauses result in the use of indexes. A **SELECT** command without a **WHERE** clause will return all rows of the specified tables joined in a Cartesian product.

➤ **ORDER BY** Forces ordering of the returned rows to either ascending (**ASC**), from least to most, which is the default order, or descending, from highest to lowest, with the descending (**DESC**) operator. The **ORDER BY** clause doesn't restrict rows but only orders the returned data set. The **ORDER BY** can use the column name, column order specifier, or column alias to identify the columns to be used in the sort. The columns specified for a sort are sorted in left-to-right order, so the values returned are first sorted by the leftmost, by the next, and so forth, until all columns have been sorted.

➤ **START WITH CONNECT BY** Returns rows in an hierarchical order.

➤ **GROUP BY** Groups the rows based on the specified column's values. The *expr* for the statement must include at least one grouping function, such as **COUNT()**, and all columns not participating in the grouping functions must be included in the **GROUP BY** column list. **GROUP BY** does not restrict values, it merely groups them. A **GROUP BY**, unless overridden with the **ORDER BY** sort option **DESC**, always returns values sorted in ascending order. A **GROUP BY** can use the column name but not the column positional specification or the column alias.

➤ **HAVING** Restricts the **GROUP BY** to those groups for which the **HAVING** condition is **TRUE**. You can't have a **HAVING** clause without a **GROUP BY** clause.

➤ **UNION, UNION ALL, INSERSECT, MINUS** Specify the set operation for the **SELECT** commands specified.

➤ **ASC, DESC** Determines ordering of the returned set of values.

➤ **FOR UPDATE** Locks the selected rows.

➤ **OF** Only locks the rows of the specified table.

➤ **NOWAIT** Returns control to you if the **SELECT** command attempts to lock a row that is locked by another user. Otherwise, the **SELECT** waits for any locked rows to be free and returns the results when they are free.

If two or more tables have column names in common in a **SELECT**, the table name or table alias must be used to differentiate them.

Column aliases can be used in **ORDER BY** but in no other clauses.

If **DISTINCT** is used, the total number of bytes selected in all select list expressions is limited to the size of a data block minus some overhead.

Hints can be used to tell the Oracle optimizer how to optimize the query, thus forcing query behavior to what you want instead of what the optimizer thinks it should be.

If all you could do with a **SELECT** was look at data from one table, it would be pretty useless. We'll take a look at joins and subqueries in the following subsections.

Joins

Joins are **SELECT** commands that retrieve data from two or more tables. One thing to remember is that a table can be joined to itself as well. The **WHERE** clause usually gives the join conditions that determine how data is selected from each table in the join to fill in the specified columns in the **SELECT** list. The minimum number of joins required to relate a set of tables is the number of tables in the join minus one.

An equijoin uses any of the equality operators. Depending on the optimizer algorithm chosen, the total size of the columns in the equijoin may be limited to **DB_BLOCK_SIZE** bytes in size. An equijoin is generally used to display data from two (or more) tables that have common values existing in corresponding columns.

A self-join joins a table to itself. Employing this option requires that table aliases be used.

A Cartesian product results if two tables are specified in a **SELECT** without a qualifying **WHERE** clause and join condition. This generates a result set with all possible combinations of the rows in the tables such that the number of rows returned is equal to the product of the number of rows in each table (that is, if table A has 10 rows and table B has 20 rows, 200 rows will be returned).

An outer join extends the results of a simple query. It returns all rows that satisfy the join condition and those rows from one of the tables for which no rows from the other satisfy the join condition. The outer join operator is (+) (the plus sign surrounded by parentheses) placed on the side of the join statement deficient in information. The outside join operator can only appear in the **WHERE** clause applied to a column name. If the specified tables have multiple join conditions, the operator must be present in all of the specified conditions. The outer join can't be used in an **OR** expression, and the outer join operator can't be applied to a column compared using an **IN** condition or subquery.

Subquery

Subqueries are used to return one or more values or sets of values to be used for comparison purposes. One using a single-row comparison operator can return only a single value. A subquery can't use ordering clauses such as **ORDER BY** or **GROUP BY**. It must return a single value if used in an equality comparison, but if used with **IN**, a subquery can return multiple values.

Exam Prep Questions

Question 1

Evaluate this command:

```
SELECT manufacturer_id
"Manufacturer Identification Code", SUM(price)
FROM inventory
WHERE price > 6.00
GROUP BY "Manufacturer Identification Code"
ORDER BY 2
```

Which clause will cause an error?

❍ a.
```
SELECT manufacturer_id
"Manufacturer Identification Code", SUM(price)
```

❍ b.
```
FROM inventory
```

❍ c.
```
WHERE price >  6.00
```

❍ d.
```
GROUP BY "Manufacturer Identification Code"
```

❍ e.
```
ORDER BY 2
```

The correct answer is d. Answer d is correct because you can't use the column alias in a **GROUP BY**. The rest of the clauses shown are correct in their syntax.

Question 2

You query the database with this command:

```
SELECT manufacturer_id
FROM inventory
WHERE manufacturer_id LIKE
'%N\%P\%O%' ESCAPE \;
```

For which character pattern is the **LIKE** operator searching?

○ a. NPO

○ b. N\%P\%O

○ c. N\P\O

○ d. N%P%O

The correct answer is d. This question almost falls within the realm of a trick question. When evaluating a **LIKE** statement, always check to see if it includes the **ESCAPE** clause. If there's an **ESCAPE** clause, take note of what character it specifies to treat as an escape. Any character that's preceded by the escape character will be treated as a normal character and will have no special meaning. In this case, with answer d, the percent signs in front of the P and O characters have been escaped, indicating they're to be treated as a part of the search string and not as wildcards. The leading and trailing percent signs have not been escaped, so they're treated as wildcards. The other answers are incorrect because they're not what the specified string translates into.

Question 3

Which **SELECT** is an outer join?

○ a.
```
SELECT i.id_number, m.manufacturer_id
  FROM inventory i, inventory m
  WHERE i.manufacturer_id = m.id_number;
```

○ b.
```
SELECT i.id_number, m.manufacturer_name
  FROM inventory i, inventory m
  WHERE i.manufacturer_id(+) = m.id_number;
```

○ c.
```
SELECT i.id_number, m.manufacturer_name
  FROM inventory i, inventory m
  WHERE i.manufacturer_id = m.id_number;
```

○ d.
```
SELECT i.id_number, m.manufacturer_id
  FROM inventory i, inventory m
  WHERE i.price BETWEEN m.avg_price
  AND m.max_price;
```

The proper answer to this question is b. Answer a, although correct in format, doesn't specify the outer join operator (+). Answer c is identical to answer b, except that, as with answer a, no outer join operator is specified. Again, although answer d is a syntactically correct **SELECT** statement, it has no outer join symbol.

Question 4

You query the database with this command:

```
SELECT price
FROM inventory
WHERE price * .25 = 4.00
AND manufacturer_id = 25001 OR
manufacturer_id = 25050 OR price > 25.00;
```

Which operator is evaluated first?

○ a. *

○ b. **AND**

○ c. **OR**

○ d. >

The proper answer is a. Answer b is incorrect because logical operators are at a lesser precedence than mathematical operators and inequality operators. Answer c is incorrect for the same reason as answer b. Answer d is incorrect because inequality operators are at a lesser precedence than mathematical operators.

Question 5

Which command is used to add new rows to an existing table?

○ a. **UPDATE**

○ b. **INTO**

○ c. **INSERT**

○ d. **CREATE**

○ e. **ADD**

The correct answer is c. Answer a is incorrect because the **UPDATE** command is used to alter existing rows, not insert new ones. Answer b is incorrect because **INTO** is actually a required part of the **SELECT** command when it is used in PL/SQL and has nothing to do with **INSERT**. Answer d is incorrect because the **CREATE** command is a DDL and not a DML command and has nothing to do with putting data into a table. Answer e is incorrect because **ADD** is a part of the DDL command **ALTER** and has nothing to do with insertion of data into tables.

Question 6

Which command would change the **contact_name** of the Gofco Company from Marilyn to Sheila?

○ a. **INSERT**

○ b. **SELECT**

○ c. **UPDATE**

○ d. **DELETE**

○ e. **ALTER**

The correct answer is c. Answer a is incorrect because you can't alter existing rows with an **INSERT** command. Answer b is incorrect because a **SELECT** by definition can't cause data to be modified. Answer d is incorrect because a **DELETE** removes data, it doesn't alter it. Answer e is incorrect because **AL-TER** is a DDL command used to modify object structure, not object content.

Question 7

You need to display the date data type column **order_date** in this format:

25TH OF FEBRUARY 1997

Which **SELECT** statement could you use?

○ a.
```
SELECT order_date('fmDD "OF" MONTH YYYY')
FROM inventory;
```

○ b.
```
SELECT
TO_CHAR(order_date,'fmDDTH "OF" MONTH YYYY')
FROM inventory;
```

○ c.
```
SELECT
TO_CHAR(order_date,('fmDDspth "OF" MONTH YYYY')
FROM inventory;
```

○ d.
```
SELECT
order_date('fmDDspth "OF" MONTH YYYY')
FROM inventory;
```

Answer b is correct. Answer a is incorrect because it's syntactically incorrect; it doesn't include the **TO_CHAR** function. Answer c is incorrect because its format line is incorrect and can't produce the desired output. Answer d is incorrect for the same reason as answer a.

Question 8

> Which clause restricts the groups of rows returned to those groups meeting a specified condition?
>
> ○ a. **SELECT**
> ○ b. **FROM**
> ○ c. **WHERE**
> ○ d. **GROUP BY**
> ○ e. **HAVING**
> ○ f. **ORDER BY**

Answer e is the correct response. Answer a is incorrect because a **SELECT** by itself doesn't group results, for that matter, a **SELECT** is a command, not a clause. Answer b is incorrect because the **FROM** clause tells **SELECT** where to get its data and has nothing to do with ordering or grouping. Answer c is incorrect because the **WHERE** clause has nothing to do with sorting or grouping, it deals with what data to retrieve. Answer d, although concerned with grouping, doesn't by itself restrict the groups; it returns to a specified set but returns all groups meeting the **SELECT** criteria. Answer f is incorrect because an **ORDER BY** only orders returned data, it doesn't restrict values returned.

Question 9

> You query the database with this command:
>
> ```
> SELECT id_number, 100/quantity
> FROM inventory;
> ```
>
> Which value is displayed when the quantity value is null?
>
> ○ a. 0
> ○ b. **NULL**
> ○ c. The keyword **NULL**
> ○ d. 100

The correct answer is b. Answer a is incorrect because any operation involving a **NULL** value results in a **NULL** value. Answer c is incorrect because a null response is a blank space, not any special keyword. Answer d is incorrect for the same reason as answer a.

Question 10

Which operator would it be most appropriate to use to search through a list of values?

○ a. **LIKE**

○ b. **=**

○ c. **BETWEEN**

○ d. **IN**

The correct answer is d. Answer a is incorrect because the **LIKE** operator only compares a value against a single template value using one or more wildcards. Answer b is incorrect because an equality can only be used to compare against a single value, not a list of values. Answer c in incorrect because **BETWEEN** is used to find values inside a specified minimum and maximum value, not inside a list of possible values.

Need To Know More?

Oracle7 Server SQL Reference Manual, Release 7.3. Oracle Corporation, February, 1996. Part No. A32538-1. This is the source book for all Oracle SQL for version 7.3. It can be found on the Web, at the time of writing, at http://www.nw.mdx.ac.uk/oracle.htm, http://is.dal.c/~oracle/, and http://www.techiesinc.com/oracledocs/DOC/products.htm. I found these sites using the Alta Vista search engine, with a search of "oracle+online+documentation". Due to the ephemeral nature of the Web, these sites may not always be available.

PL/SQL

Terms you'll need to understand:

√ Anonymous PL/SQL block

√ Procedure

√ Function

√ Package header

√ Package body

√ Implicit cursor

√ Explicit cursor

√ Flow control

Techniques you'll need to master:

√ Creating anonymous PL/SQL blocks

√ Creating procedures

√ Creating functions

√ Creating packages

√ Using flow control statements

√ Using implicit and explicit cursors

One of the most important additions to Oracle has been PL/SQL. In normal SQL, you deal with single- or multiple value sets only. In SQL, there's no way to conditionally insert, update, or select values based on multiple-condition sets (for example, if value A is 6, then make B currentcount+1, or if A is 7, make B currentcount-1). There's also no way to do single-line processing of a set of values in SQL. All of this functionality, conditional processing, flow control, and single-line set processing came along when Oracle added PL/SQL. Both directly support DML commands; special Oracle-provided packages must be employed to use DDL commands in PL/SQL. Unlike SQL, PL/SQL also allows for exception handling routines.

The PL/SQL Engine

The PL/SQL engine processes PL/SQL blocks submitted from the Server Manager. The PL/SQL blocks are parsed into the procedural statements and SQL statements. These parsed statements are processed by passing the procedural statements to the Procedural Statement Executor inside the engine, which also processes data that is local to the application and then passes the SQL statements, as needed, to the Oracle7 server SQL Statement Executor.

Memory Use And PL/SQL

Another time-saving feature of PL/SQL is that it allows a correctly written, parsed program to be used many times. A PL/SQL package, function, procedure, and, now, trigger once used will remain in memory until it's no longer frequently accessed. Hence, PL/SQL objects are collectively known as *stored objects*. In addition, PL/SQL uses the advantageous block structure that allows for compartmentalization of programs by function. By wrapping many SQL lines into one PL/SQL program, client/server applications reduce network traffic because a PL/SQL program is sent as one transaction to the database, not as multiple, smaller transactions. The PL/SQL engine can also be incorporated into other program sets, such as those involving forms and reports, thereby reducing transaction processing in these programs as well. A PL/SQL subprogram must contain a header, executable section, and an **END** command.

PL/SQL Basics

PL/SQL uses the block concept contained within a **BEGIN...END;** construct. An unnamed PL/SQL block that's used either as a standalone in SQL*Plus or as part of a trigger is known as an *anonymous PL/SQL block*. These anonymous blocks can be used in all Oracle environments. The **BEGIN...END;**, usually called the *executable section*, is the only required part of a PL/SQL program; it must begin with the keyword **BEGIN** and end with the keyword **END** followed by a semicolon. All **BEGIN...END;** keywords must be balanced.

A database trigger is a PL/SQL program (actually an anonymous PL/SQL block) that's associated with a table and is executed (or fired) automatically based on a predefined action such as **INSERT**, **UPDATE**, or **DELETE** against the table.

A complete PL/SQL program consists of the following:

➤ **A declaration section** Where variables, cursors, and constants are defined

➤ **An executable section** Where the program logic is performed

➤ **An exception handling section** Where errors are handled

An anonymous PL/SQL program can consist of just a **BEGIN...END;** block, a **DECLARE** section and **BEGIN...END;** block, or a **DECLARE**, **BEGIN...END;**, and **EXCEPTION** section. Anonymous PL/SQL programs can be as short as a single line or span dozens of pages and be as complex as any procedure, function, or trigger. There must be an executable statement within the **BEGIN...END;** statements for a block to be valid. The most simple anonymous PL/SQL block would be:

```
BEGIN
NULL;
END;
```

Of course it doesn't do anything. (**NULL** is an executable statement in PL/SQL and is used to fill in when you don't have any processing to do but must have a PL/SQL block, such as in some exception situations.)

By definition, any stored PL/SQL block (that is, the PL/SQL program is stored in the data dictionary tables and doesn't need to be read from an external file) is a named PL/SQL block. A named PL/SQL block can be a procedure or a function. Beginning with version 7.3, trigger definitions are now stored objects even though they contain anonymous PL/SQL blocks. The most simple PL/SQL named object (hence, a stored object) would be:

```
PROCEDURE start_it IS
BEGIN
NULL;
END start_it;
```

Although the purpose of such a stored object isn't really clear right now, I'll show you what it can be used for in a little bit.

Related PL/SQL procedures and functions can be combined into stored structures called *packages*. PL/SQL packages consist of a header section that declares all publicly available contents of the package and their variables and the package body, which contains the actual package definitions and any private objects, not usable outside of the package. When any publicly available part of a package is used, the entire package is read into memory and made available.

In some cases, a package may be used by multiple users who access the same application. In this situation, the package should be read into memory and *pinned* (removed from the aging algorithm) to keep it in memory. To prevent shared pool fragmentation, this preloading of packages should be done before any ad hoc SQL generation occurs. To this end, a procedure similar to the **start_it** procedure shown in the earlier snippet should be included in all packages, so a simple call to the **start_it** procedure inside the package loads the entire package into memory where it can be pinned using the **DBMS_SHARED_POOL** package.

PL/SQL Procedures

PL/SQL procedures are stored, named objects that can return zero, one, or many values to the calling process. However, only one row of values can be returned from a single procedure call. Procedure variables used for sending variables into the program and for receiving values from the program are specified at the start of the program and designated as **IN** (input variables that can't have their values altered by the program, so they're treated as constants), **OUT** (output variables that are set by the program during execution), and **IN OUT** (variables that are used for both input and output of values).

When creating procedures, the next line after the end of the procedure definition must be a forward slash (/) to tell Oracle to compile the procedure. The last statement of a PL/SQL procedure must end with a semicolon.

As was demonstrated with the **start_it** procedure, neither input nor output is required from a procedure. A procedure also doesn't require a declarative section. In fact, the only required part of a procedure is the **PROCEDURE** line and the executable block.

Procedures are created using the **CREATE PROCEDURE** command. The syntax for the **CREATE PROCEDURE** command is shown in Figure 7.1.

The clauses and variables for the **CREATE PROCEDURE** command are defined as:

➤ **CREATE [OR REPLACE]** Causes SQL to create a procedure. If **OR REPLACE** is not used and if the procedure exists, an error will result. The **OR REPLACE** allows for in-place altering of a procedure without

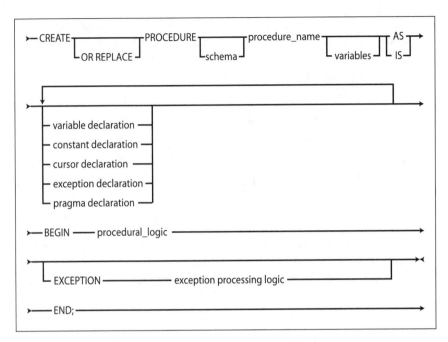

Figure 7.1   Syntax for the **CREATE PROCEDURE** command.

affecting any of its grants or dependencies. The **CREATE [OR RE-PLACE]** must be at the beginning of the statement for the procedure to be created or replaced in SQL*Plus.

➤ **schema** Name of owner for the procedure. Defaults to current user.

➤ **procedure_name** Name for the procedure (must follow standard table naming conventions).

➤ **variables** Variable declarations in a comma-separated list. A variable declaration has the format:

```
variable_name  variable_characteristic variable_type
```

For example:

```
(role_name IN VARCHAR2, newpass IN VARCHAR2)
```

Notice that no size information is specified, only the datatype of the variable, and that each variable is declared independently. Multiple declarations can't be attached to a single-type specification; each variable must have its own type of specification. The *variable_characteristic* is one of **IN, OUT**, and **IN OUT**. An **IN** variable acts as a constant and can be an expression; an **OUT** variable can only be written to and is used to return a value to the calling process; and **IN OUT** is used to pass in a value, then after the value has been changed, return it to the calling process. The *variable_type* must be specified or an error will result. If the variable characteristic isn't defined, it defaults to **IN**.

➤ **IS or AS** Some tools will balk at using **IS**, some will balk at using **AS**, and some don't care, so be watchful when using coding tools. One of these keywords must be specified or an error will result.

➤ **variable declaration** A variable declaration of the form:

```
variable_name  datatype;
```

Variable names must follow the rules for table names, with only one variable name per datatype declaration. The datatype is any allowed PL/SQL datatype. The declaration must end with a semicolon. For example:

```
Test_date   DATE;
Test_score   NUMBER;
Retest_date   DATE;
```

Multiple variable declarations per a single datatype line are not allowed. For example

```
Test_date, retest_date      DATE;
```

is not allowed.

➤ **constant declaration** Similar to a variable definition except the keyword **CONSTANT** must be declared. A constant's value can't be changed once it is set unless it's redeclared inside a subsequent block. A constant declaration looks like this:

```
passing_score CONSTANT NUMBER := 68;
```

In this example, the variable **passing_score** is assigned the value of *68* as a numeric datatype. The := compound symbol in PL/SQL is used to show assignment, the = sign is used to show equality only.

➤ **cursor declaration** If a SQL statement will retrieve multiple values, you should set it as a cursor using a cursor declaration. The cursor declaration has the form:

```
CURSOR cursor_name (input_variables) IS
executable_sql_statement;
```

For example:

```
CURSOR get_stat(stat IN VARCHAR2) IS
      SELECT name,value
      FROM v$sysstat
      WHERE name = stat;
```

The input variables to a cursor can't have a dimension specified. **CHAR, VARCHAR2**, and **NUMBER** are allowed, but **CHAR(2), VARCHAR2(20)**, or **NUMBER(10,2)** would be rejected with a format error if you tried to use them.

➤ **exception declaration** An exception is an error handling routine. Numerous predefined exceptions don't need to be declared in your program, but any user-defined exceptions must be declared in this section. An exception declaration looks like this:

```
exception_name EXCEPTION;
```

The exception name follows the naming guidelines. User-defined exceptions must be explicitly called using the **RAISE** command. Implicit exceptions are invoked automatically when they occur.

➤ **pragma declaration** A **PRAGMA EXCEPTION_INIT** declaration usually goes hand in hand with the exception declaration. A *pragma* is a PL/SQL interpreter directive that remaps standard Oracle errors into user-defined errors. The pragma call is formatted like this:

```
PRAGMA EXCEPTION_INIT(exception_name, error_number);
```

For example:

```
PRAGMA EXCEPTION_INIT(table_not_found, -904);
```

➤ **procedural_logic** The procedural logic (also known as the executable section) is the collection of SQL and PL/SQL statements used to manipulate data in the database wrapped in **BEGIN...END;** blocks. These blocks can be nested to any depth up to the maximum allowed size of a stored procedure. (It should be noted that on some systems there was a limit of 32K to 64K for a single stored procedure.) The **RAISE** command for use in exceptions can only be used in the procedural logic or executable section of a PL/SQL program. Remember that the last line of any PL/SQL program must end in a semicolon.

➤ **exception processing logic** In the final section of a PL/SQL procedure (or an individual block), you process exceptions. The exception handling, although a good practice, isn't required. The exception section of a procedure performs error trapping. All user-defined exceptions must be defined in the declaration section of the procedure before they can be raised or used. An exception processing section is formatted like this:

```
EXCEPTION
       WHEN exception_name THEN
       Error_handling_code
    END;
```

For example:

```
EXCEPTION
       WHEN table_not_found THEN
       INSERT INTO error_log
              VALUES (SYSDATE,'Table '||table_name
                     ||' not found');
    END;
```

Procedures allow complex processing to be reduced to a single procedure call statement. Procedures also enforce uniform processing techniques and ensure good standards are followed. By forcing use of procedures, you'll encourage code reuse and allow reuse of stored code from the shared pool, thus improving performance. In a client/server environment, use of procedures forces processing to the server and reduces network traffic.

PL/SQL Functions

PL/SQL functions allow multiple inputs and must return a single value. This characteristic of functions, that they must return a value, is the major difference between a function and a procedure. Functions can either be standalone or they can be placed in packages. If a function is to be used outside of its package, it must have its purity defined to the Oracle system through use of the **PRAGMA RESTRICT_REFERENCES** call in the package header right after the functions declaration. The **CREATE FUNCTION** command syntax is shown in Figure 7.2.

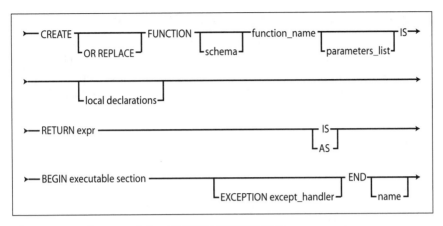

Figure 7.2 Syntax of the **CREATE FUNCTION** command.

The following are the definitions for the clauses and variables in the **CREATE FUNCTION** command:

➤ **schema** Name of the function owner.

➤ **parameter_list** List of parameters specified as follows:

```
param_name [IN|OUT|IN OUT] datatype [{:=|DEFAULT} expr]
```

The datatype specification must not have a dimension specified (for example **CHAR** not **CHAR(3)**).

➤ **local declarations** Any locally defined variables, constants, exceptions, or cursors.

➤ **executable section** Contains code used for processing in the function.

➤ **exception_handler** Exception handling code for the function.

➤ **name** Same as the name specified for the function.

➤ **expr** Expression to be returned to the calling user. The expression can be as simple as a local variable name or as complex as a mathematical equation that returns a value calculated for input values.

Functions are used to manipulate data and return a single value. Functions by definition can't alter a package's, program's, or data item's state. This means functions can't be used to write data or change the state of the system or database. A function must contain a **RETURN** statement.

Creating Anonymous PL/SQL Blocks

Anonymous PL/SQL blocks are used inside SQL routines, triggers, or directly from operating system files. Anonymous PL/SQL blocks can be used to do virtually anything that procedures and functions can, with the exception that they aren't stored in the database. An anonymous PL/SQL block has the general form:

```
DECLARE
    Declarations
BEGIN
    Executable section
EXCEPTION
    Exception handlers
END;
```

The only required portion of an anonymous PL/SQL block is the **BEGIN...END;** block with the executable section. Notice there's no **CREATE OR REPLACE** command; anonymous blocks are built directly in SQL*Plus or directly as a text file using a system editor. Anonymous PL/SQL blocks can be called from any of Oracle's executable environments and are executed by either reading them into the SQL*Plus buffer with a **GET** command and then executing a **RUN, R,** or forward slash (/) command followed by an enter or return keystroke.

Anonymous PL/SQL is especially useful in SQL*Plus scripts where complex processing is required, but the frequency of use doesn't warrant a stored procedure or function. Of course, triggers are built using anonymous PL/SQL blocks.

Exception Handling

By proper coding techniques, such as the use of exception processing, you can eliminate application hangs due to errors. Any user-defined exception or error must be implicitly invoked by use of the **RAISE** command. For example:

```
BEGIN
    ---- processing ----
    IF inventory_count < min_stocking_value THEN
        RAISE need_to_reorder;
    END IF;
    ---- processing ----
END;
```

A special form of exception is known as the **OTHERS** exception. The **OTHERS** exception should be a part of any set of exceptions. It traps any nonspecific error that happens so you can exit gracefully from your routine. The **WHEN**

OTHERS clause is only allowed in an exception section of a procedure, function, or anonymous PL/SQL block.

Using Cursors

Explicit cursors are predefined, multirow-returning SQL statements. Cursors are processed explicitly through the use of OPEN, FETCH, and CLOSE commands or through the use of cursor loops. An OPEN command parses the cursor code and calls the rows identified by the query. FETCH processes the cursor code to retrieve one row from the selected set of rows, and the values are inserted into a record or set of variables specified with an INTO clause. CLOSE closes the cursor, releasing any memory assigned to the cursor. A cursor loop has the format:

```
FOR rec_id IN cursor_id LOOP
-- processing --
END LOOP;
```

One advantage of the cursor FOR loop is that no OPEN, FETCH, or CLOSE commands are required for cursor control. That's all handled by the loop logic.

The *rec_id* must be a suitably defined record structure or properly typed variable to hold what is returned from the cursor. The *cursor_id* is the name of the cursor. The effect of issuing this type of command is to open and parse, then fetch rows from the cursor until no more records are found, at which time the cursor loop ends.

Implicit Cursors

An implicit cursor is automatically defined when any SQL statement is issued. An implicit cursor will result in two fetches against the database: one to get an indication if more than one row will be returned (if there is, you get an implicit exception raised) and the next to actually get the row. Implicit cursors can only be used to process one row at a time.

Cursor Attributes

Explicit cursors have built-in attributes that allow tracking of their status. These cursor attributes are:

➤ *Cursor_name*%FOUND Before the first fetch on an opened cursor, this is NULL and if the latest fetch is successful, %FOUND becomes TRUE. This shouldn't be checked until after a fetch has executed.

➤ *Cursor_name*%ISOPEN Before a cursor is opened, this is FALSE. If the cursor has been opened and if it's still open, this will yield TRUE.

➤ *Cursor_name*%NOTFOUND If the last fetch yields a row, this is **FALSE** and if the last fetch was unsuccessful, this becomes **TRUE**.

➤ *Cursor_name*%ROWCOUNT Returns the count for the number of rows fetched thus far. Before a cursor is opened, this yields a **NULL**. Before the first fetch, this yields zero. If **%ROWCOUNT** is checked before a cursor is opened, it will raise the **INVALID_CURSOR** exception. Until a cursor is closed, the **%ROWCOUNT** will contain the last valid count of records fetched.

Cursor attributes can also be used with the most current SQL statement (implicit cursor) by appending "SQL" to the front of their name instead of the name of the cursor. With the exception that no **OPEN** or **FETCH** logic is needed, the attributes work the same with an implicit or explicit cursor.

Controlling Flow In PL/SQL

Flow control, the use of loops and logic control such as **IF...THEN...ELSE**, was the primary reason PL/SQL was created. SQL, though great for set processing, was found lacking when it came to structure. Indeed, it wasn't designed to be structured.

PL/SQL loop control is executed through several types of loop control statements; the easiest is the **LOOP...END LOOP;**. This simple structure is augmented through additional control clauses such as **WHILE, EXIT,** and **EXIT WHEN**. PL/SQL also supports the **FOR...LOOP...END LOOP;** construct that allows iteration control, as well as the **WHILE...LOOP...END LOOP;** for conditional control.

IF...THEN...ELSE Structures

The **IF...THEN...ELSE** structure allows a single-pass conditional statement to be created. The conditions are always evaluated against the Boolean **TRUE** to determine if processing should be done or if control should pass to the next section. The full syntax for the **IF...THEN...ELSE** construct is:

```
IF condition1 THEN
    Sequence of statements
ELSIF condition2 THEN
    Sequence of statements
ELSE
    Final sequence of statements
END IF;
```

The condition statements can be simple or complex equalities or Boolean values. If the condition in the statement yields a **TRUE**, the following sequence of statements is executed. If the condition is **FALSE**, the processing passes down the decision tree of **ELSIF**s to the final **ELSE** and **END IF**. The only required part of the structure is the **IF...END IF;**. Be sure that the **END IF** is two separate words or an error will result. Notice also that the term is **ELSIF**, not ELSEIF. Finally, the final **ELSE**, if present, has no condition associated with it; it shows the final decision in the decision tree if all others are **FALSE**. If the **ELSE** isn't present, the control passes back into the program body.

A Simple *LOOP...END LOOP; Construct*

The most simple loop structure is the **LOOP...END LOOP;**. Note that unless control is passed either from an **EXIT**, **EXIT WHEN**, or exception generation, a **LOOP...END LOOP** is an infinite loop. Never depend on an exception to throw you out of a loop. The actual structure of a **LOOP...END LOOP;** looks like the following:

```
<<label_name>>
LOOP
    Sequence of statements
END LOOP label_name;
```

The *label_name* is not required; but for a nested loop structure, its use makes debugging easier.

By using the **EXIT** command, simple loops become more controllable, as seen here:

```
<<label_name>>
LOOP
    Sequence of statements
    IF condition THEN EXIT label_name;
END LOOP label_name;
```

The condition can also be built into the **EXIT** using the **WHEN** statement:

```
<<label_name>>
LOOP
    Sequence of statements
    EXIT label_name WHEN condition;
END LOOP label_name;
```

Alternate forms of the **EXIT** and **WHEN** can be used such as:

```
WHEN condition EXIT;
```

The **WHILE** Loop

Another useful form of the loop is the **WHILE** loop. The **WHILE** loop allows specification of a condition at the start of the loop, and until the condition is met, the loop executes. Unlike an **IF** statement, which only processes its set of statements if the condition it tests is **TRUE**, a **WHILE** loop will execute its contained statements until its limiting condition is **FALSE**. The **WHILE** loop should be used when an exact count of items to be processed is not available, which means the loop must continue until finished. The form for a **WHILE** loop is:

```
WHILE condition LOOP
    Sequence of statements
END LOOP;
```

Always be sure that the limiting condition will be reached. A statement inside the **WHILE** loop must itself initiate the setting of the Boolean condition or you've created an infinite loop. Note that you can also use the **WHILE NOT** condition **LOOP** form.

The **FOR** Loop

The **FOR** loop is used to process a specific number of iterations. The order of iteration can be set to either the default ascending order (1,2,3) or to reverse order (3,2,1). A specialized form of the **FOR** loop is the cursor loop that we've already discussed in previous sections. The format of the **FOR** loop is:

```
FOR index IN [REVERSE] lower_bound..higher_bound LOOP
    Sequence of statements
END LOOP;
```

Notice that there's no **STEP** command like there is in some languages that allow alteration of the iteration interval. In PL/SQL, the iteration interval is always 1. To use intervals, the **MOD(m,n)** command can be used within an **IF...END IF** structure or some other means of iteration control implemented. The lower or upper bounds can be replaced with variables. Note that the **EXIT** command and its alternative structures using **WHEN** can be used inside the **FOR** loop structure to force a premature exit from the loop.

The **GOTO** And **NULL** Statements

The **GOTO** is also present in PL/SQL. Luckily it's seldom used and it's not a crucial statement. A **GOTO** is an unconditional branch. You can't use **GOTO** into an **IF**, **LOOP**, or sub-block.

The **NULL** is the only executable command that doesn't do anything. In fact, not doing anything is its purpose. I already showed you one possible use of the **NULL** in the **start_it** procedure. Another is for testing and also for placement inside an exception block where you want to handle an exception that's been raised, but other than exiting the block, you don't want to take any other action. A common use of the **NULL** is in a **WHEN OTHERS** exception block.

DML And PL/SQL

All of the flow control, structure, and other PL/SQL is useless unless it can be used in the processing of data. PL/SQL uses Data Manipulation Language (DML) statements just like standard SQL to process the data in the database. Some functions or highly specialized procedures may contain no DML, but this is the exception rather than the rule. In general, there are four DML statements that are used in PL/SQL; these are **INSERT, UPDATE, DELETE,** and **SELECT**.

Use Of INSERT In PL/SQL

The **INSERT** command is used in an identical fashion in PL/SQL as it's used in normal DML processing in SQL sessions. However, you can also use **INSERT** with user-defined storage types created using the **%TYPE** and **%ROWTYPE** calls against the database or from the **TYPE** declarations in the declaration section. The **SQL%ROWCOUNT, SQL%FOUND,** and **SQL%NOTFOUND** attributes can be used after an **INSERT** statement to determine the status of the insert operation. If the transaction is successful (that is, rows are inserted), **%FOUND** will be **TRUE, %NOTFOUND** will be **FALSE,** and **%ROWCOUNT** will show the number of rows inserted. If the transaction is unsuccessful (that is, no rows are inserted), **%FOUND** will be **FALSE, %NOTFOUND** will be **TRUE,** and **%ROWCOUNT** will be zero.

Use Of UPDATE In PL/SQL

The **UPDATE** command is used in PL/SQL the same as it's used in normal DML processing in SQL sessions. However, you can also use **UPDATE** with user-defined storage types created using the **%TYPE** and **%ROWTYPE** calls against the database or from the **TYPE** declarations in the declaration section. The **SQL%ROWCOUNT, SQL%FOUND,** and **SQL%NOTFOUND** attributes can be used after an **UPDATE** statement to determine the status of the update operation. If the transaction is successful (that is, rows are updated), **%FOUND** will be **TRUE, %NOTFOUND** will be **FALSE,** and **%ROWCOUNT** will show the number of rows updated. If the transaction is unsuccessful (that is, no rows are updated), **%FOUND** will be **FALSE, %NOTFOUND** will be **TRUE,** and **%ROWCOUNT** will be zero.

The only addition to standard SQL for the **UPDATE** command is the **WHERE CURRENT OF** clause. This clause is used to specify the name of a cursor whose **SELECT** statement includes the **FOR UPDATE** qualifier.

Use Of DELETE In PL/SQL

The **DELETE** command is used in PL/SQL the same as it's used in normal DML processing in SQL sessions. However, you can also use **DELETE** with user-defined storage types created using the **%TYPE** and **%ROWTYPE** calls against the database or from the **TYPE** declarations in the declaration section. The **SQL%ROWCOUNT**, **SQL%FOUND**, and **SQL%NOTFOUND** attributes can be used after a **DELETE** statement to determine the status of the delete operation. If the transaction is successful (that is, rows are deleted), **%FOUND** will be **TRUE**, **%NOTFOUND** will be **FALSE**, and **%ROWCOUNT** will show the number of rows deleted. If the transaction is unsuccessful (that is, no rows are deleted), **%FOUND** will be **FALSE**, **%NOTFOUND** will be **TRUE**, and **%ROWCOUNT** will be zero.

The only addition to standard SQL for the **DELETE** command is the **WHERE CURRENT OF** clause. This clause is used to specify the name of a cursor whose **SELECT** statement includes the **FOR UPDATE** qualifier.

Use Of SELECT In PL/SQL

Of the four commands, (**INSERT, UPDATE, DELETE,** and **SELECT**) **SELECT** has the most differences between how it's used in PL/SQL and how it's used in SQL. In SQL, a **SELECT** is expected to return sets of rows that satisfy a specified condition from one or more tables. In PL/SQL, the command must only return one row unless it's placed in a cursor. The format for a **SELECT** statement that's not in a cursor adds the **INTO** keyword and requires a list of variables or types into which the retrieved row is to be inserted. For example, the following code would generate an error

```
SELECT ename FROM emp WHERE emp_number = 1;
```

while this code is perfectly acceptable (assuming **my_ename** has been declared):

```
SELECT ename INTO my_ename WHERE emp_number = 1;
```

If a **SELECT** returns more than one row, it must be placed in a cursor to be used in PL/SQL, as seen here:

```
CURSOR get_ename IS
    SELECT ename FROM emp;
```

To use a **SELECT** placed inside a cursor, either use the **OPEN, FETCH,** or **CLOSE** set of commands, or use a cursor loop to process the return sets of data, as seen here

```
BEGIN
   -- processing --
   OPEN get_ename;
   FETCH get_ename INTO my_ename;
   WHILE get_ename%FOUND LOOP
   -- processing --
      FETCH get_ename INTO my_ename;
   END LOOP;
   CLOSE get_ename;
   -- more processing --
END;
```

or with a cursor loop, as seen here:

```
BEGIN
   -- processing --
   FOR my_ename IN get_ename LOOP
   -- processing --
   END LOOP;
   -- more processing --
END;
```

In either case, the multirow-returning SQL **SELECT** must be inside a cursor. Remember that for every item in the **SELECT** list, there must be a corresponding item in the **INTO** list. A record specification or a type specification can be used as the target for the **INTO** clause. A type is specified using the **%TYPE** and a record is either implicitly created in the **FOR** loop or can be explicitly created using the **%ROWTYPE** or **TYPE** and **RECORD** declarations. The SQL%FOUND, SQL%NOTFOUND, and SQL%ROWCOUNT can be used to determine the status of a noncursor **SELECT** statement. If the transaction is successful (that is, a row is selected), **%FOUND** will be **TRUE**, **%NOTFOUND** will be **FALSE**, and **%ROWCOUNT** will show a value of 1. If the transaction is unsuccessful (that is, no row is selected), **%FOUND** will be **FALSE**, **%NOTFOUND** will be **TRUE**, and **%ROWCOUNT** will be zero.

The **FOR UPDATE** clause can be added to the **SELECT** command to lock the row or rows selected to allow for update or deletion.

COMMIT And ROLLBACK In PL/SQL

PL/SQL is transaction based. Just as in SQL, a transaction can be *committed* (made permanent), using **COMMIT** or *rolled back* (removed), using **ROLLBACK**. When a **COMMIT** is issued inside a PL/SQL block, all pending transactions inside the block are committed and made permanent, ending the current transaction. Similarly, if a **ROLLBACK** is issued, then all pending transactions are rolled back and forgotten, also ending the current transaction. A **ROLLBACK** can also be used to roll back to a **SAVEPOINT** to preserve a portion of a large, complex transaction.

ALTER And DROP Commands In PL/SQL

The only option allowed for an **ALTER** command for packages, package bodies, procedures, and functions is the **COMPILE** option. The **COMPILE** option forces a recompilation of the object and is used to recompile packages that may have been made invalid by temporary unavailability of something it was dependent upon. To alter an object's contents, use the **CREATE OR REPLACE** command.

The **DROP** command will remove the specified object from the database. A procedure or function inside a package can't be dropped. The package itself must be rebuilt without the object using the **CREATE OR REPLACE** command.

Procedure Builder

Oracle has provided a new tool to help with the creation, debugging, and testing of PL/SQL code. This tool is called Procedure Builder. A major limitation with Procedure Builder is that it only supports PL/SQL version1.x, so if you want to use PL/SQL version 2.x features, you can't use Procedure Builder. However, Procedure Builder allows for online debugging, object dependency viewing, and online testing of PL/SQL objects. Procedure Builder also allows for the generation of more than just PL/SQL files. In the following sections, I will discuss these features of Procedure Builder and the important aspects of these features.

Files Generated By Procedure Builder

Procedure Builder generates several types of files, including:

➤ **PLS** PL/SQL source text for a single program unit.

➤ **PLD** Interpretable script containing a mixture of PL/SQL source text, SQL statements, and Interpreter commands.

➤ **PLL** A compiled PL/SQL library.

➤ **LOG** An interpreter log file.

Components Of Procedure Builder

Procedure Builder is a GUI-type tool. It consists of numerous components, which are discussed in the following subsections.

The Interpreter

The PL/SQL Interpreter is the central debugging workspace for Procedure Builder. It's a two-pane window used to define, display, and debug PL/SQL program units. The PL/SQL Interpreter can be either *modal* or *modeless*. Modal means it's displayed by an Oracle product while executing an application; modeless is when the Procedure Builder is manually invoked. The PL/SQL Interpreter window contains:

➤ **The menu bar** Used in modeless mode to provide access to commands.

➤ **The control bar** Contains accelerators (wizards) for most common tasks.

➤ **The source pane** Displays a program unit's source code.

➤ **The navigator pane** Displays the object hierarchy for the current session and debugging nodes only when used in modal mode. The navigator pane can be hidden when the PL/SQL interpreter is used in a modeless state.

➤ **The interpreter pane** Used to enter and evaluate any PL/SQL construct, procedure builder, or SQL commands.

When in modal state, the PL/SQL interpreter contains additional buttons for accessing functions that are available in menus in the modeless state.

The Object Navigator

As a standalone application, the Object Navigator is displayed as a separate window or as an overlay in the interpreter window. The Navigator provides icon-based access to the objects you have access to from the current session. It displays information about dependencies, references made to other objects, parameter values, and so forth, and it also provides access to any defined debug actions for a specific object. The Object Navigator provides the simplicity of drag-and-drop movement of program units from the server side to the client side for debugging and editing, and it's also used to edit the properties of database objects.

The Object Navigator uses the concept of nodes to access Navigator capabilities. For example, the **STACK** node is used to change parameter values; other nodes are:

➤ **PROGRAM UNITS** Shows the current session's accessible PL/SQL program units.

➤ **LIBRARIES** Shows PL/SQL libraries available for the current session.

➤ **ATTACHED LIBRARIES** Shows all attached libraries.

➤ **BUILT-IN PACKAGES** Shows available Procedure Builder built-in functions.

➤ **DEBUG ACTIONS** Shows debug actions for the current program unit.

➤ **STACK** Shows current PL/SQL stack details such as variables, functions, and procedures.

➤ **DATABASE OBJECTS** Shows database objects available to the current session.

The Object Navigator provides access to several other editor or parameter entry windows. Examples of available editors are the Database Trigger and Stored Procedure editors. The Database Trigger Editor allows for the selection, viewing, editing, and compilation of database triggers. The Stored Procedure Editor allows for the selection, viewing, editing, and recompilation of stored program units. The PL/SQL submitted from the Database Trigger Editor or Stored Program Unit Editor are compiled on the server side.

The Program Unit Editor

The Program Unit Editor is used to create and edit PL/SQL program units. The Program Unit Editor compiles the program unit and allows troubleshooting of errors generated directly in the editor.

Procedure Builder Debug Actions

Debug Actions are commands that are entered into your PL/SQL program units. Debug Actions are of two general types—breakpoints and debug triggers.

Breakpoints suspend execution at a specific source line of a program unit and control is passed to the Interpreter. A breakpoint suspends operation just before a specific line of code, allowing you to step through the rest of the program unit. The **GO to STEP** command is used to resume execution of the program unit after a breakpoint is reached.

A breakpoint can also automatically invoke a breakpoint trigger. That breakpoint trigger is a PL/SQL block that's executed when a breakpoint is reached.

A debug trigger is a trigger that's fired when a specific line of PL/SQL code is reached. Note that the debug trigger is executed before the specified line executes.

Exam Prep Questions

Question 1

> What does the Procedural Statement Executor within the PL/SQL
> engine do?
>
> ○ a. Separates the SQL statements and sends them to the
>   SQL Statement Executor.
>
> ○ b. Processes server-side data.
>
> ○ c. Processes data that is local to the application.
>
> ○ d. Passes blocks of PL/SQL to the Oracle7 server.

The correct answer is c. Answer a is incorrect because this is a function of the
PL/SQL engine but not the Procedural Statement Executor inside the en-
gine. Answer b is incorrect because the server-side data is processed by the
Oracle7 server. Answer d is incorrect because this is a function of the Server
Manager, not the PL/SQL engine or its subcomponent, the Procedural State-
ment Executor.

Question 2

> Evaluate this procedure:
>
> ```
> PROCEDURE price_increase
>     (v_quota    IN BOOLEAN,
>      v_stock    IN BOOLEAN,
>      v_approval    IN OUT BOOLEAN)
> IS
> BEGIN
>     v_approval:= v_quota AND v_stock;
> END;
> ```
>
> If **v_quota** equals **NULL** and **v_stock** equals **NULL**, which value is
> assigned to **v_approval**?
>
> ○ a. **TRUE**
>
> ○ b. **FALSE**
>
> ○ c. **NULL**
>
> ○ d. None of the above

The proper response is c, because any combination involving a **NULL** results in a **NULL**. The answer a is incorrect because to evaluate to **TRUE**, both would have to be **TRUE**. Answer b is incorrect because to evaluate to **FALSE**, one value would be **TRUE** and the other **FALSE** or both would be **FALSE**. Answer d is incorrect because a Boolean value is only allowed to be **TRUE**, **FALSE**, or **NULL**.

Question 3

In which section of a PL/SQL block is a **WHEN OTHERS** clause allowed?

○ a. Header

○ b. Declarative

○ c. Executable

○ d. Exception

○ e. None of the above

The proper answer is d. The **WHEN OTHERS** clause is an exception handling clause. Answer a is incorrect because the **WHEN OTHERS** clause is only allowed in an exception section and is used to process implicit exceptions that aren't specifically covered by **WHEN** statements in the exception section. Answers b and c are incorrect for the same reason as answer a.

Question 4

Evaluate this cursor statement:

```
DECLARE
    CURSOR price_cursor
        (v_price NUMBER(8,2)) IS
        SELECT id_number, description,
        manufacturer_id
        FROM inventory
        WHERE price > v_price;
```

Why will this statement cause an error?

○ a. A parameter isn't defined.

○ b. The size of the variable can't be specified.

○ c. A **WHERE** clause can't be used in a cursor statement.

○ d. The **SELECT** statement is missing the **INTO** clause.

The proper answer is b, because only a variables type and not any size information is specified in the input variable section. Answer a is incorrect because all required parameters are specified. Answer c is incorrect because a **WHERE** clause is allowed in cursor statements. Answer d is incorrect because, in a cursor statement, the **INTO** clause must *not* be specified. The **INTO** clause is only specified in a **SELECT** statement used as an implicit cursor in PL/SQL; this is an explicit cursor.

Question 5

When will a **SELECT** statement in a PL/SQL block raise an exception?

- ○ a. When it retrieves only one row
- ○ b. When it retrieves more than one row
- ○ c. When the datatypes within the **SELECT** statement are inconsistent
- ○ d. When the **SELECT** statement is missing a required clause
- ○ e. None of the above

Answer b is the correct answer. An exception will be raised if an implicit cursor retrieves more than one row. Answer a is incorrect because an implicit cursor (a **SELECT** statement in a PL/SQL block) by definition is only allowed to return a single row. Answers c and d are incorrect because this type of error will not allow the PL/SQL program unit to be successfully compiled. If you can't compile the code, it can't execute, and if it can't execute, it can't raise an exception.

Question 6

Which type of commands are supported by PL/SQL?

- ○ a. DDL
- ○ b. DCL
- ○ c. DML
- ○ d. No commands are supported by PL/SQL

The answer to this question is c, DML (or Data Manipulation Language). Answer a, DDL, is incorrect because Data Definition Language is not directly supported in PL/SQL. To use DDL you must use one of the special support packages, such as DBMS_SQL or DBMS_UTILITY. Answer b, DCL, is incorrect. As far as I can research, DCL is Digital Control Language used in the VAX-VMS/OpenVMS system for job control. Answer d is incorrect because answer c is correct.

Question 7

> Which PL/SQL program construct must return a value?
>
> ○ a. Anonymous block
>
> ○ b. Stored function
>
> ○ c. Stored procedure
>
> ○ d. Database trigger
>
> ○ e. Application trigger

The correct answer is b. Answer a is incorrect because an anonymous PL/SQL block is incapable of returning a value; there's no syntax for it. Answer c is incorrect because the major difference between a function and a procedure is that a function must return a value whereas a procedure doesn't have to. Answers d and e are incorrect because, again, the syntax and functionality of a trigger doesn't permit the return of values.

Question 8

> Which three PL/SQL subprogram components are required?
>
> ❒ a. Header
>
> ❒ b. Declarative
>
> ❒ c. Executable
>
> ❒ d. Exception handling
>
> ❒ e. End

The correct answers are a, c, and e. Answer b is incorrect because a declarative section is not required. Answer d is incorrect because you aren't required to put exception handing into your application (even though it's a good idea). Remember, our simplest procedure would be:

```
CREATE PROCEDURE start_it AS    < This is the header
BEGIN
    NULL;
END;            < From the BEGIN to
                  the END is the executable
                  section. Every block must
                  have a BEGIN and END.
```

Question 9

Using SQL*Plus, you attempt to create this procedure:

```
    PROCEDURE price_increase
    (v_percent_increase    NUMBER)
IS
BEGIN
    UPDATE inventory
    SET price = price * v_percent_increase;
    COMMIT;
END;
```

Why does this command cause an error?

○ a. A parameter mode was not declared.

○ b. The procedure does not return a value.

○ c. The **CREATE OR REPLACE** clause is missing.

○ d. A datatype is not specified.

This is a trick question because many people will not understand what the question is asking. Remember, if it isn't shown in the question, then it isn't there. In this case, the **CREATE OR REPLACE** command line is not shown. Answer c is the correct answer. Answer a is incorrect because the mode will default to IN if not specified. Answer b is incorrect because procedures don't have to return values, only functions have to return values. Answer d is incorrect because a datatype (**NUMBER**) is clearly specified.

Question 10

Which PL/SQL program construct is associated with a database table and is fired automatically?

○ a. Anonymous block

○ b. Stored function

○ c. Stored procedure

○ d. Database trigger

○ e. Application trigger

○ f. Application procedure

Answer d is the correct answer. Answer a is incorrect because an anonymous block, although used to create the code in a trigger, can't by itself be invoked by an action taken against a database table. Answer b is incorrect because a stored function must be explicitly called from another program unit or from the command line; it can't be tied to a table to happen automatically. Answer c is incorrect for the same reasons as answer b. Answer e is incorrect because an application trigger is fired by an application action, not a table action. Answer f is incorrect because an application procedure must be explicitly called from an application.

Question 11

Which clause is required in a **SELECT** statement within a PL/SQL block?

○ a. **WHERE**

○ b. **INTO**

○ c. **GROUP BY**

○ d. **HAVING**

○ e. **ORDER BY**

The correct answer is b, **INTO**. Answer a is incorrect because a **WHERE** clause isn't required for a **SELECT** statement. Answer c is incorrect because the **GROUP BY** clause isn't allowed in an implicit cursor (a PL/SQL **SE-LECT** statement) because a **SELECT** statement inside a PL/SQL returns only one value by definition. Answer d is incorrect because a **SELECT** statement inside a PL/SQL returns only one value by definition and the **HAVING** clause is used with the **GROUP BY**, which is for a multivalue return. Answer e is incorrect because by definition a **SELECT** statement inside a PL/SQL block only returns one value.

Question 12

Using SQL*Plus, you create this procedure:

```
CREATE OR REPLACE PROCEDURE price_increase
    (v_manufacturer_id IN NUMBER,
     v_percent_increase IN NUMBER)
IS
    v_rows_update BOOLEAN;
BEGIN
  . UPDATE inventory
         SET price = price * v_percent_increase
         WHERE manufacturer_id =
              v_manufacturer_id;
    v_rows_updated := SQL%NOTFOUND;
END;
```

What value will be assigned to **v_rows_updated**?

○ a. **TRUE**, if any prices were changed

○ b. **TRUE**, if no prices were changed

○ c. **FALSE**, if no prices were changed

○ d. **NULL**

The correct answer is b. Answer a is incorrect because **%NOTFOUND** will evaluate to **TRUE** only if no prices were changed. Answer c is incorrect because if prices weren't changed, the value would be **TRUE**. Answer d is incorrect because **%NOTFOUND** will be set to either **TRUE** or **FALSE**, based on the results of the **UPDATE** command that precedes it.

Question 13

What causes a PL/SQL **WHILE** loop to terminate?

○ a. A Boolean variable or expression evaluates to **TRUE**.

○ b. A Boolean variable or expression evaluates to **FALSE**.

○ c. A Boolean variable or expression evaluates to **NULL**.

○ d. Control is passed to the **EXIT** statement.

○ e. The specified number of iterations have been performed.

The correct response is b. Answer a is incorrect because a **WHILE** condition must evaluate to **FALSE** for the loop to terminate. Answer c is incorrect for the same reason as answer a. Answer d is incorrect because a **WHILE** loop doesn't have an **EXIT** statement. Answer e is incorrect because only a **FOR** loop terminates on a specified number of iterations, and we're talking about a **WHILE** loop.

Question 14

Evaluate this incomplete loop:

```
LOOP
    INSERT INTO inventory (id_number,
                           description)
        VALUES (v_id_number, v_description);
    v_counter := v_counter + 1;
```

Which statement will need to be added to conditionally stop the execution of the loop?

○ a. **END LOOP**

○ b. **EXIT**

○ c. **EXIT WHEN**

○ d. **END**

The correct answer is c. Answer a is incorrect because although **END LOOP** ends the loop structure, it doesn't end loop processing. Answer b is incorrect because although **EXIT** will terminate loop processing, it won't do it conditionally unless paired with **WHEN**. Answer d is incorrect because just placing an **END** at this point without an **END LOOP** will cause a syntax error. Answer e is incorrect because an **EXIT WHEN** is required.

Question 15

> Which Procedure Builder component would you use to drag a copy of a server-side program unit to the client side for debugging?
>
> ○ a. Object Navigator
>
> ○ b. PL/SQL Interpreter
>
> ○ c. Program Unit Editor
>
> ○ d. Stored Program Unit Editor

The correct answer is a, the Object Navigator. Answer b is incorrect because the PL/SQL Interpreter is used to enter and edit PL/SQL; it has no drag-and-drop capabilities from the server to the client. Answer c is incorrect because although the Program Unit Editor may be used to edit a PL/SQL program unit, it must first be dragged-and-dropped over to the client side. Answer d is incorrect for the same reason as answer c.

Need To Know More?

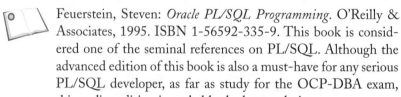

Feuerstein, Steven: *Oracle PL/SQL Programming*. O'Reilly & Associates, 1995. ISBN 1-56592-335-9. This book is considered one of the seminal references on PL/SQL. Although the advanced edition of this book is also a must-have for any serious PL/SQL developer, as far as study for the OCP-DBA exam, this earlier edition is probably the better choice.

Owens, Kevin: *Building Intelligent Databases with Oracle PL/SQL, Triggers, and Stored Procedures*. Prentice-Hall PTR, 1996. ISBN: 0-13-443631-8. An excellent reference for all phases of PL/SQL use and development.

Urman, Scott and Tim Smith: *Oracle PL/SQL Programming*. Osborne McGraw-Hill, 1996. ISBN: 0-07882-176-2. This is a good Oracle PL/SQL reference from Oracle Press.

Oracle7 Server SQL Reference Manual, Release 7.3. Oracle Corporation, February 1996. Part No. A32538-1. This is the source book for all Oracle SQL and Embedded SQL, including SQL for use in PL/SQL.

Oracle7 Server Concepts Manual, Release 7.3. Oracle Corporation, February 1996. Part No. A32534-1. This book discusses how the various parts of Oracle SQL, PL/SQL, and the database engine function together.

PL/SQL User's Guide and Reference, Release 7.3. Oracle Corporation, 1996. Part No. A32542-1. This discusses the flow and logic control statements for use in PL/SQL, as well as how to build and use anonymous blocks, functions, procedures, packages, and triggers.

PL/SQL Knowledge Base, Online Reference, Version 98.1, 1998, RevealNet, Inc., available from http://www.revealnet.com/. This online knowledge base provides for instant lookup of topics, examples, syntax, and good practices information.

Users
And Grants

Terms you'll need to understand:

√ Users

√ Grants

√ System privileges

√ Object privileges

√ Roles

Techniques you'll need to master:

√ Understanding how to create and manage users

√ Understanding the use of roles

√ Understanding the types of privileges

Database access begins with the creation of users. The users are then assigned specific rights to perform actions either directly or through roles. The rights to perform actions are called *system and object privileges*. System privileges are rights to perform actions in the database and object privileges are access rights to an object (table, index, synonym, procedure, and so on) within the database, including the columns within tables.

In this chapter, I'll explain how Oracle uses object and system privileges, along with roles, to manage users and objects.

Users

To access your database, an account must be created in the Oracle database for the user. The exceptions to this are the SYS and SYSTEM users that are created by Oracle when the database is created. In the sections that follow, I will discuss the creation, alteration, and dropping of users for the Oracle database.

Creating Users

To create a user, you must have the **CREATE USER** privilege. You can create users with Server Manager or at the command line in SQL*Plus. The command syntax for creating a user is illustrated in Figure 8.1.

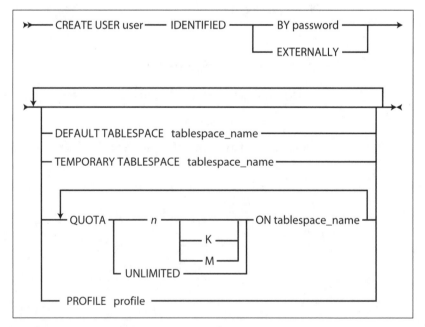

Figure 8.1 Syntax for creating a user.

Here is an example:

```
CREATE USER  james  IDENTIFIED BY    abc1
DEFAULT TABLESPACE  users
TEMPORARY TABLESPACE  temp
QUOTA  1M ON  users
QUOTA unlimited ON temp
PROFILE  enduser  ;
```

You need to assign each new user a password or indicate that operating system authentication will be used. Passwords are stored in the database in encrypted format and cannot be read by any user. The use of operating system authentication means that once your user has logged in at the operating system level, no username or password will be required when logging into the Oracle database. Users who are not assigned an Oracle password are designated as **IDENTIFIED EXTERNALLY**. Oracle depends on the operating system for authentication of the user. To use external authentication, you must set the **OS_AUTHENT_PREFIX** in the database parameter file.

When you create a user, you can designate a specific tablespace to be the default tablespace for that user. The designation of a default tablespace means that all the objects created by that user will be placed in that tablespace unless the user specifically indicates that the database object be placed in another tablespace. If no default tablespace is indicated for a user, the system tablespace will be the default for that user.

When you create a user, you can also designate a specific tablespace to be the temporary tablespace. This designation of a temporary tablespace specifies the tablespace that will be used for any database actions, which require use of a workspace for storage of intermediate results for actions such as sorting.

If no temporary tablespace is indicated for a user, the system tablespace will be used. When you designate a default tablespace, temporary tablespace, or quota on a tablespace, this does not implicitly grant any system or object privileges. You can give a user permission to create objects in tablespaces with the **QUOTA** clause.

As the DBA, you can access the **DBA_USERS** view for information on all users. Each user can access the **USER_USERS** view for information related to them. Table 8.1 shows the data stored in **DBA_USERS** and **USER_USERS**.

To enable a user to create objects in a tablespace, you need to specify a quota for that user on that tablespace. The tablespace quota may be limited to a specific amount of kilobytes or megabytes, or may be designated as unlimited.

Table 8.1	Data dictionary views for user data.
Column	**Definition**
DBA_USERS	
username	Oracle login name for the user
password	An encrypted password or IDENTIFIED EXTERNALLY
default_tablespace	Tablespace assigned as the default for the user
temporary_tablespace	Tablespace assigned for actions requiring a workspace
created	Date the user was created within the Oracle database
USER_USERS	
username	Oracle login name for the user
user_id	ID assigned by Oracle to the user
default_tablespace	Tablespace assigned as the default for the user
temporary_tablespace	Tablespace assigned for actions requiring a workspace
created	Date the user was created within the Oracle database

An unlimited quota indicates that the user can have any portion of a tablespace that is not already in use by another user. If the user is not assigned the **UN-LIMITED TABLESPACE** system privilege and the assigned limit is reached, the user will no longer be able to create additional objects or insert rows into any objects he owns in that tablespace. One thing to remember is that the role **RESOURCE** automatically grants **UNLIMITED TABLESPACE**, so only use it when absolutely required.

The **DBA_TS_QUOTAS** view provides tablespace quota information for all users in the database. The **USER_TS_QUOTAS** view provides tablespace quota information for the current user. When you query **DBA_TS_QUOTAS** or **USER_TS_QUOTAS**, a designation of -1 in the **max_bytes** and **max_blocks** columns indicates that the user has unlimited quota on that tablespace. Table 8.2 shows the data dictionary views associated with quotas.

Altering Users

To create a user, you must have the **ALTER USER** privilege. You can alter users with Server Manager or at the command line in SQL*Plus. The command line syntax for altering a user is shown in Figure 8.2.

Here is an example:

```
ALTER  USER bill IDENTIFIED BY  xyz2
```

Table 8.2	Quota data dictionary views.
Column	**Definition**
DBA_TS_QUOTAS	
tablespace_name	Name of the tablespace
username	Name of the user
bytes	Number of bytes assigned to that user
blocks	Number of blocks assigned to that user
max_bytes	Maximum number of bytes allowed for the user or -1 for unlimited
max_blocks	Maximum number of blocks allowed for the user or -1 for unlimited
USER_TS_QUOTAS	
tablespace_name	Name of the tablespace
bytes	Number of bytes assigned to that user
blocks	Number of blocks assigned to that user
max_bytes	Maximum number of bytes allowed for the user or -1 for unlimited
max_blocks	Maximum number of blocks allowed for the user or -1 for unlimited

```
DEFAULT TABLESPACE  users
TEMPORARY TABLESPACE temp
QUOTA  1M  ON  users
QUOTA unlimited ON temp
PROFILE  enduser
DEFAULT ROLE ALL ;
```

After a user is created, the only thing that you cannot alter for that user is the username. The password, default tablespace, temporary tablespace, the quota on a tablespace, profile, and default role can all be altered by someone with the **ALTER USER** system privilege.

Each user can alter the Oracle password you initially assigned to that user when you created him, provided the user is not identified externally (via the operating system). In addition to the end user, users with the **ALTER USER** system privilege can issue the **ALTER USER** command to change the user's password. The use of operating system authentication can also be changed by a user with the **ALTER USER** system privilege. Any changes to the password will take effect the next time that user logs into Oracle.

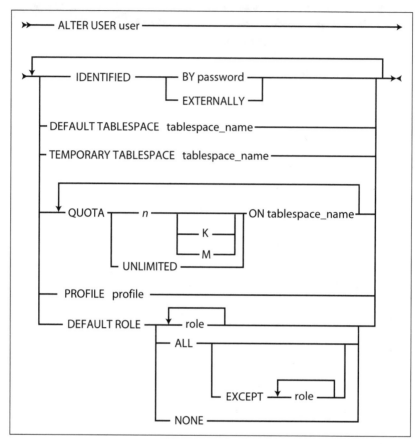

Figure 8.2 Syntax for altering a user.

When you change the default tablespace for a user, all future objects created by that user will be created in the new default tablespace you designated (unless otherwise specified by the user at the time the object is created). Remember the user must have a quota in the tablespace to create new objects in that tablespace. If a user reaches the maximum number of bytes assigned (specified in the quota), only a user with the **ALTER USER** system privileges will be able to increase the quota limit on the user.

Dropping Users

To drop a user, you must have the **DROP USER** system privilege. You can drop users with Server Manager or at the command line in SQL*Plus. The command line syntax for dropping a user is illustrated in Figure 8.3.

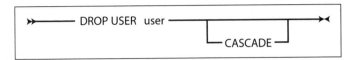

Figure 8.3   The syntax for the **DROP USER** command.

Here is an example:

```
DROP  USER  edward  CASCADE;
```

If a user owns any database objects, you can only drop that user by including the **CASCADE** keyword in the **DROP USER** command. The **DROP USER** command with the **CASCADE** keyword drops the user and all objects owned by that user. If you are using Server Manager to drop a user, you need to indicate that the associated schema objects be included in the command to drop the user. If a user owns objects and you fail to include **CASCADE**, you will receive an error message and the user will not be dropped. If a user is currently connected to the database, you cannot drop that user until he exits. After a user is dropped, all information on that user and all objects owned by that user are removed from the database.

After you have issued the command to drop a user, you cannot perform a rollback to re-create the user and his objects. **DROP USER** is a DDL command, which cannot be rolled back.

If you need the objects created by that user, you can revoke the **CREATE SESSION** system privilege to prevent the user from logging on, instead of dropping the user. You can also copy the objects to another user by importing the objects from an export made before the user was dropped. To avoid the problem of dropping a user without losing your application tables, all application tables should be owned by a separate application schema instead of an actual database user schema.

Grants

There are two types of privileges that can be granted:

➤ System privileges

➤ Object privileges

System privileges enable a user to perform a particular systemwide action or to perform a particular action on a particular type of object. For example, the privilege to create a table (**CREATE TABLE**) or insert rows into any table (**INSERT ANY TABLE**) are system privileges.

Object privileges enable a user to perform a particular action on a specific object, including tables, views, sequences, procedures, functions, and packages. For example, the privilege to insert rows into a particular table is an object privilege. Object privilege grants always include the name of the object for which the privilege is granted. Object privileges extend down to the level of individual columns in a table. These privileges are discussed in the following sections.

System Privileges

All users require the **CREATE SESSION** privilege to access the database. This privilege is automatically granted to all users when you perform the grants using Server Manager. If you create the user in command-line mode, you must remember to explicitly grant each user the **CREATE SESSION** system privilege either directly or through a role. Figure 8.4 shows the syntax for the **GRANT** command used to grant **CREATE SESSION**.

Here is an example:

```
GRANT        create session, create table
TO   annie
WITH ADMIN OPTION;
```

System privileges can be granted to other users when the grant made includes the **WITH ADMIN OPTION**.

There are over 80 distinct privileges. Most of these are self-explanatory. Table 8.3 lists of all the system privileges, as listed in RevealNet's Oracle Administration product (used with their permission).

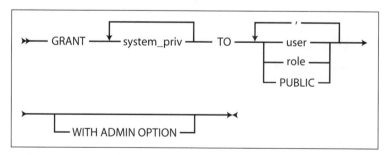

Figure 8.4   The syntax for **GRANT** command to grant **CREATE SESSION**.

Table 8.3 Oracle database system privileges.	
Privilege	**Description**
ANALYZE	
ANALYZE ANY	Allows the user to analyze any table, cluster, or index in the database.
AUDIT	
AUDIT ANY	Allows the user to audit any object in the database.
AUDIT SYSTEM	Allows the user to enable and disable statement and privilege audit options.
CLUSTER	
CREATE CLUSTER	Allows the user to create a cluster in his own schema.
CREATE ANY CLUSTER	Allows the user to create a cluster in any schema; behaves like the CREATE ANY TABLE privilege.
ALTER ANY CLUSTER	Allows the user to alter any cluster in the database.
DROP ANY CLUSTER	Allows the user to drop any cluster in the database.
DATABASE	
ALTER DATABASE	Allows a user to alter the database and add files to the operating system via Oracle regardless of operating system privileges.
DATABASE LINK	
CREATE DATABASE LINK	Allows the user to create database links in his own schema.
INDEX	
CREATE ANY INDEX	Allows the user to create an index anywhere on any table.
ALTER ANY INDEX	Allows the user to alter any index in the database.
DROP ANY INDEX	Allows the user to drop any index in the database.
PRIVILEGE	
GRANT ANY PRIVILEGE	Allows the user to grant any system privilege (not object privilege).

(continued)

Table 8.3 Oracle database system privileges *(continued)*.

PROCEDURE

CREATE PROCEDURE	Allows the user to create stored procedures, functions, and packages in his own schema.
CREATE ANY PROCEDURE	Allows the user to create stored procedures, functions and packages in any schema. (Requires that the user also have ALTER ANY TABLE, BACKUP ANY TABLE, DROP ANY TABLE, LOCK ANY TABLE, COMMENT ANY TABLE, SELECT ANY TABLE, INSERT ANY TABLE, UPDATE ANY TABLE, DELETE ANY TABLE, or GRANT ANY TABLE.)
ALTER ANY PROCEDURE	Allows the user to compile any stored procedures, functions, and packages in any schema.
DROP ANY PROCEDURE	Allows the user to drop any stored procedures, functions, and packages in any schema.
EXECUTE ANY PROCEDURE	Allows the user to execute any stored procedures, functions, and packages in any schema.

PROFILE

CREATE PROFILE	Allows the user to create profiles.
ALTER PROFILE	Allows the user to alter any profile in the database.
DROP PROFILE	Allows the user to drop any profile in the database.
ALTER RESOURCE COST	Allows the user to set costs for resources used in all user sessions.

PUBLIC DATABASE LINK

CREATE PUBLIC DATABASE LINK	Allows the user to create public database links.
DROP PUBLIC DATABASE LINK	Allows the user to drop public database links.

PUBLIC SYNONYM

CREATE PUBLIC SYNONYM	Allows the user to create public synonyms.
DROP PUBLIC SYNONYM	Allows the user to drop public synonyms.

ROLE

CREATE ROLE	Allows the user to create roles.
ALTER ANY ROLE	Allows the user to alter any role in the database.
DROP ANY ROLE	Allows the user to drop any role in the database.
GRANT ANY ROLE	Allows the user to grant any role in the database.

(continued)

Table 8.3   Oracle database system privileges *(continued)*.

ROLLBACK

CREATE ROLLBACK SEGMENT	Allows the user to create rollback segments.
ALTER ROLLBACK SEGMENT	Allows the user to alter rollback segments.
DROP ROLLBACK SEGMENT	Allows the user to drop rollback segments.

SESSION

CREATE SESSION	Allows the user to connect to the database.
ALTER SESSION	Allows the user to issue the ALTER SESSION command.
RESTRICTED SESSION	Allows the user to connect when the database has been started up using the STARTUP RESTRICT command. (The OSOPER and OSDBA roles contain this privilege.)

SEQUENCE

CREATE SEQUENCE	Allows the user to create a sequence in his own schema.
CREATE ANY SEQUENCE	Allows a user to create any sequence in any schema.
ALTER ANY SEQUENCE	Allows the user to alter any sequence in any schema.
DROP ANY SEQUENCE	Allows the user to drop any sequence in any schema.
SELECT ANY SEQUENCE	Allows the user to reference any sequence in any schema.

SNAPSHOT

CREATE SNAPSHOT	Allows the user to create snapshots in his own schema. (Must also have CREATE TABLE.)
CREATE ANY SNAPSHOT	Allows the user to create snapshots in any schema. (Must have CREATE ANY TABLE.)
DROP ANY SNAPSHOT	Allows the user to drop snapshots in any schema. (Must also have DROP ANY TABLE.)

SYNONYM

CREATE SYNONYM	Allows the user to create synonyms in his own schema.
CREATE ANY SYNONYM	Allows the user to create any synonym in any schema.
DROP ANY SYNONYM	Allows the user to drop any synonym in any schema.

(continued)

Table 8.3   Oracle database system privileges *(continued)*.

SYSTEM

ALTER SYSTEM	Allows the user to issue the ALTER SYSTEM command.

TABLE

CREATE TABLE	Allows the user to create tables in his own schema. This also allows the user to create indexes (including those for integrity constraints) on tables in his own schema. (The grantee must have a quota for the tablespace or the UNLIMITED TABLESPACE privilege.)
CREATE ANY TABLE	Allows the user to create tables in any schema.
ALTER ANY TABLE	Allows the user to alter any table in any schema and to compile any view in any schema.
BACKUP ANY TABLE	Allows the user to back up, via incremental export, any table in any schema.
DROP ANY TABLE	Allows the user to drop any table in any schema.
LOCK ANY TABLE	Allows the user to lock any table or view.
COMMENT ANY TABLE	Allows the user to enter a comment for any table, view, or column in any schema.
SELECT ANY TABLE	Allows the user to query any table, view, or snapshot in the database.
INSERT ANY TABLE	Allows the user to insert rows into any table or view in the database.
UPDATE ANY TABLE	Allows the user to update rows in any table or view in the database.
DELETE ANY TABLE	Allows the user to delete rows in any table or view in any schema.

TABLESPACE

CREATE TABLESPACE	Allows the user to create tablespaces. Also allows addition of files to the operating system regardless of the user's operating system privileges.
ALTER TABLESPACE	Allows the user to alter tablespaces. Also allows addition of files to the operating system regardless of the user's operating system privileges.
MANAGE TABLESPACE	Allows the user to take any tablespace offline, create any tablespace online, and perform hot backups.
DROP TABLESPACE	Allows the user to drop any tablespace.

(continued)

Table 8.3	**Oracle database system privileges** *(continued)*.
UNLIMITED TABLESPACE	Allows the user to use an unlimited amount of space in any tablespace overriding any quota set. This can only be granted to users, but not roles. This should not normally be granted.

TRANSACTION

FORCE TRANSACTION	Allows the user's process to force the commit or rollback of its own in-doubt distributed transactions in the database.
FORCE ANY TRANSACTION	Allows the user's process to force the commit or rollback of any distributed transactions in the local database.

TRIGGER

CREATE TRIGGER	Allows the user to create a trigger in his own schema.
CREATE ANY TRIGGER	Allows the user to create a trigger in any schema.
ALTER ANY TRIGGER	Allows the user to alter a trigger in any schema.
DROP ANY TRIGGER	Allows the user to drop a trigger in any schema.

USER

CREATE USER	Allows a user to create other users.
BECOME USER	Allows a user to become another user. This privilege must be granted to users that perform full database imports.
ALTER USER	Allows a user to alter other users in the following ways: passwords, quotas, default and temporary tablespaces, profiles, and default roles. This privilege is not required to alter the user's own password.
DROP USER	Allows a user to drop any other user.

VIEW

CREATE VIEW	Allows a user to create views in his own schema.
CREATE ANY VIEW	Allows a user to create views in any schema. (Requires that user also have: ALTER ANY TABLE, BACKUP ANY TABLE, DROP ANY TABLE, LOCK ANY TABLE, COMMENT ANY TABLE, CONNECT ANY TABLE, INSERT ANY TABLE, UPDATE ANY TABLE, DELETE ANY TABLE, or GRANT ANY TABLE.)
DROP ANY VIEW	Allows the user to drop any view in any schema.

Table 8.4	Contents of the DBA_SYS_PRIVS data dictionary view.
Column	**Definition**
grantee	Oracle login name or role that received the privilege
privilege	The system privilege granted to the user or role
admin_option	Indicates YES if the grantee can pass along the privilege and NO if the grantee cannot pass along the system privilege

As the DBA, you can access the **DBA_SYS_PRIVS** view for information on the system privileges granted to users. The format of this view is shown in Table 8.4.

Users can see information related to them by accessing the corresponding user view: **USER_SYS_PRIVS**.

Object Privileges

Object privileges define a user's rights on existing database objects. All grants on objects take effect immediately.

To grant an object privilege, you must be the owner of the object, have been granted **WITH GRANT OPTION** on that object for that privilege, or have the system privilege **GRANT ANY PRIVILEGE**. You can also grant access to all users by granting the privilege to **PUBLIC**. Figure 8.5 shows the syntax for the **GRANT** command used to grant a table-level object privilege.

Here is an example:

```
GRANT select
ON   bob.emp
TO   derek;
```

As the DBA, you can access the **DBA_TAB_PRIVS** view for information on the object privileges granted to users. You should note that although it is named **DBA_TAB_PRIVS**, it also includes information on views and sequences, as well as tables. Table 8.5 shows the contents of this view.

Users can see information on objects where they are the owner, grantor, or grantee by accessing the corresponding user view **USER_TAB_PRIVS**. Users can see information for all objects where that user or **PUBLIC** is the grantee with the **ALL_TAB_PRIVS** view. The **ALL_TAB_PRIVS** view is slightly different than the **USER_TAB_PRIVS** or **DBA_TAB_PRIVS** view. The contents of the **ALL_TAB_PRIVS** view are shown in Table 8.6.

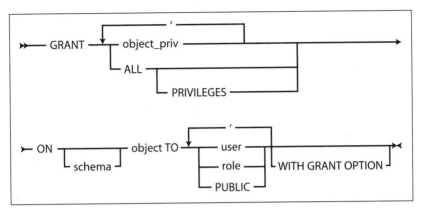

Figure 8.5 Syntax for the **GRANT** command used for a table-level grant.

Table 8.5	Contents of the DBA_TAB_PRIVS data dictionary view.
Column	**Definition**
grantee	Oracle login name or role that received the privilege
owner	Owner of the table
table_name	Name of the table, view, or sequence
grantor	Oracle login name of the person granting the privilege
privilege	System privilege granted to the user
grantable	Indicates YES if the grantee can pass along the privilege and NO if the grantee cannot pass along the system privilege

Table 8.6	Contents of the ALL_TAB_PRIVS data dictionary view.
Column	**Definition**
grantee	Oracle login name or role that received the privilege
grantor	Oracle login name of the person granting the privilege
owner	Owner of the table
table_schema	Schema of the object owner
table_name	Name of the table, view, or sequence
privilege	System privilege granted to the user
grantable	Indicates YES if the grantee can pass along the privilege and NO if the grantee cannot pass along the system privilege

A table owner can grant the following object privileges to other users:

➤ ALTER

➤ DELETE

➤ INDEX

➤ INSERT

➤ REFERENCES

➤ SELECT

➤ UPDATE

➤ EXECUTE (for stored functions, procedures, and packages)

All grants on objects and revoking of those grants are valid immediately, even if a user is currently logged into the database. The **SELECT** privilege can only be granted on tables, views, and snapshots. The **EXECUTE** privilege is used for packages, procedures, and functions. Remember that packages, procedures, and functions are always executed with the permissions of the owner of that package, procedure, or function.

By granting other users **INSERT, UPDATE, DELETE,** and **SELECT** privileges on your table, you allow them to perform that action on the table. By granting the **ALTER** privilege, you can allow another user to modify the structure of your table or create a trigger on your table. By granting users the **INDEX** privilege, you can allow them to create indexes on your table.

The **REFERENCES** privilege differs from the other privileges in that is does not actually grant the capability to change the table or data contained in the table. The **REFERENCES** privilege allows users to create foreign key constraints that reference your table.

Users can access the **USER_TAB_PRIVS_RECD** for information on table privileges where that user is the grantee. The corresponding **ALL_TAB_PRIVS_RECD** view includes all grants on objects where that user or **PUBLIC** is the grantee. Table 8.7 shows the contents of the **USER_TAB_PRIVS_RECD** view.

Users can access the **USER_TAB_PRIVS_MADE** for information on table privileges that they have granted to others. The corresponding **ALL_TAB_PRIVS_MADE** view includes information on all the grants that user has made, as well as grants by others on that user's objects. Table 8.8 shows the contents of the **USER_TAB_PRIVS_MADE** view.

Table 8.7	Contents of the USER_TAB_PRIVS_RECD data dictionary view.
Column	**Definition**
owner	Owner of the table
table_name	Name of the table, view, or sequence
grantor	Oracle login name of the person granting the privilege
privilege	System privilege granted to the user
grantable	Indicates YES if the grantee can pass along the privilege and NO if the grantee cannot pass along the object privilege

Column Privileges

Only **INSERT**, **UPDATE**, and **REFERENCES** privileges can be granted at the column level. When granting **INSERT** at the column level, you must include all the not null columns in the row. Figure 8.6 shows the syntax for granting object privileges at the column level.

Here is an example:

```
GRANT  update
ON  edwin.emp
TO  joan;
```

As the DBA, you can access the **DBA_COL_PRIVS** view for information on the column-level object privileges granted to users. Table 8.9 shows the contents of the **DBA_COL_PRIVS** view.

Users can access the **USER_COL_PRIVS_RECD** for information on column-level object privileges that have been granted to them. The **ALL_COL_PRIVS_RECD** includes information on all column privileges that have

Table 8.8	Contents of the USER_TAB_PRIVS_MADE data dictionary view.
Column	**Definition**
grantee	Oracle user granted the privilege
table_name	Name of the table, view, or sequence
grantor	Oracle login name of the person granting the privilege
privilege	System privilege granted to the user
grantable	Indicates YES if the grantee can pass along the privilege and NO if the grantee cannot pass along the object privilege

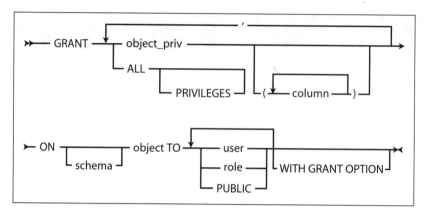

Figure 8.6 Syntax for the **GRANT** command used for column-level privilege grants.

been granted to them or to **PUBLIC**. The format of the **USER_TAB_PRIVS_RECD** view is shown in Table 8.10.

Users can access the **USER_COL_PRIVS_MADE** for information on column privileges that they have granted to others. The corresponding **ALL_COL_PRIVS_MADE** includes information on all columns where the user is the owner or the grantor. The contents of the **USER_COL_PRIVS_MADE** view are shown in Table 8.11.

Users can access information on all columns where they are the grantor, grantee, or owner, or where access has been granted to **PUBLIC** with the corresponding **ALL_TAB_PRIVS_MADE** and **ALL_TAB_PRIVS_RECD** views.

Table 8.9   Contents of the DBA_COL_PRIVS data dictionary view.

Column	Definition
grantee	Oracle login name or role that received the privilege
owner	Owner of the table
table_name	Name of the table
column_name	Name of the column
grantor	Oracle login name of the person granting the privilege
privilege	System privilege granted to the user
grantable	Indicates YES if the grantee can pass along the privilege and NO if the grantee cannot pass along the object privilege

Table 8.10   USER TAB_PRIVS_RECD data dictionary view.

Column	Definition
owner	Owner of the table
table_name	Name of the table, view, or sequence
column_name	Name of the column
grantor	Oracle login name of the person granting the privilege
privilege	System privilege granted to the user
grantable	Indicates YES if the grantee can pass along the privilege and NO if the grantee cannot pass along the column-level object privilege

Revoking Grants

When system privileges are passed to others using the **WITH ADMIN OP-TION**, revoking the system privileges from the original user will not cascade. The system privileges granted to others must be revoked directly. In contrast, when object privileges are passed on to others using the **WITH GRANT OP-TION**, the object privileges are revoked when the grantor's privileges are revoked.

It is important to note that only object privileges will cascade when revoked; system privileges will not.

When the **WITH ADMIN OPTION** or **WITH GRANT OPTION** has been included in a grant to another user, the privilege cannot be revoked directly. You must revoke the privilege and then issue another grant without the **WITH ADMIN OPTION** or **WITH GRANT OPTION**.

Table 8.11   USER_COL_PRIVS_MADE data dictionary view.

Column	Definition
grantee	Oracle user granted the privilege
table_name	Name of the table
column_name	Name of the column
grantor	Oracle login name of the person granting the privilege
privilege	System privilege granted to the user
grantable	Indicates YES if the grantee can pass along the privilege and NO if the grantee cannot pass along the column-level object privilege

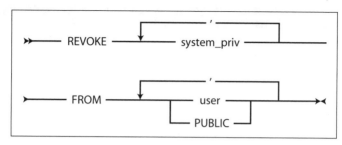

Figure 8.7 Syntax for revoking a system privilege.

The command line syntax for revoking a system privilege is seen in Figure 8.7. Here is an example:

```
REVOKE   create table
FROM   judy;
```

To revoke an object privilege, you must either be the owner of the object, have granted that privilege to that user with the **WITH GRANT OPTION**, or have the **GRANT ANY PRIVILEGE** system privilege.

You can revoke object and system privileges with Server Manager or at the command line in SQL*Plus. The command line syntax for revoking an object privilege is seen in Figure 8.8.

Here is an example:

```
REVOKE   select
ON   mike.emp
FROM   stan;
```

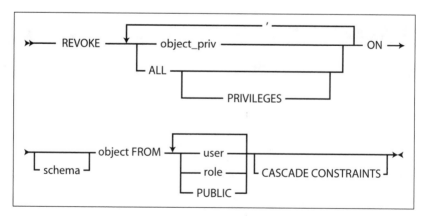

Figure 8.8 Syntax for revoking an object privilege.

When the object privilege **REFERENCES** has been granted, you must specify **CASCADE CONSTRAINTS** to drop the foreign key constraints that where created.

Use Of Roles

Using roles has several benefits, including:

➤ Reducing the number of grants and thereby making it easier to manage security.

➤ Dynamically changing the privileges for many users with a single grant or revoke.

➤ Selectively enabling or disabling depending on the application.

Roles can be used for most system and object privileges. Privileges granted through a role cannot be used for creating an object (views, packages, procedures, and functions). You need to grant privileges directly to the user for this.

Creating Roles

You need to create the role first and then grant system and object privileges to that role. When you create the role, there are three password options available:

➤ No authentication

➤ Operating system authentication

➤ Password authentication

You can set operating system authentication either when the role is created or by using the database initialization parameters **OS_ROLES=TRUE** and **REMOTE_OS_ROLES=TRUE**. If you are using the multithreaded server option, you cannot use operating system authentication for roles.

To create a role, you must have the **CREATE ROLE** system privilege. You can create roles with Server Manager or at the command line in SQL*Plus. The command syntax for creating a role is seen in Figure 8.9.

Here is an example:

```
CREATE ROLE  appusers
NOT  IDENTIFIED;
```

To alter a role, you must have the **ALTER ANY ROLE** system privilege or have been granted the role with the **WITH ADMIN OPTION**. The creator of any role automatically has the **WITH ADMIN OPTION** for that role.

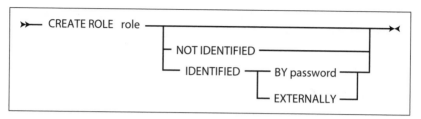

Figure 8.9 Syntax for creating a role.

Grants To Roles

To grant a role to a user, you must either be the creator of that role or have the **GRANT ANY ROLE** privilege. You can grant roles to users with Server Manager or at the command line in SQL*Plus. Grants to roles will not take effect for a user if that user is currently logged into the database with that role. When the user exits or sets another role, the changes will take effect. Once roles have been granted to a user, they can be enabled and disabled.

The command-line syntax for granting privileges to a role is the same as the syntax for granting privileges to a user. Figure 8.10 is the syntax is for granting roles to users.

Here is an example:

```
GRANT   enduser
TO   patrick ;
```

Figure 8.11 is the syntax for granting system privileges to roles.

Here is an example:

```
GRANT   create   session
TO   enduser;
```

Figure 8.12 is the following syntax for granting object privileges to roles.

Here is an example:

```
GRANT   select
ON   john.emp
TO   enduser;
```

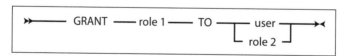

Figure 8.10 The syntax for granting roles to users.

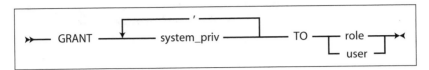

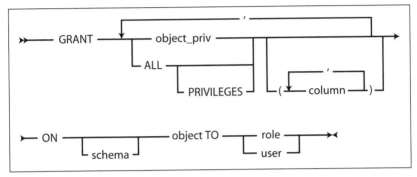

Figure 8.11 Syntax for granting system privileges to roles.

Figure 8.12 Syntax for granting object privileges to roles.

System privileges can be granted to roles with the exception of the **UNLIM-ITED TABLESPACE** system privilege. Grants on objects can be passed to other users or to roles if the grantee has been given the **WITH GRANT OPTION**. However, you cannot assign a privilege that includes the **WITH GRANT OPTION** to a role. The **INDEX** and **REFERENCES** privileges cannot be granted to a role; they must be granted only to a user. You can grant that role to a user or to another role. However, you cannot grant a role to itself.

You can look at the data dictionary tables shown in Table 8.12 for information on views for roles.

The **ROLE_TAB_PRIVS** view shown in Table 8.13 provides information on tables and column grants to roles.

Setting Roles

When a user is created, the default for active roles is set to **ALL**. The default **ALL** means that all the roles granted to a user are active. The DBA can change the default with an **ALTER USER** command. A user can enable multiple roles at one time and use the **SET ROLE** command to switch between roles or activate all roles with the command **SET ROLE ALL**. The **SET ROLE ALL** command will not work if any of the roles assigned to that user requires either a password or operating system authentication.

The command-line syntax for setting roles is shown in Figure 8.13.

Table 8.12	Data dictionary views for roles.
Column	**Definition**
DBA_ROLES	
role	Name of the role
password_required	Yes, No, or External for operating system authentication
DBA_ROLE_PRIVS	
grantee	Name of the user or role receiving the grant
granted_role	Name of the role
admin_option	Y if it was granted with the admin option
default_role	Y if this is the grantee's default role
ROLE_ROLE_PRIVS	
role	Name of the role receiving the role grant
granted_role	Name of the role granted the role
admin_option	Indicates the role was granted with the admin option
ROLE_SYS_PRIVS	
role	Name of the role receiving the system privilege
privilege	System privilege being granted
admin_option	Indicates the grant was with the admin option

Table 8.13	Contents of the ROLE_TAB_PRIVS data dictionary view.
Columns	**Definition**
role	Name of the role
owner	Owner of the table, view, or sequence
table_name	Name of the table, view, or sequence
column_name	Name of the column within the table, if applicable
privilege	Object privilege granted to that role
grantable	YES if it was granted with the admin option; NO otherwise

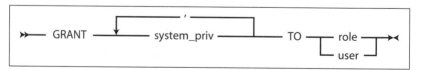

Figure 8.13 Syntax for setting roles.

Users can look at the **SESSION_ROLES** view to find the roles that are currently enabled for them. Users can look at **SESSION_PRIVS** view to see the privileges available to their session.

If you determine that all control of roles will be at the operating system level, you can set the database initialization parameter **OS_ROLES** equal to **TRUE**. All roles must still be created first in the database. Any grants you previously made using the database command line or Server Manager are still listed in the data dictionary, but they cannot be used and are not in effect. If the use of roles is determined at the operating system level, the multithreaded server option cannot be used.

You can use the **MAX_ENABLED_ROLES** parameter in the database initialization file to set the number of roles that you will allow any user to have enabled at one time.

Special Roles

Oracle creates the following two roles when you install the Oracle executables:

➤ OSOPER

➤ OSDBA

Oracle creates the following three roles when you create the database:

➤ CONNECT

➤ RESOURCE

➤ DBA

When you execute the catalog.sql script, the following two roles are created:

➤ EXP_FULL_DATABASE

➤ IMP_FULL_DATABASE

In the following section, I'll explain these special roles and how they are used for database maintenance.

OSOPER And OSDBA

The OSOPER and OSDBA roles are created at the operating system level when Oracle is installed. They cannot be granted. The OSOPER and OSDBA roles are needed to perform database operations when the database is not mounted and therefore the data dictionary is not accessible. It is the OSOPER and OSDBA roles that are used when you use **CONNECT INTERNAL** to connect to the database using Server Manager.

The OSOPER role can perform the following database management commands:

➤ STARTUP

➤ SHUTDOWN

➤ ALTER DATABASE OPEN/MOUNT

➤ ALTER DATABASE BACKUP CONTROLFILE

➤ ALTER TABLESPACE BEGIN/END BACKUP

➤ ARCHIVE LOG

➤ RECOVER

The OSDBA role has the OSOPER role. The OSDBA role also has **WITH ADMIN OPTION** to enable it to grant system privileges to other users. The OSDBA role is the role that is used to create the database and for time-based recovery processes. Both the OSOPER and OSDBA roles include the **RE-STRICTED SESSION** system privilege.

If you intend to allow remote users to use **CONNECT INTERNAL,** you need to set the **REMOTE_LOGIN_PASSWORDFILE** option in your database parameter file to either **EXCLUSIVE** or **SHARED**. The user will then connect in Server Manager with the **AS SYSDBA** or **AS SYSOPER** clause at the end of the **CONNECT** command. For instance:

```
CONNECT SYS AS SYSDBA
```

The privileges assigned to SYSDBA correspond to those for OSDBA. The privileges assigned to SYSOPER correspond to OSOPER. The operating system verifies the provided password using an external operating system file. This external file is generated using the ORAPWD utility. When the password for the INTERNAL or SYS accounts are changed with the **ALTER USER** command, the changes are mapped to the operating system password file. The **V$PWFILE_USERS** view lists users with the SYSDBA and SYSOPER privileges.

CONNECT, RESOURCE, And DBA Roles

The CONNECT, RESOURCE, and DBA roles are predefined roles that are available for backward compatibility. These are created by Oracle when the database is created. When you create a user with Server Manager, the CONNECT role is automatically granted to that user.

The following system privileges are granted to the CONNECT role:

➤ ALTER SESSION

➤ CREATE CLUSTER

➤ CREATE DATABASE LINK

➤ CREATE SEQUENCE

➤ CREATE SESSION

➤ CREATE SYNONYM

➤ CREATE TABLE

➤ CREATE VIEW

When you grant a user the RESOURCE role, that user is granted the **UN-LIMITED TABLESPACE** system privilege as well. The following system privileges are granted to the RESOURCE role:

➤ CREATE CLUSTER

➤ CREATE PROCEDURE

➤ CREATE SEQUENCE

➤ CREATE TABLE

➤ CREATE TRIGGER

The DBA role includes all system privileges, the capability to grant those system privileges to others, and **UNLIMITED TABLESPACE**. If the EXP_FULL_DATABASE and IMP_FULL_DATABASE roles have been created, they are granted implicitly with the DBA role.

You can grant additional privileges to or revoke privileges from the CONNECT, RESOURCE, and DBA roles just as you would any other role that you created.

Export/Import Roles

Oracle provides a script entitled catexp.sql. This script creates the EXP_FULL_DATABASE and IMP_FULL_DATABASE roles. You can grant these to a user who will be executing the export and import utilities.

The EXP_FULL_DATABASE role has the **SELECT ANY TABLE** and **BACKUP ANY TABLE** system privileges. In addition, this role has **INSERT**, **DELETE**, and **UPDATE** privileges on the **SYS.INCVID**, **SYS.INCFIL**, and **SYS.INCEXP** tables.

The IMP_FULL_DATABASE role has the **BECOME USER** system privilege.

Exam Prep Questions

Question 1

> Which **SHUTDOWN** method is an alternative to killing a user's session?
>
> ○ a. **NORMAL**
>
> ○ b. **IMMEDIATE**
>
> ○ c. **ABORT**

The correct answer is b, **IMMEDIATE.** This answer requires some judgment. Because you cannot shut down the database normally if even one user session is active, eliminate a as the correct answer. Both **SHUTDOWN IMMEDI-ATE** and **SHUTDOWN ABORT** will terminate all user sessions, but you avoid the **SHUTDOWN ABORT** whenever possible because the database will be closed in an inconsistent state. **SHUTDOWN IMMEDIATE** is the best answer.

Question 2

> What is displayed when you query **USER_USERS**?
>
> ○ a. Information about all users of the database
>
> ○ b. Information about the current user
>
> ○ c. Tablespace quotas for all users
>
> ○ d. Tablespace quotas for the current user

The correct answer is b. Views prefixed with **USER** will give information relevant to the current user only.

Question 3

> Which keyword when added to a **DROP USER** command will re-move all objects contained in a user's schema?
>
> ○ a. **DEFAULT**
>
> ○ b. **QUOTA**
>
> ○ c. **CASCADE**
>
> ○ d. **EXCEPT**

The correct answer is c. A user cannot be dropped if he owns objects unless you explicitly include the **CASCADE** option of the **DROP USER** command. It is not possible to drop a user and keep the user's objects in the database. You can export the user's objects and import them into another user or another user can use his **SELECT** privileges on the objects to copy them before the user is dropped. Once a **DROP USER** statement is issued, it cannot be rolled back.

Question 4

> Which view would you query to display the number of bytes charged to each user?
>
> ○ a. **USER_USERS**
>
> ○ b. **ALL_USERS**
>
> ○ c. **DBA_USERS**
>
> ○ d. **USER_TS_QUOTAS**
>
> ○ e. **DBA_TS_QUOTAS**

The correct answer is e. The number of bytes is listed for each user in the **DBA_TS_QUOTAS** view. This view also includes the maximum bytes as set by the quota assigned to the user. Note the wording of this question. It asks how you would obtain tablespace usage information for each user. You can eliminate **USER_TS_QUOTAS** because it will give tablespace usage information on the current user only. Pay special attention to whether the question asks for statistics on the current user or all users.

Question 5

> Evaluate this command:
>
> ```
> ALTER USER jennifer
> QUOTA 0 ON SYSTEM;
> ```
>
> Which task will this command accomplish?
>
> ○ a. Remove user Jennifer
>
> ○ b. Drop user Jennifer's objects
>
> ○ c. Revoke user Jennifer's tablespace
>
> ○ d. Allocate tablespace to user Jennifer

The correct answer is c. However, this answer is vague. Jennifer may have quotas on several tablespaces and this command will only revoke Jennifer's usage on the **SYSTEM** tablespace. A process of elimination is used. The command in this question will not remove or drop the user Jennifer. It will not allocate tablespace to Jennifer. The only applicable answer is c, revoke user Jennifer's tablespace.

Question 6

> When creating a user, which step could be skipped if the user will not be creating any objects?
>
> ○ a. Assign a username and password
>
> ○ b. Assign a default tablespace
>
> ○ c. Assign a tablespace for temporary tables
>
> ○ d. Assign a default profile

The correct answer is b. Be sure to read this question carefully. Notice the words "will not be creating any objects." If a default tablespace is not explicitly assigned, the **SYSTEM** tablespace will be the implicit default. However, if a user will not be creating objects, he will not actually be placing anything in the **SYSTEM** tablespace. It is also true that if a profile is not created, the default profile is implicitly assigned; but that is true regardless of whether the user is going to create objects.

Question 7

> Who needs a usage quota?
>
> ○ a. The owner of an object that is read only
>
> ○ b. A user who is about to create a table
>
> ○ c. A user who only reads data from an object owned by another user
>
> ○ d. A user who is inserting data into an object owned by another user

The correct answer is b. Inserting data into an object owned by another user will use the quota of the user who owns the object.

Question 8

What does the option **EXTERNALLY** do when creating a user with the **CREATE USER** command?

○ a. Allow the user remote access.

○ b. Allow the user network access.

○ c. Allow the user to access the database without a password.

○ d. Requires that the user's password be verified by the operating system.

The correct answer is d. When you create a user with **IDENTIFIED EXTERNALLY**, you do not specify a password. The username and password are verified by the operating system.

Question 9

Jennifer granted a privilege using **WITH GRANT OPTION** to Sharon. Sharon granted the privilege to Jacob. If Jennifer's privilege is revoked, who else will lose their privileges?

○ a. Only Sharon

○ b. Only Jacob

○ c. Both Sharon and Jacob

○ d. No one else will lose their privileges

The correct answer is c. **WITH GRANT OPTION** indicates that an object privilege was granted. Remember that when an object privilege is revoked, it cascades to all the users who received the privilege from that user.

Question 10

Jennifer granted a privilege using **WITH ADMIN OPTION** to Sharon. Sharon granted the privilege to Jacob. If Jennifer's privileges are revoked, who else will lose their privileges?

○ a. Only Sharon

○ b. Only Jacob

○ c. Both Sharon and Jacob

○ d. No one else will lose their privileges

The correct answer is d. **WITH ADMIN OPTION** indicates that a system privilege was granted. Revoking system privileges from a user does not cascade to others.

Question 11

> Which characteristic describes a role?
>
> ○ a. Can only consist of object privileges
>
> ○ b. Is owned by the DBA
>
> ○ c. May be granted to any role
>
> ○ d. May be granted to itself

The correct answer is c. Both system and object privileges can be granted to a role and a role can be granted to another user. However, recursive grants of a role to itself are not allowed.

Question 12

> Which command could you use to set a default role for a user?
>
> ○ a. **CREATE ROLE**
>
> ○ b. **ALTER USER**
>
> ○ c. **CREATE USER**
>
> ○ d. **SET ROLE**

The correct answer is b. It is correct that you can set a default role for a user when the user is created. However, the question implies that the user and role are already created.

Need To Know More?

 Ault, Michael R.: *Oracle 7.0 Administration & Management.* John Wiley & Sons, 1994. ISBN 0-47160-857-2. Chapters 2, 3, and 4 deal with object, privilege, and user administration.

Honour, Edward: *Oracle How-To.* Waite Group Press, 1996. ISBN 1-57169-048-4. Chapters 2 and 3 deal with users and security.

Loney, Kevin: *Oracle DBA Handbook, 7.3 Edition.* Oracle Press, 1996. ISBN 0-07882-289-0. Chapter 9 covers users and security.

For more information, check out the *Oracle7 Administrator's Guide* and the *Oracle7 Server Reference Manual.*

Database Utilities

Terms you'll need to understand:

√ Server Manager line mode

√ SQL* Plus

√ SQL* Loader

√ OSDBA

√ OSOPER

√ SYSDBA

√ SYSOPER

√ SQL buffer

√ Direct path load

√ Conventional path load

√ Discarded records

√ Rejected records

√ Control file

Techniques you'll need to master:

√ Connecting to an Oracle database using Server Manager

√ Starting up an Oracle database using Server Manager

√ Shutting down an Oracle database using Server Manager

√ Executing line-mode commands

√ Executing batch scripts

√ Creating Oracle password file using ORAPWD utility

√ Working with the SQL buffer

√ Entering SQL*Plus commands

√ Changing the SQL*Plus environment

√ Setting up PRODUCT_USER_PROFILE

√ Using conventional path loading

√ Using direct path loading

In this chapter, I'll explain the Server Manager command line interface and show the syntax for Server Manager commands. In addition, I will give example questions that show how understanding Server Manager commands will help you succeed on the OCP-DBA exams.

In the second half of this chapter, I'll discuss SQL*Plus. SQL*Plus is the basic tool used to interact with an Oracle database. Unlike Server Manager, which is for database administrators, SQL*Plus is normally used by DBAs, developers, and users. Within SQL*Plus, users can execute DDL, DML, Dynamic SQL scripts, and reports.

Finally, I'll delve into the SQL*Loader, which loads data from files into Oracle databases.

Server Manager

Server Manager is the database administration tool that replaced SQLDBA in Oracle version 6 and 7.0. Server Manager can be run in line mode, which is a command line interface, or in a GUI mode prior to Oracle version 7.3.3. Oracle's new GUI administration tool, Oracle Enterprise Manager (OEM), replaces the GUI version of Server Manager in all releases of Oracle starting with version 7.3.3. Although many new GUI tools, including OEM, can be used to manage an Oracle database, it is important for a DBA to be familiar with the line mode version of Server Manager.

Why Line Mode When You Can GUI?

GUI tools such as OEM are very helpful with interactive database management. To automate database administration tasks such as **STARTUP**, **SHUTDOWN**, and **BACKUP**, a command interface is needed that can run batch scripts. All of Oracle's installation scripts, as well as the scripts for automatic startup and shutdown of the database, use Server Manager in line mode.

The syntax for starting Server Manager is platform-specific and executed from the operating system prompt. On Unix platforms, the command is svrmgrl. On the Windows platform, the command is svrmgrXX (the XX is replaced with the version of Server Manager installed). The Server Manager version shipped with Oracle7.3 is svrmgr23. Server Manager can also start in line mode and execute a script all in one command, as follows:

```
svrmgrl command=@dbstart
```

Executing Commands Using Server Manager In Line Mode

In addition to Server Manager commands like **CREATE DATABASE,** **STARTUP,** and **SHUTDOWN,** you can execute SQL statements and PL/SQL code while in line mode. Many Server Manager commands are single-line commands that do not require a command line terminator. These commands can be continued to more than one line by using a backslash (\) at the end of each line.

SQL statements or PL/SQL code can be entered and executed in Server Manager the same as in SQL*Plus. Use a semicolon (;) to terminate and execute SQL statements and a slash (/) by itself on the last line of PL/SQL code. SQL scripts can be run by using the @ command. For example, to run the script dbstart.sql, the command would be as follows:

```
SVRMGR> @dbstart
```

If you do not supply a file name with the @ command, Server Manager will prompt for one, as follows:

```
SVRMGR> @
Name of script file:
```

Server Manager Commands

The Server Manager program takes the place of the old SQL*DBA program that was used in older version 7 and version 6 systems. The Server Manager uses a number of commands, such as the at symbol (@), **ARCHIVE LOG,** **CONNECT, RECOVER, SET, SHOW, STARTUP,** and **SHUTDOWN.** The following sections discuss these commands.

The @ Command

The @ command (or at command) is used to execute a script stored as an operating system file. The full path name must be given unless the file is in the current directory. A double at symbol (@@) can be used within an executing script to call other scripts. The use of the @@ assumes the script file is in the same directory as the calling script. Here is an example:

```
svrmgr> @/u01/sql/begin_bk.sql
```

The *ARCHIVE LOG* Command

The **ARCHIVE LOG** command is used to control automatic archiving or redo log files. Here is its syntax:

```
>--ARCHIVE LOG ------------------------->>
              |--START TO 'location'--|
              |--STOP----------------|
              |--NEXT----------------|
              |--ALL-----------------|
              |--LIST----------------|
              |--integer-------------|
```

The following are the explanations for the **ARCHIVE LOG** command options:

➤ **START** Begins automatic archiving of the database. If no location is given for the archive files, the database will use the initialization parameter **LOG_ARCHIVE_DEST**. If a location is given, it overrides the initialization parameter and starts archiving in the new location. On non-Windows NT platforms, the **ARCH** background process will start. Under Windows NT, the **ARCH** will start as a thread of the Oracle.exe process.

➤ **STOP** Stops automatic archiving. This does not take the database out of archive log mode. After all redo log file groups are full, database operations will stop until the full redo log files are archived.

➤ **NEXT** Performs a manual archive of the next online redo log file group that is full and has not been archived.

➤ **ALL** Performs a manual archive of all online redo log file groups that are full and have not been archived.

➤ *integer* Archives the online redo log file group with the log sequence number equal to the integer even if the log file group is not full. For example:

```
SVRMGR> ARCHIVE LOG 33840
Archives log sequence 33840 to the current
LOG_ARCHIVE_DEST
```

➤ **LIST** Displays current archive log mode information.

Here is an example:

```
SVRMGR> ARCHIVE LOG LIST
```

```
Database log mode              Archive Mode
Archive destination            /u01/app/
                               oracle/admin/
                               DB1/arch/log
Oldest online log sequence     33838
Next log sequence to archive   33840
Current log sequence           33840
```

The *CONNECT* Command

The **CONNECT** command is used to log on a user to a local or remote database. Its syntax is as follows:

```
CONNECT username/password
CONNECT username/password@instance alias
CONNECT username/password AS SYSOPER or SYSDBA
CONNECT INTERNAL
CONNECT username/as SYSDBA
```

The **CONNECT** command has the following parameters and options:

➤ **username** Any usernames currently defined to the database.

➤ **password** The password for the username given.

➤ **instance alias** The instance alias used to connect to a remote database.

➤ **AS SYSOPER or SYSDBA** Enables users granted access to the database through OS authentication or through the Oracle password file to connect with system privileges. **SYSOPER** will log the user in with OSOPER database role and **SYSDBA** will log the user in with OSDBA database role. OSOPER allows database startup, shutdown, and general maintenance, whereas OSDBA allows database creation as well as all of the other operations.

➤ **INTERNAL** Connects to the database as the SYS account.

➤ **Slash (/)** Connects with OS authentication.

Two operating system roles are used to control administrator connections when OS authentication is used: OSOPER and OSDBA. These roles are granted at the operating system level and not through an Oracle grant. The method for granting these privileges is operation system-specific.

OSOPER allows the user to perform the following actions and grants the **RESTRICTED SESSION** privilege:

➤ **STARTUP**

➤ SHUTDOWN

➤ ALTER DATABASE

➤ OPEN/MOUNT

➤ ALTER DATABASE BACKUP

➤ ARCHIVE LOG

➤ RECOVER

OSDBA grants the user all system privileges with the **ADMIN OPTION** as well as the OSOPER role. A user granted the OSDBA role can also execute **CREATE DATABASE** and time-based recover commands.

To use password file authentication, a password file must first be created using the **ORAPWD** command. This command is executed at an operating system prompt. Users are added to the password file when they are granted the SYSDBA or SYSOPER roles in Oracle. Here is an example:

```
ORAPWD FILE=filename PASSWORD=password \
ENTRIES=max number of users in file
```

In addition to the password file, the initialization parameter **REMOTE_LOGIN_PASSWORDFILE** must be set to the correct value described here:

➤ **NONE** This is the default value and causes Oracle not to use user password files.

➤ **EXCLUSIVE** The **EXCLUSIVE** parameter causes the password file to be used by only one database. Any database user can be added to an exclusive password file.

➤ **SHARED** The **SHARED** parameter causes the password file to be shared by more than one database. In this case, only the SYS and INTERNAL users can be added to the password file.

Following are some example connections:

➤ To connect to the database using the schema and privileges associated with the username, use the following:

```
CONNECT john/doe
```

➤ To connect using a password file as user john but with the SYS schema and administrator privileges, use the following:

```
CONNECT john/doe AS SYSDBA
```

➤ To connect using OS authentication, use the following:

```
CONNECT / AS SYSDBA
```

The *RECOVER* Command

The **RECOVER** command performs media recovery on the database, tablespaces, or datafiles. To issue the **RECOVER** command, you must be connected to Oracle as SYSDBA, SYSOPER, or INTERNAL. The **RECOVER** command cannot be used when you are connected to Oracle using the multithreaded server. Figure 9.1 illustrates the syntax of the **RECOVER** command.

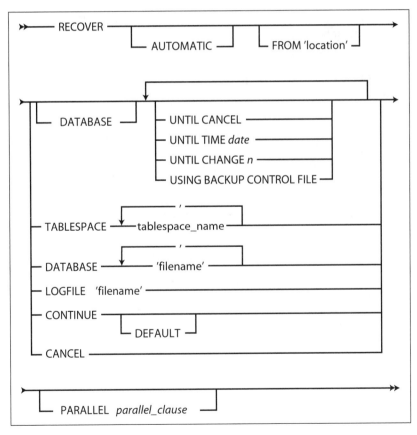

Figure 9.1 The **RECOVER** command's syntax.

The **RECOVER** command uses the following parameters:

➤ **DATABASE** Used to recover the entire database.

➤ **USING BACKUP CONTROL FILE** Indicates the backup control file will be used instead of the active control file for the recovery.

➤ **TABLESPACE** Indicates a tablespace will be recovered and is followed by the tablespace name.

➤ **DATAFILE** Indicates the datafiles to be recovered and is followed by the datafile names.

➤ **UNTIL CANCEL** Indicates an incomplete recovery. Recovery is completed when you specify **CANCEL** instead of the archive log filename.

➤ **UNTIL CHANGE** Indicates an incomplete recovery. **UNTIL CHANGE** is followed by the system change number (SCN) to which you want to recover.

➤ **UNTIL TIME** Indicates an incomplete point in time recovery. Use the following format:

```
'YYYY-MM-DD:HH24:MI:SS'
```

➤ **PARALLEL** Sets the number of parallel recovery processes to use in applying redo entries. If you use the **DEFAULT DEGREE** clause, the recovery uses twice the number of processes as the number of datafiles being recovered. **INSTANCES** indicates how many instances will be used for parallel recovery.

➤ **NOPARALLEL** Indicates the recovery will be done serially.

For a more detailed information of the **RECOVER** command, see the *Oracle7 Server Administrator's Guide*.

The **SET** Command

The **SET** command is used in both the Server Manager and SQL*Plus to alter the sessions environment. Here is the syntax:

```
>--SET----------------------------------------------->>
          |--AUTORECOVERY    ON/OFF---------------|
          |--CHARWIDTH       integer--------------|
          |--COMPATIBILITY   V6/V7/NATIVE---------|
          |--DATEWIDTH       integer--------------|
```

```
|--ECHO              ON/OFF---------------|
|--INSTANCE          Instance alias/local--|
|--LOGSOURCE         Path-----------------|
|--LONGWIDTH         integer--------------|
|--MAXDATA           integer--------------|
|--NUMWIDTH          integer--------------|
|--RETRIES           integer/infinite------|
|--SERVEROUTPUT      ON/OFF   size---------|
|--STOPONERROR       ON/OFF---------------|
|--TERMOUT           ON/OFF---------------|
|--TIMING            ON/OFF---------------|
```

The **SET** command options have the following definitions:

➤ **AUTORECOVERY** Setting **AUTORECOVERY** to **ON** will cause the **RECOVER** command to automatically apply archive log files during recovery. The archive log files will be applied based on the initialization parameters **LOG_ARCHIVE_DEST** and **LOG ARCHIVE_FORMAT**.

➤ **CHARWIDTH** Sets the column display width for **CHAR** data. The default is 80 characters.

➤ **COMPATIBILITY** Changes database compatibility. Native compatibility matches the database.

➤ **DATAWIDTH** Sets the column display width for **DATE** data.

➤ **ECHO ECHO ON** will echo commands from scripts that are run.

➤ **INSTANCE** Changes the default instance to which you are connected.

➤ **LOGSOURCE** Sets the location from where archive logs are retrieved during recovery. This parameter overrides the initialization parameter **LOG_ARCHIVE_DEST**.

➤ **LONGWIDTH** Sets the column display width for **LONG** data. The default is 80 characters.

➤ **MAXDATA** Sets the maximum number of bytes a **SELECT** statement can return in a fetch. The default is 20,480 bytes.

➤ **NUMWIDTH** Set the column display width for **NUMBER** data. The default is 10 single-place numeric characters (including any decimals).

➤ **RETRIES** Affects the **STARTUP** command if the **RETRY** option is used. The **STARTUP** command will retry the specified number of times. The default number of tries is infinite.

➤ **SERVEROUTPUT SERVEROUPUT ON** enables output from the **DBMS_OUTPUT PUT** and **PUT_LINE** commands.

➤ **STOPONERROR STOPONERRPOR ON** causes command files to stop execution if an error occurs.

➤ **TERMOUT TERMOUT OFF** stops output from SQL command coming back to the screen. The default is **ON**, which allows output to come to the terminal.

➤ **TIMING ON** gives timing feedback on parse, execute, and fetch times.

The *SHOW* Command

The **SHOW** command is used to show the current value of all the **SET** commands with the addition of the **ERRORS, PARAMETERS, SGA,** and **SPOOL** parameters. Its syntax is as follows:

```
>--SHOW----------------------->>
         |--AUTORECOVERY---|
         |--CHARWIDTH------|
         |--COMPATIBILITY--|
         |--DATEWIDTH------|
         |--ECHO-----------|
         |--INSTANCE-------|
         |--LOGSOURCE------|
         |--LONGWIDTH------|
         |--MAXDATA--------|
         |--NUMWIDTH-------|
         |--RETRIES--------|
         |--SERVEROUTPUT---|
         |--STOPONERROR----|
         |--TERMOUT--------|
         |--TIMING---------|
         |--ERRORS---------|
         |--PARAMETERS-----|
         |--SGA------------|
         |--SPOOL----------|
```

The **SHOW** command has the following three options that are most important for the exam:

➤ **ERRORS** Shows the errors from the last procedure, package, or function that was compiled.

➤ **PARAMETERS** Displays the value of initialization parameters.

➤ **SGA** Shows the current instance's system global area. Here is an example:

```
SHOW SGA
Total Shared Global Area     32420880
Fixed size                   38944
Variable Size                11869168
Database Buffers             20480000
Redo Buffers                 32768
```

The *STARTUP* Command

The **STARTUP** command starts the Oracle instance, mounts the database, and opens it for use. **STARTUP** can also be combined with any of the following options to perform maintenance or other activities. When you issue a **STARTUP OPEN** command, the database goes through a **NOMOUNT** and **MOUNT** phase before being in an **OPEN** state. Here are all the options:

```
>--STARTUP----------------------->>
            |--FORCE-----------|
            |--RESTRICT--------|
            |--PFILE=filename--|
            |--MOUNT-----------|
            |--NOMOUNT---------|
            |--OPEN------------|
            |--RECOVER---------|
            |--database_name---|
            |--EXCLUSIVE-------|
            |--PARALLEL--------|
            |--SHARED----------|
            |--RETRY ----------|
```

The **STARTUP** command has the following options:

➤ **FORCE** Performs a **SHUTDOWN ABORT** followed by a **STARTUP OPEN**, used only in emergencies. This option is also used with certain undocumented initialization parameters to force open a corrupted database.

➤ **RESTRICT** Performs a **NOMOUNT, MOUNT,** and **OPEN,** leaving the database in restricted user mode. The restricted user mode allows only users (usually DBAs) with **RESTRICTED SESSION** privilege to log in to the instance.

➤ **PFILE** This option uses a parameter file to start the instance.

➤ **MOUNT** Used for certain maintenance operations. This option is performed automatically by **STARTUP, STARTUP OPEN, STARTUP FORCE, STARTUP RESTRICT,** and **STARTUP RECOVER** command options. It performs a startup of instance processes and mounts the database, leaving it accessible only to the Server Manager process.

➤ **NOMOUNT** The **NOMOUNT** state starts the instance but doesn't mount any database files. This option is only used for creation of a database, and is performed automatically by all other options. This option cannot be used with **OPEN, MOUNT, SHARED, EXCLUSIVE,** or **PARALLEL** options.

➤ **OPEN** Used to **NOMOUNT, MOUNT,** and **OPEN** a database, the same as issuing a **STARTUP** command with no options.

➤ **RECOVER** Used when it is known that a database will need recovery. Note that instance recovery will be performed automatically on instance startup. This option is only needed to force media recovery.

➤ **database_name** This is the database name to mount or open. If a database name is not given, **STARTUP** uses the name in the parameter file (init<SID>.ora).

➤ **EXCLUSIVE** When opened it this mode, a database can only be mounted or opened by one Oracle instance. This parameter cannot be used with the **SHARED** or **PARALLEL** options.

➤ **PARALLEL** This option is used only when mounting the database for use in a parallel server configuration (one where multiple instances use the same set of database files). This is also known as the **SHARED** option.

➤ **RETRY** This option can only be used with instances in **PARALLEL** mode. If the database is busy being recovered by another instance, the **RETRY** command will make Oracle attempt to open the database every five seconds. The number of attempts can be set with the **SET RETRIES** command in Server Manager.

Following are some examples of when to use the **STARTUP** command:

➤ To start an Oracle instance, mount the database in **EXCLUSIVE** mode, and open the database using the default init<SID>.ora file, enter

```
SVRMGR> STARTUP
```

or:

```
SVRMGR> STARTUP OPEN database_name EXCLUSIVE
```

To start up the same database in parallel mode, enter

```
SVRMGR> STARTUP PARALLEL
```

or:

```
SVRMGR> STARTUP OPEN database_name PARALLEL
```

➤ To shut down the database immediately and restart it without mounting or opening for DBA connections only, enter:

```
SVRMGR> STARTUP FORCE NOMOUNT RESTRICT
```

To start up a database using a parameter file initdb1.ora, enter:

```
SVRMGR> STARTUP PFILE=initdb1.ora
```

The *SHUTDOWN Command*

The **SHUTDOWN** command has a similar syntax to the **STARTUP** command; however, as you can imagine the command's options are different:

➤ **NORMAL** This is the default if the **SHUTDOWN** command is issued with no options. It is the most polite of the shutdown options in that it waits patiently for all users to log off before shutting down the instance, whether they are actively engaged in transactions or just sitting idle. **NORMAL** is also the safest shutdown and is suggested as the only option to use prior to a cold backup. However, I have never experienced a problem recovering from a shutdown using the next option, **IMMEDIATE**. **SHUTDOWN NORMAL** is the slowest shutdown option. A startup from a **SHUTDOWN NORMAL** will be the fastest startup because no instance recovery is performed.

➤ **IMMEDIATE** This is the next most polite shutdown option. It waits until pending transactions are complete, then logs users off and shuts down the instance. **SHUTDOWN IMMEDIATE** is faster than **SHUTDOWN NORMAL**. Instance recovery may be performed on startup from a **SHUTDOWN IMMEDIATE**. **SHUTDOWN**

IMMEDIATE provides an alternative to killing user sessions and then performing a **SHUTDOWN NORMAL.**

➤ **ABORT** This is the rude shutdown option. It immediately stops the Oracle processes and should only be used when all other options have failed to shut down the instance. It will leave the database in an inconsistent state, which means that the database may not be able to be recovered from if this state is used to take a cold backup from. **SHUTDOWN ABORT** is the fastest of all the shutdown options, but will always require instance recovery and in some rare cases may cause database corruption that is not recoverable. You should always follow a **SHUTDOWN ABORT** with a **STARTUP NORMAL** and **SHUTDOWN NORMAL.**

Here are some examples of the **SHUTDOWN** command:

```
SVRMGR> SHUTDOWN
SVRMGR> Database closed
SVRMGR> Database dismounted
SVRMGR> Oracle instance shut down
```

SQL*Plus

Although many new GUI tools, including Oracle's Enterprise Manager tool, can be used to manage an Oracle database, it is important for a DBA to be familiar with SQL*Plus. Knowledge of basic SQL*Plus commands is necessary for success on the OCP-DBA exams.

In previous chapters, I have covered SQL and PL/SQL but not the utility SQL*Plus, which in most cases is where SQL and PL/SQL is tested and developed. Learning how to manipulate commands and change the SQL*Plus environment can aid in the development process. This section will review basic SQL*Plus commands.

The SQL Buffer

Oracle stores the last SQL command or PL/SQL block entered in a memory area called the *SQL buffer*. The SQL buffer can only hold one command at a time. To rerun a command or PL/SQL block, just type any of the following at the SQL*Plus prompt:

```
SQL> r
SQL> run
SQL> /
```

To list the contents of the buffer, type "list" or "L". SQL*Plus commands, like the **SET** command, are not stored in the SQL buffer. Input to the SQL buffer can be terminated three ways:

➤ Enter a slash (/)

➤ Enter a semicolon (;)

➤ Press the Enter key twice

Entering SQL*Plus Commands

The syntax for SQL*Plus commands are different from SQL or PL/SQL. SQL*Plus commands are not terminated with a colon or a slash. Instead, you just press the Enter key at the end of the command line. If you want to continue the command to the next line, use a hyphen (-) as the continuation character. For example:

```
SQL> COLUMN price FORMAT $999,999.99 -
> HEADING Cost
```

Table 9.1 summarizes the SQL*Plus commands.

If you are not familiar with these commands, refer to Oracle's *SQL*Plus User's Guide and Reference*. The most complex is probably the **SET** command.

Table 9.1   The SQL*Plus commands.

Command	Description
@	Runs the specified command file.
@@	Runs a nested command file.
/	Executes a SQL command or PL/SQL block.
ACCEPT	Reads a line of input and stores it in a variable.
APPEND	Adds specified text to the end of the current line in the buffer.
BREAK	Specifies where and how formatting will change in a report, or lists the current break definition.
BTITLE	Places and formats a specified title at the bottom of each report page, or lists the current BTITLE definition.
CHANGE	Changes text on the current line in the buffer.
CLEAR	Resets or erases the current value or setting for the specified option, such as BREAKs or COLUMNs.

(continued)

Table 9.1	The SQL*Plus commands *(continued)*.
Command	**Description**
COLUMN	Specifies display attributes for a column, or lists the current display attributes for a single column or for all columns.
COMPUTE	Calculates and prints summary lines, using various standard computations, on subsets of selected rows, or lists all COMPUTE definitions.
CONNECT	Connects Oracle with username given.
COPY	Copies data from a query to a table in a local or remote database.
DEFINE	Specifies a user variable and assigns it a CHAR value, or lists the value and variable type of a single variable or all variables.
DEL	Deletes one or more lines of the buffer.
DESCRIBE	Lists the column definitions for the specified table, view, or synonym or the specifications for the specified function or procedure.
DISCONNECT	Commits pending changes to the database and logs the current username off Oracle, but does not exit SQL*Plus.
EDIT	Invokes a host operating system text editor on the contents of the specified file or on the contents of the buffer.
EXECUTE	Executes a single PL/SQL statement.
EXIT	Terminates SQL*Plus and returns control to the operating system.
GET	Loads a host operating system file into the SQL buffer.
HELP	Accesses the SQL*Plus help system.
HOST	Executes a host operating system command without leaving SQL*Plus.
INPUT	Adds one or more new lines after the current line in the buffer.
LIST	Lists one or more lines of the SQL buffer.
PAUSE	Displays an empty line followed by a line containing text, then waits for the user to press Enter, or displays empty lines and waits for the user's response.
PRINT	Displays the current value of a bind variable.
PROMPT	Sends the specified message or a blank line to the user's screen.
REMARK	Begins a comment in a command file.

(continued)

Table 9.1   The SQL*Plus commands *(continued)*.

Command	Description
REPFOOTER	Places and formats a specified report footer at the bottom of each report, or lists the current REPFOOTER definition.
REPHEADER	Places and formats a specified report header at the top of each report, or lists the current REPHEADER definition.
RUN	Lists and executes the SQL command or PL/SQL block currently stored in the SQL buffer.
SAVE	Saves the contents of the SQL buffer in a host operating system file.
SET	Sets a system variable to alter the SQL*Plus environment for your current session.
SHOW	Shows the value of a SQL*Plus system variable or the current SQL*Plus environment.
SPOOL	Stores query results in an operating system file and, optionally, sends the file to a printer with the SPOOL OUT command.
SQLPLUS or sqlplus	Starts SQL*Plus from the operating system prompt.
START	Executes the contents of the specified command file.
STORE	Saves attributes of the current SQL*Plus environment in a host operating system file.
TIMING	Records timing data for an elapsed period of time, lists the current timer's title and timing data, or lists the number of active timers.
TTITLE	Places and formats a specified title at the top of each report page, or lists the current TTITLE definition.
UNDEFINE	Deletes one or more user variables that you defined either explicitly (with the DEFINE command) or implicitly (with an argument to the START command).
VARIABLE	Declares a bind variable that can be referenced in PL/SQL.
WHENEVER OSERROR	Exits SQL*Plus if an operating system command generates an error.
WHENEVER SQLERROR	Exits SQL*Plus if a SQL command or PL/SQL block gets an error.

The SQL*Plus **SET** command is very similar to the Server Manager **SET** command. Here are a few of the SQL*Plus **SET** command options:

```
>--SET------------------------------------------------>>
            |--CHARWIDTH       integer-------------|
            |--DATEWIDTH       integer-------------|
            |--ECHO            ON/OFF--------------|
            |--LONGWIDTH       integer-------------|
            |--MAXDATA         integer-------------|
            |--NUMWIDTH        integer-------------|
            |--SERVEROUTPUT    ON/OFF    size--------|
            |--STOPONERROR     ON/OFF--------------|
            |--TERMOUT         ON/OFF--------------|
            |--TIMING          ON/OFF--------------|
            |--VERIFY          ON/OFF--------------|
            |--AUTOTRACE       ON/OFF EXPLAIN-------|
```

The **SET** command options have the following definitions:

➤ **CHARWIDTH** sets the column display width for **CHAR** data. The default is 80 characters.

➤ **DATAWIDTH** sets the column display width for **DATE** data.

➤ **ECHO ECHO ON** will echo commands from scripts that are run.

➤ **LONGWIDTH** sets the column display width for **LONG** data. The default is 80 characters.

➤ **MAXDATA** sets the maximum number of bytes a **SELECT** statement can return in a fetch. The default is 20,480 bytes.

➤ **NUMWIDTH** sets the column display width for **NUMBER** data. The default is 10 single place numeric characters (including any decimals).

➤ **SERVEROUTPUT SERVEROUPUT ON** enables output form the **DBMS_OUTPUT PUT** and **PUT_LINE** commands.

➤ **TERMOUT TERMOUT OFF** stops output from SQL command coming back to the screen. The default is **ON**, which allows output to come to the terminal.

➤ **TIMING ON** gives timing feedback on parse, execute, and fetch times.

➤ **VERIFY VERIFY ON** (the default) shows both the before change and after change image of a line where a substitution has occurred.

➤ **AUTOTRACE AUTOTRACE ON** turns on tracing information for commands, used with the **EXPLAIN** option will also generate an explain plan for the commands entered after the **AUTOTRACE** command is executed.

SQL*Plus is started using the **SQLPLUS** or **sqlplus** command depending upon the system on which you run. The full syntax to start SQL*Plus is:

```
SQLPLUS username/password@connect @file p1, p2...pn
```

The **SQLPLUS** (or **sqlplus**) command has the following options:

➤ **username/password** The username and password with which to connect to the database. For OS authorized logins (OPS$), a single slash (/) is accepted.

➤ **@connect** Specification of the proper connection alias if the database is not the default instance or is a remote instance (as defined in the tnsnames.ora file).

➤ **@file** The full path name of a SQL command file to execute immediately upon sign on to the database.

➤ **p1, p2...pn** List of arguments expected by the SQL command file. (Note that according to Oracle, a maximum of nine arguments can be used. However, I have used more, so it may be platform-dependent.)

PRODUCT_USER_PROFILE Table

The **PRODUCT_USER_PROFILE** table is used to disable selected SQL and SQL*Plus commands while in SQL*Plus on a user-by-user basis. This security is enforced by SQL*Plus, not Oracle. The **PRODUCT_USER_PROFILE** table should be created from the system account by running the PUPBLD.sql file. If this table is not created, all users except SYSTEM will see a warning when connecting to SQL*Plus stating that the **PRODUCT_USER_PROFILE** table is not created. Any SQL or SQL*Plus command can be disabled for a user by inserting a row for the user into the **PRODUCT_USER_PROFILE** table.

SQL*Loader

SQL*Loader loads data from files into an Oracle database. It is the only Oracle utility designed to load data into Oracle. Alternative methods of loading data would be coding load programs in 3GL languages like C++ or using direct file reads using the UTL_FILE set of stored procedures.

SQL*Loader can do the following:

➤ Load data from multiple files.

➤ Load delimited data, fixed-length data, and variable-length data.

➤ Use SQL functions on data before inserting it into Oracle.

➤ Load many datatypes that are not native to Oracle by converting them to Oracle datatypes.

➤ Combine more than one physical record into a single logical record.

➤ Break a single physical record into multiple logical records.

➤ Generate unique keys via a sequence generator.

➤ Load from disk or tape drives.

➤ Load data directly into Oracle for faster loads.

Direct Path Load

Direct path loads are much faster than conventional path loads. This is because a direct path load writes directly to the database files, bypassing the overhead of the database. Because direct path loads write directly to datafiles, they do not compete for database resources with other user processes.

Conventional Path Load

The conventional path load uses the same method as all other Oracle tools for inserting data. Conventional path load does a SQL insert with a bind array buffer. In addition, conventional path loads will look for and try to fill partially filled blocks. While under normal database operations this helps performance of the database, the search for partially filled blocks slows downloads.

SQL*Loader Files

SQL*Loader can have up to five files associated with a load:

➤ Control file

➤ Log file

➤ Bad file

➤ Discard file

➤ Datafile

The Control File

The control file contains the DDL definitions that show the format of the data, the location of the datafile, and the Oracle table that will be loaded to. The control file is normally created with a text editor. The control file can also contain the data to be loaded instead of using a separate datafile.

The keywords used with SQL*Loader control files are:

➤ **LOAD DATA** Must be the first line of the control file.

➤ **INFILE** 'load_file.dat' Used only when data is not in the control file. **INFILE** * is used if the data is in the control file.

➤ **INTO TABLE** table_name The Oracle table to load into.

➤ **BEGINDATA** Used to denote the beginning of data in the control file.

➤ **POSITION** Used with fixed-length data to define column positions.

➤ **FIELDS TERMINATED BY** ',' Defines the delimiting character in a delimited file.

➤ **APPEND** Data will be loaded into Oracle tables even if they are not empty.

➤ **SEQUENCE** Generate unique numbers sequentially for the load.

➤ **DISCARDFILE** 'file_name.dsc' Discard the file for load.

➤ **DISCARDMAX** The maximum number of discards allowed before stopping the load.

➤ **REPLACE** If there is data in the Oracle table, delete the data before starting the load.

➤ **BADFILE** 'file_name.bad' File for bad records.

The Log File

SQL*Loader will create a log file when it is started. The log file contains detailed information about the load, including the number of records loaded, not loaded, error messages, and so on. If SQL*Loader cannot create a log file, the program will abort.

The Bad File

Records are put in the bad file when they are rejected by Oracle. Oracle may reject a record because it is missing a data for a **NOT NULL** field or perhaps because of a duplicate key in a unique index. The bad file is in the same format as the original datafile. After the data is corrected, the same control file can be used to load the bad file. The infile file name would be changed to the bad file name.

The Discard File

The discard file is only created if there are discarded records. Records in the discard file are discarded by SQL*Loader because they do not match the record selection criteria of the control file. The discard file is also written in the same format as the original datafile, so the same control file can be used to load it.

The Datafile

The datafile contains the data to be loaded. The data can be fixed-length records or comma (or some other character) delimited. The datafile can even be EBCDIC (IBM) format. For small amounts of data, the control and data portions can be combined into a single file.

SQL*Loader Command Line

SQL*Loader can be started from the OS command line. Parameters given on the command line override the parameters in the control file. On Unix systems, the command is:

```
sqlldr "command line parameters"
```

On Windows systems running Oracle7.3.x, the command is:

```
sqlldr73 "command line parameters"
```

The command line parameters for the command line (or loaded into a parameter file) are:

➤ **USERID** Oracle username/password.

➤ **CONTROL** Control file name.

➤ **LOG** Log file name.

➤ **BAD** Bad file name.

➤ **DATA** Data file name.

➤ **DISCARD** Discard file name.

➤ **DISCARDMAX** Maximum number of discards allowed (default is infinite).

➤ **SKIP** The number of records to skip in the datafile (default is 0).

➤ **LOAD** The number of records to load (default is all).

➤ **ERRORS** The number of errors allowed before the load is terminated (default is 50).

➤ **ROWS** The number of rows in the conventional path bind array or between saves in direct path.

➤ **BINDSIZE** The size in bytes of the conventional path bind array.

➤ **SILENT** No terminal feedback is generated during load.

➤ **DIRECT** Use direct path load.

➤ **PARFILE** The name of a file that holds parameters for the load.

➤ **PARALLEL** Performs a parallel load (default is false).

➤ **FILE** Database file from which to allocate extents. This is used only with a **PARALLEL** load.

Here is an example of a SQL*Loader command line:

```
Sqlldr userid=john/doe control=testload.ctl log=testload.log
```

Exam Prep Questions

Question 1

> When starting an Oracle instance and opening a database, what is the first state the database goes through?
>
> ○ a. **MOUNT**
>
> ○ b. **NOMOUNT**
>
> ○ c. **OPEN**

The correct answer is b, the **NOMOUNT** state. During the **NOMOUNT** state, the init<SID>.ora file is read, control files are identified, the SGA is created and initialized, and the background processes are started.

Question 2

> When connected in Server Manager as SYSDBA, SYSOPER, or INTERNAL, what is the first step in starting an instance?
>
> ○ a. Start Oracle background processes
>
> ○ b. Initialize the SGA
>
> ○ c. Issue the **STARTUP** command
>
> ○ d. Mount the database

The correct answer is c, issue the **STARTUP** command. The **STARTUP** command will start the Oracle instance and optionally mount and open the database.

Question 3

> Before a create database statement is issued, what state should the instance be in?
>
> ○ a. **OPEN**
>
> ○ b. **MOUNT**
>
> ○ c. **NOMOUNT**
>
> ○ d. **ABORTED**

The answer to this question is c, **NOMOUNT**. The instance must be started with no database mounted. Answer a is incorrect because a database must exist for it to be opened. Answer b is incorrect because a database must be created before it can be mounted. Answer d is incorrect because if you aborted the instance, it will have already been created.

Question 4

How would you start a database so it could be used by multiple instances?

○ a. By using **EXCLUSIVE**

○ b. By using **FORCE**

○ c. By using **PARALLEL**

The correct answer is c, **PARALLEL**. Answer a is incorrect because **EXCLUSIVE** is the opposite of **PARALLEL**. Answer b is incorrect because **FORCE** is used to abort, then start up a database in **EXCLUSIVE** mode.

Question 5

What action is taken when the following command is executed in SQL*Plus?

```
SAVE test_file
```

○ a. None, this is not a valid SQL*Plus command.

○ b. A file is created with the contents of the SQL buffer.

○ c. The system editor is started.

The correct answer is b. The **SAVE** command puts the SQL buffer into a file. Answer a is incorrect because this is a valid SQL*Plus command. Answer c is incorrect because the **ED[IT]** command starts the system editor.

Question 6

What will happen when you enter the following SQL*Plus command?

```
COLUMN price NULL 'Free'
```

○ a. The column price will be set to **NULL**.

○ b. The **NULL** constraint on the column price will be set.

○ c. The text string 'Free' will be displayed for **NULL** values.

○ d. The column price will be updated by setting all **NULL** values to 'Free'.

The correct answer to this question is c. For a detailed description of the **COLUMN** command, see the *SQL*Plus User's Guide and Reference*.

Question 7

What are the three ways the SQL buffer can be terminated?

❏ a. By pressing Enter

❏ b. By entering a slash (/)

❏ c. By pressing the Esc key

❏ d. By entering a semicolon (;)

❏ e. By pressing Enter twice

❏ f. By pressing the Ctrl key and the Esc key at the same time

The answers to this question are b, d, and e. Answer a is incorrect because this adds a blank line to the buffer. Answer c is incorrect because this does nothing. Answer f is incorrect because this does nothing.

Question 8

What is the maximum number of parameters that can be passed
to a SQL script file from the command line?

○ a. Infinite

○ b. 1

○ c. 5

○ d. 9

○ e. 32

The correct answer according to Oracle is c. However, I have personally tested
as many as 10 successfully in a 7.2.3 configuration.

Question 9

What happens when **VERIFY** is set to **ON**?

○ a. The SQL syntax is checked before it is sent to Oracle.

○ b. Old and new values for substitution variables are
displayed.

○ c. You are prompted to confirm changes.

The correct answer is b. Answer a is incorrect because this is done anyway.
Answer c is incorrect because this is not done by any SQL*Plus command.

Question 10

Which SQL*Loader file holds all the information needed to load a
load file?

○ a. Parfile

○ b. Log

○ c. Command

○ d. Control

The correct answer is d. The control file has all the information needed for the
load. Answer a is incorrect because a parfile has the commands and command
line options, but not the data or control file records. Answer b is incorrect
because the log file is written to, not read from. Answer c is invalid.

Question 11

> Which of the following is a characteristic of direct path loading?
>
> ○ a. Uses the SQL **INSERT** command to load row data
>
> ○ b. Writes directly to Oracle datafiles
>
> ○ c. Fills an array of rows to be inserted into the database
>
> ○ d. Can only load into clustered tables

The correct answer for this question is b. Direct path loads are fast because they load data directly to the datafiles by adding new blocks. Answer a is incorrect because answer b is correct. Answer c is incorrect because the fast path option builds blocks, not arrays. Answer d is incorrect because fast path is used against normal tables.

Need To Know More?

Oracle7 Server Administrator's Guide, Release 7.3, Oracle Corporation, February 1996, Part No. A32535-1.

Oracle7 Server Utilities User's Guide, Release 7.3, Oracle Corporation, February 1996, Part No. A32541-1.

Oracle Server Manager User's Guide, Release 2.1, Oracle Corporation, 1996, Part No. A30887-1.

Oracle Server Manager Release 2.3.2 Addendum, Release 2.3.2, Oracle Corporation, 1996, Part No. A42570-1.

SQL*Plus User's Guide and Reference, Release 3.3, Oracle Corporation, 1996, Part No. A42562-1.

Oracle Administrator Product (Software), Release 97.4, RevealNet, Incorporated, 1997, http://www.revealnet.com/. The Oracle Administrator Product has numerous, detailed examples of using SQL*Plus, SQL*Loader, and Server Manager, including a complete command reference and SQL*Loader command and file content (control and parameter as well as command line) reference with examples.

Database Design And Modeling

Terms you'll need to understand:

√ Entity

√ Relationship

√ Entity relationship diagram (ERD)

√ Function hierarchy diagram (FHD)

√ Attribute

√ Column

√ Cardinality

√ Strategy

√ Analysis

√ Transition

√ Production

√ UID

√ Primary key

√ Foreign key

√ Referential integrity

Techniques you'll need to master:

√ Understanding the process of normalization

√ Reading an entity relationship diagram (ERD)

√ Applying the five-step system development cycle

√ Converting from an ERD to tables, relations, and constraints

Ninety percent of any field is learning the *jargon*—the language specific to that field. The other 10 percent is applying techniques. With Oracle, the jargon is that of relational databases. Much of this jargon can be attributed to Dr. E.F. (Ted) Codd, who formulated the rules called *normal forms* for data. He also formulated the relational algebra upon which relational databases are designed. If you're preparing to take the OCP exams, you should already be familiar with the relational jargon. This section is only designed to be a refresher. If you're not familiar with the jargon, there's a comprehensive list of references in the "Need To Know More" section at the end of this chapter. The 10 percent attributed to applying the techniques inherent with the jargon is what experience is all about, and if you really know the jargon, the techniques are easy to learn.

The Five-Step System Development Cycle

You may see the five-step process or the seven-step process (depending on the granularity of each step) used in many books on systems and software design. Figure 10.1 shows the Oracle interpretation of the steps as a five-step process.

The five-step system development cycle consists of:

➤ Strategy and analysis

➤ Design

➤ Build and document

➤ Transition

➤ Production

Each of the steps is important, and adherence to this type of methodology has shown to produce quality systems that are easy to maintain. Oracle computer-aided design and engineering tools (CASE), such as Designer/2000 and Developer/2000, use this methodology.

Strategy And Analysis

In the strategy and analysis step, the user and system requirements are gathered and analyzed. The expected deliverables from this stage would be a set of requirements (in the form of documents) that specify the *whats* of the system, not the *hows*. A project plan and development time frame may also be specified at this time, with the understanding that if the design cycle shows problems

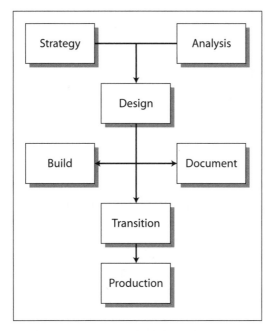

Figure 10.1   The five-step system development cycle.

with the time lines, they'll be adjusted. The documents, at this point, are high level in nature and provide the big picture.

Design

In the design step, the user requirements and system specifications are applied to create a design document consisting of an entity relationship diagram (ERD), flow charts, function decompositions, module descriptions, data flow diagrams, and so forth. (The ERD is discussed further in the section titled "Database Design" later in this chapter.) The purpose of the design step is to convey the *hows* of the application and should specify programming languages, database systems, coding, and naming standards.

Build And Document

In the build and document step, the design from the design step is converted from specifications and diagrams to actual executables and database structures. During this step, the *as-built* documents that instruct users how to use the system and production support how to support the application are written. ERDs are mapped to tables, columns, and relations; function decompositions are mapped to stored procedures; and 3GL executables and module descriptions are mapped into GUIs, screens, and executables. The build and document step will also incorporate unit testing and system test functions.

Transition

In the transition step, the application is put through user-acceptance testing. Final procedures are developed and turnover packages are prepared. Database tuning occurs at this time because true user load can't be tested without users in most environments.

Production

In the production step, the application is passed off to production support and moves into a maintenance mode where code is locked down and database changes are minimized. Once a system is "in production," the activities around it move into the support and maintenance arena. Strict change control is the rule under production-level applications and no ad hoc changes to structure or code are allowed.

Database Design

Tables, tuples, and attributes have already been discussed throughout this book, and we've also touched on relationships. Now, let's look at relationships a bit more closely and see how they apply to relational databases. Stop for a moment and consider the company where you work or perhaps for whom you're consulting. The company has employees or, let's say, the company employs workers. The reverse is also true; a worker is employed by a company. This is a *relationship*—a logical tie between information that's contained in entities. In this case, the information is from the entities: the company and the workers. Notice that a relationship must make sense from both directions. If a relationship doesn't work both ways, it isn't a proper relationship, and you should reevaluate it.

Can a worker have more than one job? Of course. Can a company have more than one worker? Yes. So let's restate the relationship. A company can employ one or more workers. A worker may be employed by one or more companies.

This is called a *many-to-many* relationship. Of course other types of relationships exist. Within a company, a worker usually only works for one department at a time, though a department may have many workers. This is called a *one-to-many relationship*. Generally speaking, most many-to-many relationships can be broken down into one-to-many relationships; and one-to-many relationships form a majority of the relationships in a relational database. A relationship occurs between two *entities*. In the earlier example, *worker* and *company* are entities. An entity is always singular in nature, and in most cases, an entity will map into a table. A diagram showing the logical structure of a relational database is called an *entity relation diagram*, or ERD for short (see Figure 10.2).

Study Figure 10.2 carefully. You will be expected to identify the symbols (such as UID and the various line types).

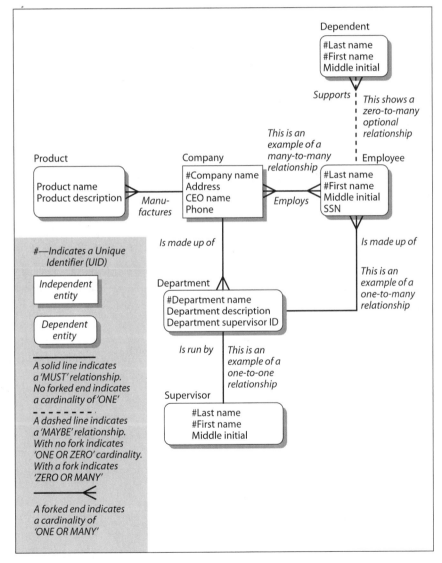

Figure 10.2   Example of a simple entity relationship diagram.

Another aspect of a relational database is its functions. Don't be confused. In this case, a *function* is a reason for a database feature, not a stored PL/SQL program. Without functions, a database would have no purpose for being. Functions start at a high level, such as providing a means of tracking and reporting the work history of employees. Functions can be broken down or, if you wish, decomposed until they are atomic in nature. An absolute purist would break down a function until it consisted of operations involving individual attributes, such as add, delete, update, or retrieve.

For example, say we wished to retrieve a record (or tuple) from a table, update one of its columns (or attributes), and then return the row to the table. In one case, it could be considered one function: update of attribute x. In a different light, it could be decomposed into the individual retrieves, modifies, and updates of the columns. In most cases, it isn't required to go into great and gory detail. The functions a database is designed to perform are shown in a function hierarchy diagram (FHD). Entities (hence, tables) and relations map into functions. Figure 10.3 shows a simple FHD.

The final aspect of a relational database is its modules. A *module* may perform one or more functions and may map into a form, a report, a menu, or a procedure. For example, a single module representing a form can handle numerous atomic functions, such as add, update, retrieve, and delete of tables or even a group of tables or data records.

Let's summarize. A relational database is made up of entities consisting of attributes. These entities and attributes can be mapped into tables and columns. Each occurrence of an entity adds a row to the table it maps to. These rows are called tuples. Each entity relates to one or more other entities by means of relationships. A relationship is defined as a named association between two things of significance (entities). Relationships must be valid in both directions and must have degree such as one-to-many or many-to-many. Relationships must also show *optimality*, such as *may be* or *must be*.

Designing A Database

Functions are used to tell what's done with the entities and relations. Entities and relations map into functions. Modules implement functions and map into forms, reports, menus, or procedures. The normal sequence of database design is:

1. Perform entity and attribute analysis.

2. Normalize entity and attribute structure to at least third normal form (discussed in the next section).

3. Identify unique identifiers (UIDs) for each entity.

4. Define entity relationships.

5. Map entities to tables.

6. Map attributes to columns.

7. Map UIDs to primary keys.

8. Map relationships to foreign keys.

This logical movement from the abstract to the concrete allows for a properly designed database. Notice that primary and foreign key relationships are only mentioned. Primary and foreign key relationships are collectively termed

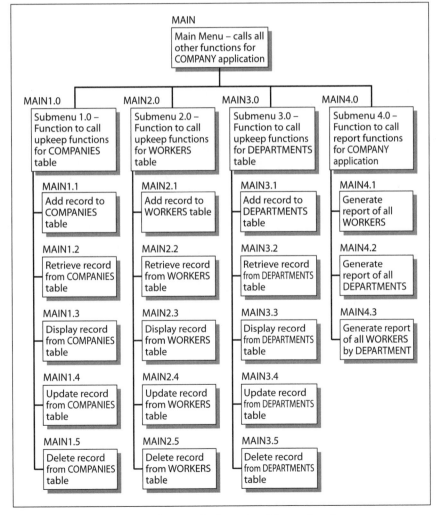

Figure 10.3   Example of a simple function hierarchy diagram.

referential integrity. Other constraints, such as user-defined or column constraints, are also available. User-defined constraints are usually specified to enforce business rules. Column constraints generally enforce typing rules (for example, a character field that can only use numbers and has a constraint to enforce this value rule in place), validate input, or enforce a **NOT NULL** restriction.

Normalization

All of relational design depends on Dr. E.F. (Ted) Codd's rules. The entire set of rules are complex and, to most of us, rather obtuse at times. Luckily, they've been used to produce the Rules of Normalization. These, simply stated, are:

➤ **Precursor** Each occurrence of an entity is uniquely identifiable by a combination of attributes and/or relationships.

➤ **First normal form** Remove repeated attributes or groups of attributes to their own entity.

➤ **Second normal form** Remove attributes dependent on only part of the unique identifier.

➤ **Third normal form** Remove attributes dependent on attributes that are not a part of the unique identifier.

In short, to be in third normal form all attributes in an entity must relate directly to the identifier and only to the identifier.

This unique identifier is called the *primary key.* It can be a unique number, (such as a social security number) or a combination of attributes called a *concatenated* or *combination key* (such as a last name and a date of birth). Generally speaking, these primary keys are used to enforce relations by mapping the keys into related entities where they become *foreign keys.*

Exam Prep Questions

Question 1

> Which symbol indicates a UID?
>
> ○ a. *
>
> ○ b. o
>
> ○ c. #
>
> ○ d. &
>
> ○ e. $

The proper answer is c, the pound sign (#). Answer a is incorrect because the asterisk (*) is used to denote a primary key value. Answer b is incorrect because the lowercase o is used to indicate a candidate key. Answer d is incorrect because the ampersand (&) isn't used in CASE nomenclature. Answer e is incorrect because the dollar sign ($) isn't used in CASE nomenclature.

Question 2

> What does a single solid line between two entities represent?
>
> ○ a. Optional
>
> ○ b. Mandatory
>
> ○ c. One or more
>
> ○ d. One and only one

The correct answer is d, one and only one. Answer a is incorrect because an optional relationship is shown by use of a dotted line. Answer b, though partially correct in that a solid line represents a mandatory relationship, doesn't completely answer the question. Answer c is incorrect because a one-or-more relation is shown with a crow's-foot on the many-end of the relationship line.

Question 3

> Which statement is a many-to-one relationship?
>
> ○ a. Each street may have one and only one sign.
>
> ○ b. Each street may must have many signs.
>
> ○ c. Many signs may be on one and only one street.
>
> ○ d. Many signs may be on many streets.

The correct answer to this question is c. In this case, the answer is contained in the wording "Many signs may be on one and only one street." Even though the normal wording is reversed (usually it would be each street may have one or more signs), it still denotes a one-to-many relationship. Answer a is incorrect because it clearly denotes a one-to-one relationship. Answer b is incorrect because it's a syntactically impossible statement. Answer d is incorrect because it's clearly a many-to-many relationship.

Question 4

> Which type of constraint is used to enforce business rules?
>
> ○ a. Column
>
> ○ b. Referential
>
> ○ c. Entity
>
> ○ d. User-defined

The proper answer to this question is d. By definition, a user-defined constraint is used to enforce business rules. Answer a is incorrect because column constraints are used to enforce validity, value, and **NULL**- and **NOT NULL**-type constraints only. Answer b is incorrect because referential constraints are used for data concurrency only. Answer c is incorrect because there's no such thing as an entity constraint.

Question 5

> Which type of integrity constraint exists if only a number value
> can be inserted into a column?
>
> ○ a. Column
>
> ○ b. Referential
>
> ○ c. Entity
>
> ○ d. User-defined

The correct answer is a. The constraint described is used to enforce typing; only column constraints are used to enforce typing. Answer b is incorrect because referential constraints are for data concurrency only. Answer c is incorrect because there are no entity constraints. Answer d is incorrect because user-defined constraints are used for business rules, not for data validity.

Question 6

> Which component of an entity relationship diagram is a named
> association between two things of significance?
>
> ○ a. Entity
>
> ○ b. Attribute
>
> ○ c. Relationship

The correct answer is c because the question is actually stating the definition of a relationship. Answer a is incorrect because an entity is a thing of significance, such as a car or person, so the question is actually asking "Which component of an entity relationship diagram is a named association between two entities?" A named association is a relationship. Answer b is incorrect because an attribute is part of an entity.

Question 7

When designing the database, which step comes first?

○ a. Map attributes to columns

○ b. Map entities to tables

○ c. Map UID to primary keys

○ d. Map relationships to foreign keys

The correct answer is b. You must first map the entities into tables or you won't have anything in which to place the attributes when you map them into columns. If you don't have columns, you can't specify primary keys; and if you don't have primary keys, you can't map out the relationships to other tables using primary key/foreign key relationships. Answer a is incorrect because you can't map attributes to columns until you've mapped entities to tables. Answer c is incorrect because you can't map UIDs to primary keys until attributes are mapped to columns. Answer d is incorrect because relationships can't be mapped to foreign keys until UIDs are mapped to primary keys.

Question 8

In which stage of the system development cycle should you complete user acceptance testing?

○ a. Strategy and analysis

○ b. Design

○ c. Build and document

○ d. Transition

○ e. Production

The answer to this question is d. The process of user acceptance testing is done during the transition phase and it would not make sense to try to do user testing before a complete system is available. Answer a is incorrect because strategy and analysis is the first step of the cycle, and there's nothing to test yet. Answer b is incorrect because this is only the design step and there's nothing to test yet. Answer c is incorrect because, at this step, we build and document, so although there are things that can be tested, they aren't ready for users until all modules are ready. Answer e is incorrect because by the time you reach the production step, you had better have tested and let the users test the application.

Question 9

> Which integrity constraint type states that foreign key values must
> match a primary key or be null?
>
> ○ a. Entity
>
> ○ b. Referential
>
> ○ c. Column
>
> ○ d. User-defined

The proper answer to this question is b because the question is actually stating
the definition of a referential integrity constraint. Answer a is incorrect because there are no entity constraints. Answer c is incorrect because column
constraints enforce validity, value, or null status. Answer d is incorrect because
user-defined constraints are used to enforce business rules.

Question 10

> What is the first stage of the system development cycle?
>
> ○ a. Build and document
>
> ○ b. Design
>
> ○ c. Transition
>
> ○ d. Strategy and analysis
>
> ○ e. Production

The correct answer is d. The first stage is strategy and analysis. You can't design a system until you understand it. The strategy and analysis stage provides
understanding used to design the system. Answer a is incorrect because you
don't build and document until you perform the strategy and analysis and design steps. Answer b is incorrect because you don't design before performing
the strategy and analysis step. Answer c is incorrect because you must perform
the strategy and analysis, design, and build and document steps before you
have anything to transition. Answer e is incorrect because production is the
final step.

Need To Know More?

Ault, Michael R.: *Oracle8 Administration and Management.* John Wiley & Sons, 1998. ISBN 0-47119-234-1. The introduction chapter provides a great review of relational theory, entity relational modeling, and normalization.

Barker, Richard: *CASE*METHOD: Entity Relationship Modelling.* Addison-Wesley Publishing Co., Inc., 1990. ISBN 0-20141-696-4.

Barker, Richard and Cliff Longman: *CASE*METHOD: Function and Process Modelling.* Addison-Wesley Publishing Co., Inc., 1992. ISBN 0-20156-525-0.

Barker, Richard: *CASE*METHOD: Tasks and Deliverables.* Addison-Wesley Publishing Co., Inc., 1990. ISBN 0-20141-697-2. This three-book set details all of Oracle's development methodologies. The three books cover the system development cycle, entity relationship diagramming, and conversion of interviews into attributes, entities, and so forth.

Brathwaite, Kenmore S.: *Relational Databases: Concepts, Design and Administration.* McGraw-Hill, Inc., 1991. ISBN 0-07007-252-3. Another excellent book covering relational database design and structure.

Date, Christopher J.: *Introduction to Database Systems Vol. 2, 4th Edition.* Addison-Wesley Publishing Co., Inc., 1982. ISBN 0-20114-474-3. Date's book may be a bit much for those not acquainted with relational theory, but it will give you all the great and gory details of relational theory.

Atre, Shaku: *Data Base: Structured Techniques for Design, Performance, and Management.* John Wiley & Sons, 1988. ISBN 0-47185-251-1. This book provides a complete overview of databases from their beginnings to relational, and it provides insights on proper normalization techniques and the *whys* behind the *hows*. Although it is now out of print, online services such as www.amazon.com offer to search for a copy.

Sample Test: SQL And PL/SQL

11

The sections that follow provide numerous pointers for development of a successful test-taking strategy, including how to choose proper answers, how to decode ambiguity, how to work within the Oracle framework, how to decide what to memorize, and how to prepare for the test. Finally, I provide a number of questions that cover the subject matter likely to appear on Test 1 of the Oracle Certified Database Administrator track, "Introduction to Oracle: SQL and PL/ SQL." Good luck!

Questions, Questions, Questions

Each exam in the DBA test series comprises 60 questions. You are allotted 90 minutes for each of the DBA exams. The questions on the exam will be of two types:

➤ Multiple choice with a single answer

➤ Multiple choice with multiple answers

Note: In my experience, I haven't seen any fill in the blank or pick the spot on the graphic questions on the exams.

Always take the time to read the question twice before selecting an answer. Not every question has only one answer. Some questions will have multiple answers, and if so, it will be clearly stated in the question how many answers you should select. There is no partial credit given for incomplete answers; if the question asks for two answers, you have to give two answers or the entire question is counted as incorrect.

When taking the test, always read all of the answers and never assume that a question can't be as easy as it looks. In some cases, they are, and second-guessing the question is one of the biggest problems with taking this type of test.

Picking Correct Answers

Obviously, the only way to pass any exam is to select the correct answers. Unfortunately, exams are written by human beings. Tests like the SAT and GRE have been run through batteries of test experts and have been standardized; the Oracle Certified Professional exams have not. Although a question might make perfect sense to the person who wrote it, the wording can be ambiguous, diabolical, or convoluted to just about anyone else. In other cases, the question may be so poorly written, or worse, even have an opinion rather than a hard fact as an answer, that unless you have an inside track you just can't divine the correct answer from your knowledge base. In cases when you have no idea what the answer is, there is almost always one or more answer out of the set of answers that can be eliminated because:

➤ The answer doesn't apply to the situation

➤ The answer describes a nonexistent issue

➤ The answer is already eliminated by the question text

After obviously wrong answers have been eliminated, you must rely on your retained knowledge to eliminate further answers. Look for what are called *distracters.* These are answers that sound perfectly plausible but refer to actions, commands, or features not present or not available in the described situation.

If you have eliminated all the answers you can through logic and knowledge and you are left with more than one choice, I suggest using *question inversion.* Question inversion is the process where you rephrase the question in terms of each remaining answer, seeking the premise of the existing question as the answer. Here is an example:

The color of a clear daytime sky is blue because:

○ a. Dust particles in the atmosphere scatter the blue components of light

○ b. The sun puts out a great deal of the blue spectrum

○ c. Oxygen absorbs most of the other spectral elements

○ d. The Van Allen belt absorbs much of the ultraviolet spectrum, thus allowing only the blue components to reach us

---

Now, say you have reduced the possible choices to answers a and c. Try rephrasing the question: "The dust in the atmosphere scattering the blue components of light cause the daytime sky to be _____ in color." Or: "Oxygen absorbing other spectral elements cause the daytime sky to be _____ in color."

Sometimes this rephrasing will jog your memory to produce the correct answer. (By the way, the correct answer is a.) Answer d is an example of a distracter: It sounds logical on the surface, unless you know that the Van Allen belt absorbs and deflects charged particle radiation, but light passes straight through (the ozone layer takes care of the ultraviolet).

Finally, if you just can't decide between two (or more) answers, guess! An unanswered question is always wrong, and at least with an educated guess you have some chance of getting the question correct.

Decoding Ambiguity

Tests are not designed to ensure everyone passes. Tests are designed to test knowledge on a given topic. A properly designed test has a bell-curve shaped distribution for the target qualified audience where a certain percent will fail. A problem with the the Oracle tests is that they have been tailored to Oracle's training materials, regardless of the fact that some of the material in the training is hearsay, some is old-DBA tales, and some is just incorrect. I have tried to point out in the previous chapters the obvious errors. For example, I have noticed that if you select the highest answer for a numeric type question, it is generally correct if the highest is the most conservative way to go, lowest if that is the most conservative. Some examples would be: the exam's insistence that the percent increase for a temporary tablespace should be 50 percent and that to be properly tuned, a rollback segment should have 20 extents as a minimum.

The only way to overcome some of the test's limitations is to be prepared. You will discover that many exam questions test your knowledge of things not directly related to the issue raised by the questions. This means that the answers offered to you, even the incorrect ones, are as much a part of the skill assessment as are the questions. If you don't know all the aspects of the test topic (in this case SQL and PL/SQL) cold, you won't be able to eliminate answers that are obviously wrong because they relate to a different aspect of the topic than the one addressed by the question.

Questions may give away the answers, especially questions dealing with commands and data dictionary topics. Read a question and evaluate the answers in light of common terms, names, and structure.

Another problem is that Oracle uses some terminology in its training materials that is found nowhere else in its documentation sets.

Working Within The Framework

The questions are presented to you in a random order. A question on SQL may follow a question on PL/SQL followed by one on database design. However, this can work to your advantage because a future question may unwittingly answer the question you are puzzling over. You will find that the incorrect answer to one question may be the correct answer to one further down the line. Take the time to read all of the answers for each question, even if you spot the correct one immediately (or should I say, especially if you spot the correct one immediately?) Also, the exam format enables you to mark questions that you want to revisit or mark those you feel may give you insight into other questions—even if you know you have answered them correctly.

Deciding What To Memorize

The amount of memorization you will have to do depends on whether you are a visual learner. If you can see the command structure diagrams in your head, you won't need to memorize as much as if you can't. The test will stretch your recollection skills through command syntax and operational command sequences used within the Oracle environment, testing not only when you should use a feature, but also when you shouldn't.

The important types of information to memorize are:

➤ The parts of procedures, functions, and packages

➤ Commands and their uses

➤ Use of anonymous PL/SQL blocks

➤ Restrictions on command use (such as with joins in **SELECT**)

➤ Use of SQL*Plus and Procedure Builder

➤ Database design and implementation topics (normalization, ERDs, and so on)

If you work your way through this book sitting in front of an Oracle database you have access to so you can try out commands, test the questions' answers, and in general, play with unfamiliar features, you should have no problem understanding the questions when they appear on the exam.

Preparing For The Test

If one is to excel in any endeavor, one must practice. The perfect musical performance looks easy, but you don't see the hours, days, and weeks of practice it took to make it look that way. Taking tests and passing them is the same. Without practice, to show you your weak areas, you go into a test with blinders on and are easily broadsided. I've included a practice exam in this chapter. You should give yourself 90 uninterrupted minutes. Use the honor system—you will gain no benefit from cheating. The idea is to see where you are weak and require further study, not to answer 100 percent of the questions correctly by looking up the answers. After your time is up or you finish, you can check your answers in Chapter 12. It might even be easier to make a copy of the sample test so you can take it multiple times.

If you want additional practice, other example exams are available from Oracle's education and certification site (http://education.oracle.com/certification) or SelfTest Software's site (http://www.stsware.com).

Taking The Test

Once you are sitting in front of the testing computer, there is nothing more you can do to increase your knowledge or preparation, so relax. Take a deep breath, stretch, and attack the first question.

Don't rush; there is plenty of time to complete each question and to return to skipped questions. If you read a question twice and are still clueless, mark it for revisit and move on. Easy and hard questions are randomly distributed, so don't take too long on hard questions or you may cheat yourself of the chance to answer some end-of-test easy questions. Hard and easy questions have the same number of points, so take care of the easy ones *first* and revisit the hard ones after answering everything that you can.

As you answer each question that you have marked to revisit, remove the mark and go on. If a question is still impossible, go on to the next you marked. On your final pass (just before time is called) guess on those that you are completely clueless on. Remember, if a question isn't answered, it is always counted wrong, but a guess just may be correct.

Sample Test: SQL And PL/SQL

Question 1

The PL/SQL executable section contains which type of statements?

- ○ a. The procedure or function name and input/output variable definitions
- ○ b. The definition of program variables, constants, exceptions, and cursors
- ○ c. SQL statements to manipulate data in the database
- ○ d. Statements to deal with error handling

Question 2

What type of constraint should be used to ensure that only a numeric value can be inserted into a column?

- ○ a. Referential
- ○ b. Column
- ○ c. Entity
- ○ d. User-defined

Question 3

Based on the exhibit, evaluate this **SELECT** statement:

```
SELECT description
FROM inventory
WHERE id_number = 'A12345'
SORT BY 1;
```

Which clause will cause an error?

- ○ a. **SELECT description**
- ○ b. **FROM inventory**
- ○ c. **WHERE id_number = 'A12345'**
- ○ d. **SORT BY 1;**
- ○ e. None of the above

Instance chart for table INVENTORY.					
Column Name:	ID_NUMBER	DESCRIPTION	MANUFACTURER_ID	QUANTITY	PRICE
Key Type:	PK		FK		
Nulls/Unique:	NN, U	NN	NN		
FK Table:			MANUFACTURER		
FK Column:			ID_NUMBER		
Datatype:	NUM	VARCHAR2	VARCHAR2	NUM	NUM
Length:	9	26	25	9	8,2

Question 4

To search a list of values, which operator would be most appropriate to use?

○ a. **LIKE**

○ b. **=**

○ c. **BETWEEN**

○ d. **IN**

Question 5

Evaluate this command:

```
ALTER TABLE product
DISABLE CONSTRAINT pk_product CASCADE;
```

Which task would this command accomplish?

○ a. Delete only the primary key values

○ b. Disable only the primary key constraint

○ c. Disable all dependent integrity constraints

○ d. Alter all dependent integrity constraint values

Question 6

Which two characters require the **ESCAPE** option to be used as literals?

☐　a. %

☐　b. _

☐　c. $

☐　d. /

Question 7

What operation is not allowed on a view created with the **WITH CHECK OPTION** clause?

○　a. **SELECT** from the view

○　b. **DELETE** from the view

○　c. Place an index on the view

○　d. **UPDATE** using the view

Question 8

You attempt to create a view with this command:

```
CREATE VIEW parts_view
AS SELECT id_number, description, quantity
FROM inventory
WHERE id_number = 1234
ORDER BY description;
```

Which clause causes an error?

○　a. **CREATE VIEW parts_view**

○　b. **AS SELECT id_number, description, quantity**

○　c. **FROM inventory**

○　d. **WHERE id_number = 1234**

○　e. **ORDER BY description;**

Question 9

Evaluate this function created with SQL*Plus:

```
CREATE OR REPLACE FUNCTION give_discount
   (start_value IN NUMBER)
IS
BEGIN
   RETURN (start_value * 0.75);
END subtract_fixed_value;
```

Why will this function cause an error?

○ a. A clause is missing.

○ b. A keyword is missing.

○ c. The parameter mode should not be specified.

○ d. The **CREATE OR REPLACE** statement is invalid.

Question 10

In the executable section of a PL/SQL block, you include this statement:

```
Product.min_inventory1 := 12;
```

Which task will this accomplish?

○ a. A composite variable will be assigned a value.

○ b. A record will be assigned a value.

○ c. A constant will be assigned a value.

○ d. An index identifier will be assigned a value.

Question 11

Using the exhibit, evaluate the following query:

```
SELECT TO_CHAR(price, $099999.99)
FROM inventory;
```

How is the price value 0.50 displayed?

○ a. .50

○ b. $.50

○ c. $00000.50

○ d. $0.50

Instance chart for table INVENTORY.

Column Name:	ID_NUMBER	DESCRIPTION	MANUFACTURER_ID	QUANTITY	PRICE
Key Type:	PK		FK		
Nulls/Unique:	NN, U	NN	NN		
FK Table:			MANUFACTURER		
FK Column:			ID_NUMBER		
Datatype:	NUM	VARCHAR2	VARCHAR2	NUM	NUM
Length:	9	26	25	9	8,2

Question 12

What is the purpose of the **ALL_** set of data dictionary views?

○ a. List all objects that the user has created of the specific type

○ b. List all objects that the user has been granted rights on of the specific type

○ c. List all objects of the specific type in the database

○ d. List all dynamic data of the specific type about the database

Question 13

You have a command with a length of three lines in the command buffer of a SQL*Plus session. At the SQL prompt you enter this command:

```
DEL
```

What is the state of the buffer?

○ a. The buffer is clear.

○ b. The buffer is holding the command **DEL.**

○ c. The buffer is holding one line of the original text.

○ d. The buffer is holding two lines of the original text.

Question 14

Using the exhibit, evaluate this command:

```
SELECT id_number
FROM inventory
WHERE price IN (8.25, 0.25);
```

Which value would be displayed?

○ a. 36025

○ b. 36023

○ c. 43081

○ d. 36028

Contents of the INVENTORY table.

ID_NUMBER	DESCRIPTION	MANUFACTURER_ID	QUANTITY	PRICE	ORDER_DATE
36025	Spike 1 in	acme0525	234	2.45	12-May-97
36027	Nail 3/8	smith0626	134	0.25	15-Oct-97
36023	Chain	Jones0426	245	8.25	20-Jun-97
36028	Canvas	packy0122	1245	2.21	26-Oct-97
43081	Rubber Sheets	rubberrus0804	334	28.31	02-Feb-98

Question 15

You query the database with this command:

```
SELECT manufacturer_desc
FROM manufacturer
WHERE manufaturer_id LIKE '%F\%B\%I%' ESCAPE \;
```

For which character pattern will the **LIKE** operator be searching?

○ a. **FBI**

○ b. **F\%B\%I**

○ c. **F\B\I**

○ d. **F%B%I**

Question 16

Evaluate this statement:

```
SELECT a.isotope, b.mass_no, b.weight_no
FROM chart_n a, chart_n b
WHERE a.isotope ='IODINE'
AND a.group_id = b.group_id
```

Which type of join is shown?

○ a. Equijoin

○ b. Non-equijoin

○ c. Self-join

○ d. Outer join

Question 17

When designing the database, which step comes last?

○ a. Map attributes to columns

○ b. Map entities to tables

○ c. Map UID to primary keys

○ d. Map relationships to foreign keys

Question 18

> What is the second stage of the system development cycle?
>
> ○ a. Build and document
>
> ○ b. Design
>
> ○ c. Transition
>
> ○ d. Strategy and analysis
>
> ○ e. Production

Question 19

> When will an exception be raised in a PL/SQL block?
>
> ○ a. When an implicit cursor retrieves only one row.
>
> ○ b. When an implicit cursor retrieves more than one row.
>
> ○ c. When the datatypes within a **SELECT** statement are inconsistent.
>
> ○ d. When an embedded **SELECT** statement is missing a required clause.

Question 20

> What are the advantages of using the **%ROWTYPE** attribute to declare a PL/SQL type? (Choose two.)
>
> ❏ a. The number and datatypes of the underlying database table columns may be unknown.
>
> ❏ b. The datatype of a unused column in the underlying table may change.
>
> ❏ c. The datatype sizes or types of the underlying table may change at runtime.
>
> ❏ d. All column constraints are applied to the variables declared using **%ROWTYPE**.

Question 21

Which statement would you use to query the database for the
id_number and description of each item that was ordered before
February 1, 1998 and whose price is less than 0.75 or greater
than 7.00?

○ a.
```
SELECT id_number, description FROM inventory
   WHERE price BETWEEN 0.75 and 7.00 OR
   order_date < '01-feb-98';
```

○ b.
```
SELECT id_number, description FROM inventory
   WHERE price < 0.75 OR
         price > 7.00 AND
   order_date > '01-feb-98';
```

○ c.
```
SELECT id_number, description FROM inventory
   WHERE price IN (0.75, 7.00) OR
   order_date < '01-feb-98';
```

○ d.
```
SELECT id_number, description FROM inventory
   WHERE (price < 0.70 OR price > 7.00) AND
   order_date < '01-feb-98';
```

Question 22

What is the purpose of the SQL*Plus command **GET**?

○ a. Get a printer assignment

○ b. Get the contents of the buffer for editing

○ c. Get the contents of a previously saved operating system
    file into the buffer

○ d. Get a storage location for the buffer contents

Question 23

Which integrity constraint type states that for each value for the specified column in the child table there must be a matching primary key value in the parent table or the value in the child must be null?

○ a. User-defined

○ b. Entity

○ c. Column

○ d. Referential

Question 24

Which two operators cannot be used in an outer join condition?

❑ a. =

❑ b. **IN**

❑ c. **AND**

❑ d. **OR**

Question 25

Which is a characteristic of a database trigger?

○ a. Can be invoked from any SQL environment

○ b. Must always return a value

○ c. May return one or more values but isn't required to

○ d. Associated with a table and is executed automatically

Question 26

What is the default length of a **VARCHAR2** column?

○ a. 38

○ b. 255

○ c. 2000

○ d. There is no default length, it must be specified

Question 27

You query the database with this command:

```
SELECT
CONCAT(LOWER(SUBSTR(description,10)),
LENGTH(product_name)) "Product ID"
FROM inventory;
```

Which function is evaluated second?

○ a. **CONCAT()**

○ b. **LOWER()**

○ c. **SUBSTR()**

Question 28

Which of the following activities would take place in the transition phase of the system development cycle?

○ a. User interviews

○ b. Develop ERDs

○ c. Code all program modules

○ d. User acceptance testing

○ e. Perform normal routine maintenance

Question 29

Which of the following could be placed in a **WHERE** clause?

○ a. List of items to retrieve from a table

○ b. List of tables to retrieve values from

○ c. An outer join condition

○ d. The columns used to group and order the returned values

Question 30

What function would you use to convert a character string representation of a date into a date?

○ a. **TO_CHAR**

○ b. **TO_NUM**

○ c. **TO_DATE**

○ d. **CHR**

Question 31

What is the purpose of the **EXCEPTION** section of a PL/SQL block?

○ a. To define procedure or function name and input/output variables

○ b. To define variable, exception, cursor, and constants for the PL/SQL block

○ c. To contain the executable SQL statements

○ d. To contain the functions for error trapping

Question 32

You query the database with this command:

```
SELECT
    isotope,
    DISTINCT group_id,mass_no,atomic_weight
FROM chart_n;
```

What values are displayed?

○ a. Distinct combinations of **isotope, group_id, mass_no**, and **atomic_weight**.

○ b. **isotope** and distinct combinations of **group_id, mass_no**, and **atomic_weight**.

○ c. **isotope** and distinct **group_id**, as well as **mass_no** and **atomic_weight**.

○ d. No values will be displayed because the statement will fail.

Question 33

For which of the following would you use the **ALTER TABLE...MODIFY** option?

- ○ a. Add a column to the table
- ○ b. Increase the precision of a numeric column
- ○ c. Disable a table constraint
- ○ d. Drop a table constraint

Question 34

Which Procedure Builder component would you use to edit the properties of your database objects?

- ○ a. Stored Program Unit Editor
- ○ b. Program Unit Editor
- ○ c. PL/SQL Interpreter
- ○ d. Object Navigator

Question 35

Evaluate this command:

```
SELECT isotope, AVG(atomic_weight)
FROM char_n
WHERE AVG(atomic_weight) > 89.00
GROUP BY group_id
ORDER BY AVG(atomic_weight);
```

Which clause will cause an error?

- ○ a.
```
SELECT isotope, AVG(atomic_weight)
```
- ○ b.
```
WHERE AVG(atomic_weight) > 89.00
```
- ○ c.
```
GROUP BY group_id
```
- ○ d.
```
ORDER BY AVG(atomic_weight);
```

Question 36

Which type of PL/SQL statement would you use to decrease the price values by 30 percent for items with more than 1,000 in stock and by 25 percent for items with more than 500 in stock?

○ a. A simple insert loop

○ b. A simple **UPDATE** statement

○ c. An **IF...THEN...ELSE** statement

○ d. A **WHILE** loop

Question 37

You query the database with this command:

```
SELECT id_number,
       (quantity + 200 / 0.25 + 25 - 10)
FROM inventory:
```

Which expression is evaluated first?

○ a. quantity +200

○ b. 200 / 0.25

○ c. 0.25 + 25

○ d. 25 - 10

Question 38

In light of the exhibit, you attempt to query the database with this command:

```
SELECT NVL(100/efficiency, none)
FROM calibrations;
```

Why does this statement cause an error when the quantity values are null?

○ a. The expression attempts to divide a null value.

○ b. The character string **none** should be in single quotes.

○ c. The datatypes in the conversion function are incompatible.

○ d. A null value used in an expression cannot be converted to an actual value.

The instance chart of the CALIBRATIONS table.

Column Name:	INSTRUMENT_ID	EFFICIENCY	CAL_DATE
Key Type:	PK		
Nulls/Unique:	NN, U	NN	
FK Table:			
FK Column:			
Datatype:	Num	Num	Date
Length:			

Question 39

What is the purpose of the PL/SQL **FETCH** command?

○ a. To define a cursor to be used later

○ b. To retrieve values from the active set into local variables

○ c. To call the rows identified by a cursor query into the active set

○ d. To release the memory used by the cursor

Question 40

After reviewing the exhibit, evaluate this command:

```
DELETE FROM inventory
WHERE
order_date>TO_DATE('07.10.1997',
                    'DD.MM.YYYY');
```

Which of the listed **ID_NUMBER** values would be deleted?

○ a. 36025

○ b. 36023

○ c. 36027

○ d. None would be deleted, because the statement will fail

Contents of the INVENTORY table.

ID_NUMBER	DESCRIPTION	MANUFACTURER_ID	QUANTITY	PRICE	ORDER_DATE
36025	Spike 1 in	acme0525	234	2.45	12-May-97
36027	Nail 3/8	smith0626	134	0.25	15-Oct-97
36023	Chain	Jones0426	245	8.25	20-Jun-97
36028	Canvas	packy0122	1245	2.21	26-Oct-97
43081	Rubber Sheets	rubberrus0804	334	28.31	02-Feb-98

Question 41

Which privilege can only be granted to a user?

○ a. **ALTER**

○ b. **DELETE**

○ c. **INDEX**

○ d. **INSERT**

Question 42

Evaluate this procedure:

```
PROCEDURE found_isotope
    (v_energy_line IN BOOLEAN,
     v_proper_ratio IN BOOLEAN,
     v_found OUT BOOLEAN)
IS
BEGIN
    v_found := v_energy_line AND v_proper_ratio;
END;
```

If **v_energy_line** equals **TRUE** and **v_proper_line** equals **NULL**, which value is assigned to **v_approval**?

○ a. **TRUE**

○ b. **FALSE**

○ c. **NULL**

○ d. None of the above

Question 43

In a **SELECT** statement, what is the purpose of the & character?

○ a. To act as an escape character

○ b. To act as a wildcard for multiple characters

○ c. To indicate a value that is passed in at execution time

○ d. To act as a wildcard for a single character

Question 44

Evaluate this command:

```
SELECT c.isotope, g.calibration
FROM chart_n i, gamma_calibrations g
WHERE c.energy = g.energy;
```

What type of join is the command?

○ a. Equijoin

○ b. Non-equijoin

○ c. Self-join

○ d. The statement is not a join query

Question 45

What is the purpose of the **LENGTH** string function?

○ a. To insert a capital letter for each new word in the string

○ b. To return a specified substring from the string

○ c. To return the number of characters in the string

○ d. To substitute a non-null string for any null values returned

Question 46

What will the following operation return?

```
SELECT
TO_DATE('01-jan-97') - TO_DATE('01-dec-96')
FROM dual;
```

○ a. A **DATE** value

○ b. A **VARCHAR2** value

○ c. An error, you can't do this with dates

○ d. A number

Question 47

You query the database with this command:

```
SELECT atomic_weight
FROM chart_n
WHERE atomic_weight (BETWEEN 1 AND 50)
OR atomic_weight IN (25, 70, 95)
AND atomic_weight BETWEEN (25 AND 75)
```

Which of the following values could the statement retrieve?

○ a. 51

○ b. 95

○ c. 30

○ d. 75

Question 48

In the executable section of a PL/SQL block, you include these statements:

```
Isotope_record.isotope := 'IODINE';
Isotope_record.group := 'HALIDE';
```

Which task did will be accomplished?

○ a. A record field will be created based on the isotope table.

○ b. A constant will be initialized.

○ c. A constant will be created.

○ d. A record field will be assigned a character string value.

Question 49

Which statement best describes a relationship?

○ a. A thing of significance

○ b. A distinct characteristic of a thing of significance

○ c. A named association between two things of significance

○ d. Describes the way data flows

Question 50

Which statement is true about the **TRUNCATE TABLE** command?

○ a. Disables constraints in the target table.

○ b. Releases the storage space used by the target table.

○ c. Removes the target table from the database.

○ d. Data removed is recoverable via the **ROLLBACK** command.

Question 51

Which of the following is a use for the **TO_CHAR** command?

○ a. Convert a **VARCHAR2** value into a **DATE** value

○ b. Convert a **DATE** value into a **VARCHAR2** value using a specified format

○ c. Convert a **VARCHAR2** value into a **NUMBER** value

○ d. Convert a specified **VARCHAR2** into a **CHAR** value

Question 52

Evaluate this command:

```
CREATE TABLE purchase_items
    (id_number     NUMBER(9),
     description   VARCHAR2(25))
AS
SELECT id_number, description
FROM inventory
WHERE quantity < 10;
```

Why will this statement cause an error?

○ a. A clause is missing.

○ b. A keyword is missing.

○ c. The **WHERE** clause cannot be used when creating a table.

○ d. The datatypes in the new table must not be defined.

Question 53

Which language allows exception handling routines?

○ a. SQL

○ b. SQL*Plus

○ c. PL/SQL

○ d. None of the above

Question 54

Examine the exhibit. Which value is displayed if you query the database with the following command?

```
SELECT COUNT(description)
FROM inventory;
```

○ a. 8

○ b. 5

○ c. 1

○ d. **COUNT** returns an error if it is not run against a primary key

Contents of the INVENTORY table.

ID_NUMBER	DESCRIPTION	MANUFACTURER_ID	QUANTITY	PRICE	ORDER_DATE
36025	Spike 1 in	acme0525	234	2.45	12-May-97
36027	Nail 3/8	smith0626	134	0.25	15-Oct-97
36023	Chain	Jones0426	245	8.25	20-Jun-97
36028	Canvas	packy0122	1245	2.21	26-Oct-97
43081	Rubber Sheets	rubberrus0804	334	28.31	02-Feb-98

Question 55

Evaluate this command:

```
CREATE FORCE VIEW isotope_groups
AS SELECT isotope, group_id
FROM chart_n
WHERE atomic_weight>50
GROUP BY group_id
ORDER BY atomic_weight;
```

Which clause will cause an error?

○ a.
```
AS SELECT isotope, group_id
```

○ b.
```
FROM chart_n
```

○ c.
```
WHERE atomic_weight>50
```

○ d.
```
ORDER BY atomic_weight;
```

Question 56

You write a **SELECT** statement with two join conditions. What is the maximum number of tables you have joined together?

○ a. 0

○ b. 4

○ c. 2

○ d. 3

Question 57

Which of the following is a purpose of the user-defined constraint?

○ a. To enforce not null restrictions

○ b. To enforce referential integrity

○ c. To enforce business rules

○ d. To take action based on insert, update, or delete to the base table

Question 58

Which character could be used in a table name?

- ○ a. #
- ○ b. %
- ○ c. *
- ○ d. @

Question 59

Use the two exhibits to evaluate this command:

```
INSERT INTO inventory (id_number,
                       description,
                       manufacturer_id)
VALUES (36023, 'Sheet Metal','beth104ss');
```

Which type of constraint will be violated?

- ○ a. Check
- ○ b. Not null
- ○ c. Primary key
- ○ d. Foreign key

Instance chart for table INVENTORY.

Column Name:	ID_NUMBER	DESCRIPTION	MANUFACTURER_ID	QUANTITY	PRICE
Key Type:	PK		FK		
Nulls/Unique:	NN, U	NN	NN		
FK Table:			MANUFACTURER		
FK Column:			ID_NUMBER		
Datatype:	NUM	VARCHAR2	VARCHAR2	NUM	NUM
Length:	9	26	25	9	8,2

Contents of the INVENTORY table.

ID_NUMBER	DESCRIPTION	MANUFACTURER_ID	QUANTITY	PRICE	ORDER_DATE
36025	Spike 1 in	acme0525	234	2.45	12-May-97
36027	Nail 3/8	smith0626	134	0.25	15-Oct-97
36023	Chain	Jones0426	245	8.25	20-Jun-97
36028	Canvas	packy0122	1245	2.21	26-Oct-97
43081	Rubber Sheets	rubberrus0804	334	28.31	02-Feb-98

Question 60

Which command would you use to remove all the rows from the
ISOTOPE table, but allow rollback?

○ a. **DROP TABLE isotope;**

○ b. **DELETE isotope;**

○ c. **TRUNCATE TABLE isotope;**

○ d. There is no way to remove all rows and allow rollback

Answer Key To SQL And PL/SQL Sample Test

1. c	19. b	37. b	55. d
2. b	20. a, c	38. c	56. d
3. c	21. d	39. c	57. c
4. d	22. c	40. c	58. a
5. c	23. d	41. c	59. c
6. a, b	24. c, d	42. c	60. b
7. c	25. d	43. c	
8. e	26. d	44. a	
9. a	27. c	45. c	
10. b	28. d	46. d	
11. d	29. c	47. c	
12. b	30. c	48. d	
13. d	31. d	49. c	
14. b	32. d	50. b	
15. d	33. b	51. b	
16. c	34. d	52. d	
17. d	35. b	53. c	
18. b	36. c	54. b	

Here are the answers to the questions presented in Chapter 11.

Question 1

The correct answer is c. This is directly from the definition of the executable section. Answer a is the definition for the header section; the executable section never contains the definitions for variables nor does it provide the name of the procedure. Answer b is incorrect because this is the function of the declarative section or a PL/SQL program. Answer d is incorrect because this is the definition of the exception section of a PL/SQL block and not the executable section.

Question 2

The correct answer is b. Column constraints are used to verify values and enforce uniqueness as well as not null. Answer a is incorrect because referential constraints are used to ensure data integrity between tables. Answer c is incorrect. There is no such thing as entity constraints (at least as far as I know). Finally, answer d is incorrect because user-defined constraints are used to enforce business rules and have nothing to do with data validation rules.

Question 3

After examining the exhibit, you should notice that the **ID_NUMBER** column is a **NUMBER** datatype column. Attempting to compare this with 'A12345' would result in an error because "A" cannot be implicitly converted to a number. Therefore the correct answer is c. The other lines are correct syntax, so all the other answers are incorrect.

Question 4

The answer is d. The **IN** operator is used to compare a value or expression to a list of values. Answer a is incorrect because the **LIKE** operator is used to compare a wildcard search value against a column or expression. Answer b is incorrect because the equal sign (=) is used to show equality as in an equijoin, not check a list of values. Answer c is incorrect because **BETWEEN** is used to compare against a range of values, not a list of values.

Question 5

The evaluation of the command results in realizing that the command disables the primary key constraint and cascades this to disable all dependent constraints. Therefore, the correct answer is c. Answer a is incorrect because no data is deleted by this statement. Answer b is incorrect because this command disables the primary key and all dependent constraints. Answer d is incorrect because, once again, no values are deleted, only constraints altered.

Question 6

The correct answers are a and b. The percent sign (%) is used as a multicharacter wildcard character just as the underscore (_) is a single-character wildcard character, so both must be escaped to be used as a literal. The dollar sign ($) and forward slash (/) can be used as literals so they do not have to be escaped.

Question 7

The correct answer is c. You cannot index a view. Assuming that the syntax rules are properly followed during creation of the view, answer c is the only answer that is always something that cannot be done to a view. **SELECT**, **UPDATE**, and **DELETE** are all allowed even with a **WITH CHECK OPTION** clause.

Question 8

Answer e is correct. An **ORDER BY** is not allowed in a view. All of the other lines are syntactically correct, so all the other answers are incorrect.

Question 9

The correct answer is a. All functions must specify their return variable type using the **RETURN** clause immediately following the **CREATE OR REPLACE** statement. All the other lines are syntactically correct, so they are all incorrect.

Question 10

The correct answer is b. The format of the declaration shows that you're dealing with a record because dot notation indicates a record type is being used. Answer a is incorrect because this is not a composite variable. Answer c is incorrect because nowhere do you see the key word **CONSTANT** in the declaration. Answer d is incorrect because you are not dealing with an index identifier.

Question 11

In reality, because there is no answer that says "the query will fail," you don't really need an exhibit to answer this question. You can safely assume that the price column is a numeric. The correct answer for this question is d, $0.50. The leading $ and zero tell Oracle to format the number such that if the leading numbers before the decimal are all zero, show one zero to the left of the decimal. Answer a is incorrect because no zero is displayed as well as no dollar sign. Answer b is incorrect because no leading zero to the left of the decimal is displayed and answer c is incorrect because the format only specifies a single leading zero, not a zero fill.

Question 12

The answer to this question is b. Answer a is incorrect because this describes the **USER_** views and not the **ALL_** views. Answer c is incorrect because this describes the **DBA_** views. Answer d is incorrect because this describes the **V$** views.

Question 13

The correct answer is d. Simply entering the **DEL** (delete) command in SQL*Plus removes the current line from the buffer. Because you have three lines in the buffer, if you remove one you have two left. Answer a is incorrect because you only deleted one line. Answer b is incorrect because the editing commands and **DESCRIBE** are not placed in the buffer. Answer c is incorrect because you only deleted the current line, thus leaving two lines still in the buffer.

Question 14

The key to evaluating the **SELECT** statement is to look at the **IN** clause. The command will only return a value if the price is either 8.25 or 0.25. Records 36023 and 36027 both meet this criteria, but the only one listed is 36023. Therefore, answer b is the correct answer. None of the other answers has a price value that is in the list of values specified in the **IN** clause.

Question 15

The correct answer is d. The backslashes are used to escape the percent signs, thus allowing them to be treated as literals. Answer a is incorrect because it doesn't include the percent signs (%) that have been escaped. Answer b is incorrect because the backslashes (\) would be ignored. Answer c is incorrect because the backslashes would be ignored and the dollar signs ($) would be shown instead.

Question 16

The correct answer is c. A self-join is when a table is joined to itself. Notice that even though two aliases are specified, only one table is used making this a self-join. Answer a is incorrect because although this is an equijoin, it is primarily a self-join. Answer b is incorrect because this is a self-join. Answer d is incorrect because the outer join symbol (+) has not been used.

Question 17

The correct answer is d. Answer a is incorrect because this is the second step. Answer c is incorrect because this is the first step and answer c is incorrect because this is the third step.

Question 18

The correct answer to this question is b. The design step is the second stage of the system development cycle. Answer a is incorrect because this is the third stage. Answer c is incorrect because transition is the fourth stage. Answer d is incorrect because this is the first stage. Answer e is incorrect because this is the last stage.

Question 19

The correct answer is b. An implicit cursor is only allowed to return one row, so it raises an exception when more than one row is returned. Answer a is incorrect because this is the correct behavior for an implicit cursor, thus it wouldn't raise an exception. Answer c is incorrect because this would prevent the PL/SQL from compiling and thus it could never raise an exception because you couldn't execute it. Answer d is incorrect because again, this would result in a syntax error, thus not allowing execution and the raising of an exception.

Question 20

The correct answers are a and c. The **%ROWTYPE** declaration allows flexibility in that it automatically allows for an increase or decrease in the number of columns in a table or for the alteration of the size or datatype of the columns. Answer b is incorrect because you don't care about unused columns. Answer d is incorrect because it is totally wrong and constraints are never applied to variables.

Question 21

The correct statement is d. Notice that the **SELECT** in answer d groups the inequalities into a single condition using a set of parentheses. Also notice that the proper inequality is expressed for the date value; only this **SELECT** will return the proper answer. Answer a is incorrect because this statement uses a **BETWEEN**, and thus doesn't check for inequality (greater or less than).

Answer b is incorrect because the inequalities aren't grouped correctly and it checks for a greater-than date rather than a less-than date as would be required for a "before" date. Answer c is incorrect because it uses an **IN** operator and not an inequality test.

Question 22

The correct answer is c. The purpose of the SQL*Plus **GET** command is to get the contents of a previously saved operating system file into the buffer. Answer a is incorrect because this is the purpose of the **SPOOL** command. Answer b is incorrect because this is the function of the **LIST** command. Answer d is incorrect because this is not a function of any SQL*Plus command.

Question 23

The correct answer to this question is d. Answer a is incorrect because a user-defined constraint is used to enforce business rules. Answer b is incorrect because entity constraints don't exist. Answer c is incorrect because a column constraint is used to validate entry.

Question 24

The correct answers are c and d. Answer a is incorrect because an equal sign (=) can be used in an outer join. Answer b is incorrect because an **IN** operator can also be used in an outer join.

Question 25

The correct answer is d. Triggers are associated with tables and are automatically fired on specified actions against the table. Answer a is incorrect because a trigger is only fired from a table interaction. Answer b is incorrect because triggers don't return values. Answer c is incorrect because a trigger doesn't return values.

Question 26

The correct answer to this question is d. All the other answers are incorrect because there is no default length for a **VARCHAR2** column.

Question 27

The correct answer to this question is c. Answer a is incorrect because **CONCAT()** is outside of the parentheses. Answer b is incorrect because **LOWER()** is not inside the innermost parentheses.

Question 28

The correct answer is d. In the transition stage, user acceptance testing is performed. Prior to the transition stage, there is nothing to test because the system is still being developed. Answer a is incorrect because this would take place in the strategy and analysis phase. Answer b is incorrect because this is done in the build and document phase. Answer c is incorrect because this is performed in the build and document phase. Answer e is incorrect because this is part of the production phase.

Question 29

The correct answer is c. Of all of the answers, only an outer join is allowed in a **WHERE** clause. Answer a is incorrect because a list of items to retrieve from a table is what is found in a **SELECT** clause. Answer b is incorrect because a list of tables from which to retrieve values is what is found in a **FROM** clause. Answer d is incorrect because this specified column list is what is found in a **GROUP** or **SORT** clause.

Question 30

The correct answer is c. The **TO_DATE** function is the only function used to convert a character string representation of a date into an internal date format. Answer a is incorrect because the **TO_CHAR** function is used to convert a date into a **VARCHAR2** or a number into a **VARCHAR2**, not the other way around. Answer b is incorrect because **TO_NUM** is used to convert a **CHAR** or **VARCHAR2** into a numeric value and has nothing to do with dates. Answer d is incorrect since **CHR** is used to return the character representation of an input numeric value based on the current character set conversion chart.

Question 31

The correct answer is d. The **EXCEPTION** section is used specifically to perform error trapping functionality. Answer a is incorrect because this function is done by the header of a stored object. Answer b is incorrect because this is done in the declaration section. Answer c is incorrect because this is the purpose of the executable section.

Question 32

The correct answer is d. The statement is syntactically incorrect and will fail. A **DISTINCT** cannot be used in this manner. Answers a, b, and c are incorrect due to the improper placement of the **DISTINCT** operator that will cause the entire statement to fail.

Question 33

The correct answer is b. The **MODIFY** option of the **ALTER TABLE** command is only used to change the characteristics or the datatype of a column. Answer a is incorrect because this operation must be done with an **ADD** clause. Answer c is incorrect because this operation is done with a **DISABLE** clause. Answer d is incorrect because this operation is done using a **DROP** clause.

Question 34

The correct answer to this question is d. The Object Navigator is the only component of the Procedure Builder product that allows access to object properties. Answer a is incorrect because this component is not used to edit properties. Answer b is incorrect because this component doesn't edit properties. Answer c is incorrect because this component acts to interpret PL/SQL code, not as an editor.

Question 35

The correct answer to this question is b. You cannot use a grouping function such as **AVG** in a **WHERE** clause. The rest of the lines are syntactically correct and thus are the incorrect answers.

Question 36

The correct answer is c. In this question, you are asked to perform conditional tests and take action based on the results of the test. The only PL/SQL structure capable of this is the **IF...THEN...ELSE**. Answer a is incorrect because a simple insert loop wouldn't use a condition complex enough to handle the conditions specified. Answer b is incorrect because a simple **UPDATE** couldn't do a conditional update as specified. Answer d is incorrect because a **WHILE** loop wouldn't properly handle the update specified.

Question 37

The correct answer is b because multiplication (*) and division (/) are evaluated first in the hierarchy of operations. All of the other operators shown are under division in the hierarchy of operations.

Question 38

The correct answer to this question is c. To use the **NVL** command, the value being tested for **NULL** and the substitution value have to be of the same datatype. In this example we are attempting to substitute a character string for a numeric, so this will generate an error. Answer a is incorrect because the division will return a **NULL**, which the **NVL** should be able to handle. Answer b is incorrect because even placing **none** in single quotes doesn't solve the conversion problem between incompatible types. Answer d is just flat out incorrect because this is the purpose of the **NVL** function.

Question 39

The correct answer is c. The **FETCH** command retrieves values returned by the cursor into the active set. Answer a is incorrect because this statement is the function of the **CURSOR** command. Answer b is incorrect because this is the function of the **OPEN** command. Answer d is incorrect because this is the function of the **CLOSE** command.

Question 40

The correct answer is c. Of the values available in the table that meet the criteria (36027, 36028, and 43081), only 36027 is listed in the answer set, so it is the correct answer. Answers a and b are incorrect because they don't meet the selection criteria. Answer d is incorrect because answer c is correct.

Question 41

The correct answer is c. Answer a is incorrect because it can be granted to a role as well as a user. Answer b is incorrect because it can be granted to a role as well as a user. Answer d is incorrect because it to can be granted to a role as well as a user.

Question 42

The correct answer is c. A combination of **NULL** and **TRUE** or **NULL** and **FALSE** will result in a **NULL**; a **TRUE** and **TRUE** will result in a **TRUE**; and a **FALSE** and **FALSE** will result in a **FALSE**. A **TRUE** and **FALSE** also results in a **FALSE**. Answer a is incorrect because both would have to be **TRUE** for the result to be **TRUE**. Answer b is incorrect because either one would be **TRUE** and the other **FALSE** or both **FALSE** for the condition to be **FALSE**. Answer d is incorrect because answer c is correct.

Question 43

The correct answer is c. The ampersand character (&), either by itself or with a second ampersand, denotes substitution at runtime. Answer a is incorrect because this value is usually a backslash (\) unless specified as something else using the **ESCAPE** keyword. Answer b is incorrect because the percent sign (%) is the multicharacter wildcard. Answer d is incorrect because the underscore (_) is used as the single-character wildcard.

Question 44

The correct answer is a. Because the **SELECT** is using an equality test (using an equal sign), this is an equijoin operation. Answer b is incorrect because this is not a not equal (!=, <>) type join. Answer c is incorrect because a self-join is a table joined to itself and this is clearly two tables being joined. Answer d is incorrect because answer a is correct.

Question 45

The correct answer is c. The entire reason for the **LENGTH** function's being is to return a number value that corresponds to the length of a character datatype's contents. Answer a is incorrect because this is the purpose of the **INITCAP** function. Answer b is incorrect because this is the purpose of the **SUBSTR** function. Answer d is correct because this is the purpose of the **NVL** function.

Question 46

The correct answer is d. When two dates are subtracted, you receive a numeric value that corresponds to the number of days between the dates. Answer a is incorrect because this type of date arithmetic returns a number. Answer b is incorrect because date arithmetic returns a date or a number, but not a **VARCHAR2**. Answer c is incorrect because answer d is correct.

Question 47

The correct answer is c. Answer a is excluded by the **BETWEEN 1 AND 50 OR** atomic_weight **IN (25, 70, 95)** clause. Answer b is excluded by the **AND** atomic_weight **BETWEEN (25 AND 75)** clause. Answer d is excluded by the atomic_weight **(BETWEEN 1 AND 50)** clause.

Question 48

The correct answer is d. Answer a is incorrect because you aren't using a **%ROWTYPE**. Answer b and c are incorrect because you aren't using the keyword **CONSTANT**.

Question 49

The correct answer is c. A relationship is a named association between two items of significance, this is the definition of a relationship. Answer a is incorrect because it describes an entity. Answer b is incorrect because it describes an attribute. Answer d is incorrect because it describes a data flow diagram.

Question 50

The correct answer is b. Answer a is incorrect because **TRUNCATE** doesn't disable constraints and can't be used with active constraints in place. Answer c is incorrect because **TRUNCATE** removes data, not tables. Answer d is incorrect because a **TRUNCATE** is a DDL statement and can't be rolled back using a **ROLLBACK** command.

Question 51

The correct answer is b. Answer a is incorrect because this describes the **TO_DATE** function. Answer c is incorrect because this describes the **TO_NUMBER** function. Answer d is incorrect because this is an implicit conversion and doesn't require a function.

Question 52

The correct answer is d. Answer a is incorrect because the statements outside of the column definitions are syntactically correct. Answer b is incorrect for the same reason as a. Answer c is incorrect because a **WHERE** clause can be used in a **CREATE TABLE** subselect.

Question 53

The correct answer is c. Answer a, SQL, allows some limited error handling, but no exception processing. Answer b, SQL*Plus, provides for formatting and environment control but no exception processing. Answer d is incorrect because answer c is correct.

Question 54

The correct answer is b. Answer a is incorrect because there aren't eight rows in the table. Answer c is incorrect because there is more than one row in the table with a description. Answer d is incorrect because you can count on any column in a table.

Question 55

The correct answer is d because you cannot use **ORDER BY** in a view. Answers a, b, and c are incorrect because they are syntactically correct.

Question 56

The correct answer is d. You can determine the minimum number of joins based on the formula $n-1$, where n is the number of tables to be joined. Therefore, with two join conditions, the maximum number of tables that could be joined is three. Answers a, b, and c are incorrect because a zero-table join is not possible, a four-table join would require three join conditions, and although you could use two join conditions to join two tables, the question specifically asks for the maximum number that could be joined.

Question 57

The correct answer is c. Answer a is incorrect because this is the purpose of a column constraint. Answer b is incorrect because this is the purpose of a referential integrity constraint. Answer d is incorrect because this is the purpose of a trigger.

Question 58

The only character that could be used would be the pound sign (#), so answer a is correct. Answer b is incorrect because the percent sign (%) is a restricted character used for multicharacter wildcards. The asterisk (*) is use to denote multiplication and thus is a reserved character. Therefore, answer c is incorrect. Answer d is incorrect because the at sign (@) is used as a special character in SQL*Plus and is thus a reserved character.

Question 59

The correct answer is c. Notice that the column in the first is the **ID_NUMBER** column, which is the primary key for the table, and the **INSERT** command is attempting to insert the value 36023, which already exists in the table, thus violating the primary key uniqueness requirement. Answer a is incorrect because none of the exhibits items show a **CHECK** constraint as being assigned. Answer b is incorrect because **ID_NUMBER, DESCRIPTION,** and **MANUFACTURER_ID** (the only **NOT NULL** columns) have all been specified. Answer d is incorrect because a value for the foreign key column **MANUFACTURER_ID** is specified and because the exhibits don't show that the value exists in the **MANUFACTURER** table, you have to assume it does.

Question 60

The correct answer is b. Answer a is incorrect because the **DROP** command would remove the entire table. Also, because it is a DDL command, it is not able to be rolled back. Answer c is incorrect because the **TRUNCATE** command, which can delete rows, does not allow rollback because it too is a DDL command. Answer d is incorrect because answer b is correct.

13

Database Administration

Terms you'll need to understand:

√ Audit trail

√ Statement auditing

√ Object auditing

√ Privilege auditing

√ Profiles

√ Resources

√ Optimal Flexible Architecture (OFA)

Techniques you'll need to master:

√ Understanding how to set up, view, and manage audit trails

√ Understanding how to use profiles for resource management

√ Understanding physical database storage concepts

In this chapter, I will cover several areas of database administration. I'll explain how to set up and manage auditing within the database. I'll cover the usage of profiles to set limits on your users. Finally, I will examine physical database design using Oracle's Optimal Flexible Architecture (OFA).

Auditing The Database

Auditing is a method of recording database activity as part of database security. It enables the DBA to track user activity within the database. The audit records provide information on who performed what database operation and when it was performed. Records are written to a SYS-owned table named **AUD$**. The **SYS.AUD$** table is commonly referred to as the *audit trail*.

Auditing information is not collected without some impact on performance and database resources. How much of an impact auditing will have on your system depends largely on the type of auditing you enable. For example, setting high-level auditing such as connection activity will not have as much of a performance impact as tracking all SQL statements issued by all users. It is best to start out with high-level auditing and then refine additional auditing as needed.

You can audit all users with the exception of SYS and CONNECT INTERNAL. Auditing can only be performed for users connected directly to the database and not for actions on a remote database.

Auditing should be enabled if the following types of questionable activities are noted:

➤ Unexplained changes in passwords, tablespace settings, or quotas

➤ Excessive deadlocks are encountered

➤ Records are being read, deleted, or changed without authorization

There are three types of auditing:

➤ Statement auditing

➤ Privilege auditing

➤ Object auditing

Enabling And Disabling Auditing

The database initialization parameter **AUDIT_TRAIL** controls the enabling and disabling of auditing. The default setting for this parameter is **NONE**, which means that no auditing will be performed, regardless of whether or not **AUDIT** commands are issued. It is important to remember that any auditing statements issued will not be performed if **AUDIT_TRAIL=NONE**. Unless auditing is enabled in the database parameter initialization file, any auditing options that have been turned on will not create records in the audit trail. Auditing is not completely disabled unless it is set to **NONE** in the database parameter initialization file.

You must set the database initialization parameter **AUDIT_TRAIL** to **DB** or **OS** to enable auditing. The **DB** setting means the audit trail records are stored in the database in the **SYS.AUD$** table. **OS** will send the audit trail records to an operating system file. The **OS** setting is operating system-dependent and is not supported on all operating systems.

Auditing can be performed based on whether statements are executed successfully or unsuccessfully. Auditing **WHEN SUCCESSFUL** inserts records into the audit trail only if the SQL command executes successfully. Auditing **WHEN NOT SUCCESSFUL** inserts records into the audit trail only when the SQL statement is unsuccessful. If a statement is unsuccessful due to syntax errors, it will not be included in the audit trail. If neither **WHEN SUCCESSFUL** nor **WHEN NOT SUCCESSFUL** is specified, both successful and unsuccessful actions will be audited.

Auditing can be set using **BY SESSION** or **BY ACCESS**. When you use the **BY SESSION** option for statement or privilege auditing, the audit process writes a single record to the audit trail when a connection is made. When the session is disconnected, that record is updated with cumulative information about the session. The information collected includes connection time, disconnection time, and logical and physical I/Os processed. Audit options set using **BY SESSION** for objects insert one record per database object into the audit trail for each session. When you set auditing using **BY ACCESS**, a record is inserted into the audit trail for each statement issued. All auditing of DDL statements will be audited using **BY ACCESS** regardless of whether you have set auditing using **BY ACCESS** or **BY SESSION**.

The **BY USER** option enables you to limit auditing to a specific user or list of users. When you do not specify **BY USER**, all users will be audited.

When you change auditing options, they become active for subsequent sessions, not current sessions. Any existing sessions will continue to use the auditing options in effect when the existing sessions log into the database.

The syntax to enable statement and privilege auditing is seen in Figure 13.1.

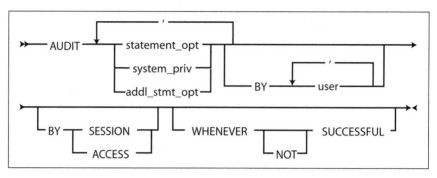

Figure 13.1 Syntax to enable statement and privilege auditing.

The following are the options listed in the syntax diagram for statement auditing:

statement_opt:

```
>>-CLUSTER------------------------------------------><
   |------------DATABASE LINK-----------------|
   |   |-PUBLIC---|                           |
   |----------EXISTS--------------------------|
   |   |--NOT--|                              |
   |----INDEX---------------------------------|
   |----PROCEDURE-----------------------------|
   |-------ROLE-------------------------------|
   |-------ROLLBACK SEGMENT-------------------|
   |-------SEQUENCE---------------------------|
   |-------SESSION----------------------------|
   |-------------------SYNONYM----------------|
   |   |---PUBLIC---|                         |
   |                                          |
   |--SYSTEM----------AUDIT-------------------|
   |          |--GRANT--|                     |
   |--TABLE-----------------------------------|
   |--TABLESPACE------------------------------|
   |--TRIGGER---------------------------------|
   |--USER------------------------------------|
   |--VIEW------------------------------------|
```

addl_stmt_opt:

```
>>--EXECUTE------PROCEDURE--------------------><
   |   |----GRANT----|                    |
   |                                       |
   |-------ALTER------------SEQUENCE------|
   |   |--GRANT---|                        |
   |   |-SELECT---|                        |
   |                                       |
```

```
|-----ALTER------------TABLE------------|
|----COMMENT-----|
|----DELETE------|
|----GRANT-------|
|----INSERT------|
|----LOCK--------|
|----SELECT------|
|----UPDATE------|
```

Here is an example:

```
AUDIT DELETE TABLE, INSERT TABLE,
EXECUTE ANY PROCEDURE
BY beth
BY ACCESS
WHENEVER SUCCESSFUL;
```

The syntax to disable statement and privilege auditing is seen in Figure 13.2.

Here is an example:

```
NOAUDIT DELETE TABLE, INSERT TABLE,
EXECUTE ANY PROCEDURE
BY beth
WHENEVER SUCCESSFUL;
```

The syntax to enable object auditing is seen in Figure 13.3.

Here is an example:

```
AUDIT SELECT, INSERT, DELETE
ON gordon.dept
WHENEVER SUCCESSFUL;
```

The syntax to disable object auditing is seen in Figure 13.4.

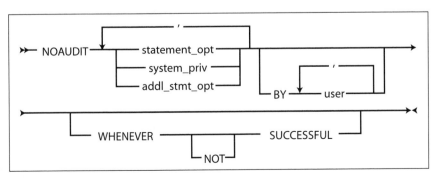

Figure 13.2   Syntax to disable statement and privilege auditing.

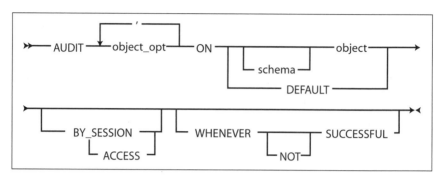

Figure 13.3 Syntax to enable object auditing.

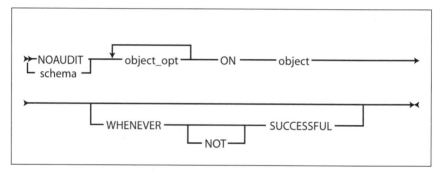

Figure 13.4 Syntax to turn off object auditing.

Here is an example:

```
NOAUDIT SELECT, INSERT, DELETE
ON gordon.dept
WHENEVER SUCCESSFUL;
```

Statement Auditing

Statement auditing is the tracking of SQL statements issued by database users. To enable or disable auditing on SQL statements, you must have the **AUDIT** system privilege. Table 13.1 shows the statements that can be audited.

In addition to the statement auditing options in Table 13.1, there are several options that will create audit records for a combination of statements. These options, sometimes referred to as *audit shortcuts*, are:

➤ CONNECT

➤ RESOURCE

➤ **DBA**

➤ **ALL**

Table 13.1 Statement auditing options.	
Option	**Commands Included**
ALTER SYSTEM	ALTER SYSTEM
CLUSTER	CREATE CLUSTER, ALTER CLUSTER, TRUNCATE CLUSTER, DROP CLUSTER
DATABASE LINK	CREATE DATABASE LINK, DROP DATABASE LINK
INDEX	CREATE INDEX, ALTER INDEX, DROP INDEX
NOT EXISTS	All SQL statements that return an Oracle error because the specified structure or object does not exist
PROCEDURE	CREATE (or REPLACE) FUNCTION, CREATE (or REPLACE) PACKAGE, CREATE (or REPLACE) PACKAGE BODY, CREATE (or REPLACE) PROCEDURE, DROP PACKAGE, DROP PROCEDURE
PUBLIC DATABASE LINK	CREATE PUBLIC DATABASE LINK, DROP PUBLIC DATABASE LINK
PUBLIC SYNONYM	CREATE PUBLIC SYNONYM, DROP PUBLIC SYNONYM
ROLE	CREATE ROLE, ALTER ROLE, SET ROLE, DROP ROLE
ROLLBACK SEGMENT	CREATE ROLLBACK SEGMENT, ALTER ROLLBACK SEGMENT, DROP ROLLBACK SEGMENT
SEQUENCE	CREATE SEQUENCE, DROP SEQUENCE
SESSION	All connections and disconnections
SYNONYM	CREATE SYNONYM, DROP SYNONYM
SYSTEM AUDIT	AUDIT, NOAUDIT
SYSTEM GRANT	GRANT SYSTEM PRIVILEGES/ROLES TO USER/ROLE, REVOKE SYSTEM PRIVILEGES/ROLES FROM USER/ROLE
TABLE	CREATE TABLE, ALTER TABLE, DROP TABLE
TABLESPACE	CREATE TABLESPACE, ALTER TABLESPACE, DROP TABLESPACE
TRIGGER	CREATE TRIGGER, ALTER TRIGGER, ENABLE (or DISABLE), ALTER TABLE with ENABLE, DISABLE, and DROP clauses
USER	CREATE USER, ALTER USER, DROP USER
VIEW	CREATE (or REPLACE) VIEW, DROP VIEW

Table 13.2 Statement auditing shortcuts.	
Shortcut Option	**Statement Equivalent**
CONNECT	Equivalent to setting auditing for SESSION
RESOURCE	Equivalent to setting auditing for ALTER SYSTEM, CLUSTER, DATABASE LINK, PROCEDURE, ROLLBACK SEGMENT, SEQUENCE, SYNONYM, TABLE, TABLESPACE, VIEW
DBA	Equivalent to setting auditing for ALTER SYSTEM, PUBLIC DATABASE LINK, PUBLIC SYNONYM, ROLE, SYSTEM GRANT, and USER.
ALL	Equivalent to auditing all statement options

Table 13.2 shows the statements audited by each of these shortcuts.

The audit shortcuts are useful for setting up auditing for multiple options with one command. For example

```
AUDIT RESOURCE
WHENEVER NOT SUCCESSFUL;
```

will audit all the commands listed for **ALTER SYSTEM, CLUSTER, DATABASE LINK, PROCEDURE, ROLLBACK SEGMENT, SE-QUENCE, SYNONYM, TABLE, TABLESPACE,** and **VIEW** for all users when the command does not successfully complete.

Be careful that you do not confuse these with the roles named CONNECT, RESOURCE, and DBA. These shortcuts are provided for compatibility with earlier versions of Oracle and may not be supported in future versions.

Privilege Auditing

Privilege auditing is the tracking of SQL statements issued by users who have been granted the right to execute that statement through a system privilege. To enable or disable auditing on SQL statements, you must have the **AUDIT** system privilege. Privilege audit options match the corresponding system privileges. (See Chapter 8 for a list of all system privileges.) For example, to audit the **DELETE ANY TABLE** system privilege, you would issue the following command:

```
AUDIT DELETE ANY TABLE
BY ACCESS
WHENEVER SUCCESSFUL;
```

Object Auditing

Object auditing is the tracking of specific SQL DML statements against objects by database users. To enable or disable auditing on objects, you must have the **AUDIT ANY** system privilege or own the object. The following objects can be audited: tables, views, sequences, packages, standalone stored procedures, and standalone functions. Because views and procedures may contain statements that reference multiple objects, views and procedures may generate multiple records in the audit trail. You cannot limit object auditing with the **BY USER** clause; all users will be audited for the object. Table 13.3 shows the statements audited for each option.

You can set a default for object auditing with the **ON DEFAULT** option. This default then will audit those actions on all objects that are created after the default auditing statement started. For example, the command

```
AUDIT delete ON DEFAULT;
```

will begin auditing all SQL statements that delete data from any new tables or views created after the **AUDIT** command is executed. You must explicitly turn

Table 13.3	Statements audited for object options.
Options	**Statements Audited**
ALTER SEQUENCE	ALTER SEQUENCE sequence_name
ALTER TABLE	ALTER TABLE table_name
COMMENT TABLE	COMMENT ON TABLE, VIEW, SNAPSHOT, COLUMN
DELETE TABLE	DELETE FROM TABLE, VIEW
EXECUTE PROCEDURE	Calls to procedures and functions
GRANT PROCEDURE	GRANT PRIVILEGE ON PROCEDURE, REVOKE PRIVILEGE ON PROCEDURE
GRANT TABLE	GRANT PRIVILEGE ON TABLE, VIEW, SNAPSHOT, REVOKE PRIVILEGE ON TABLE, VIEW, SNAPSHOT
INSERT TABLE	INSERT INTO TABLE, VIEW
LOCK TABLE	LOCK TABLE, VIEW
SELECT SEQUENCE	Reference to a sequence
SELECT TABLE	SELECT...FROM TABLE, VIEW, SNAPSHOT
UPDATE TABLE	UPDATE TABLE, VIEW

off default auditing with the **NOAUDIT...ON DEFAULT** command. For example, the command

```
NOAUDIT delete ON DEFAULT;
```

will turn off the previous **AUDIT** command. All objects will use the auditing options set at the time of their creation unless explicitly turned off.

Table 13.4 lists the types of auditing that can be performed against specific database objects.

Managing The Audit Trail

Audit records are written when the statement is executed. Even if a statement or transaction is rolled back, the audit trail record remains. Auditing by session will only write one record to the audit trail; auditing by access will write multiple records, one for each time the action is executed.

The audit trail grows according to the following factors:

➤ The number of audit options enabled

➤ The number of audited actions issued

Table 13.4	Types of auditing for objects.				
Option	**Table**	**View**	**Sequence**	**Snapshot**	**Package, Procedure, or Function**
ALTER	X	X			
AUDIT	X	X	X		
COMMENT	X	X			
DELETE	X	X			
EXECUTE					X
GRANT	X	X	X	X	
INDEX	X				
INSERT	X	X			
LOCK	X	X			
RENAME	X	X		X	
SELECT	X	X	X	X	
UPDATE	X	X			

You need to control the growth of the audit trail with the following methods:

➤ Enable and disable auditing options

➤ Be selective in deciding what auditing should be turned on

➤ Control who can perform auditing

To control auditing of objects, Oracle recommends that all objects be owned by a separate schema that does not correspond to an actual user and that schema is not granted **CONNECT SESSION**. This will prevent anyone from connecting as the owner of these objects and turning on auditing for the objects. The **AUDIT ANY** system privilege should not be granted to anyone except the security administrator. An alternative method is to have all the objects owned by the security administrator.

If the audit trail record cannot be written, the audited action will not be executed and errors will be generated. If connections are being audited and the audit trail table (**SYS.AUD$**) is full, users will not be allowed to log into the database. The DBA can use **CONNECT INTERNAL** using Server Manager in either GUI or command-line mode and clean out the audit trail.

You should develop an auditing strategy by evaluating the purpose of the auditing and be conservative in the auditing performed. When auditing is being set to investigate possible problems, begin with general auditing and then narrow this to specific actions. If the purpose of the audit is to provide a record of historical activity, remember to archive (to another table or an export file) and purge data on a regular basis. You can selectively insert records into another table if only a subset needs to be maintained.

To truncate the audit trail, it is recommend you follow these steps:

1. Copy any subset of records you may need to keep in a temporary table or export the entire **SYS.AUD$** table.

2. Connect internal.

3. Truncate the **SYS.AUD$** table.

4. Insert records from the temporary table back into **SYS.AUD$**.

To protect the audit trail, you should **AUDIT** insert, update, and delete on **SYS.AUD$ BY ACCESS** so that records cannot be added, changed, or deleted without that action being audited. Even if a user can delete records from **SYS.AUD$**, he cannot delete the records generated by his actions without creating additional audit records. In addition, users should not be granted **DELETE ANY TABLE** system privilege. Always protect the audit trail (**SYS.AUD$**).

The maximum size allowed for an audit trail written to the database is determined at the time the database is created. By default, the size reflects the system tablespace default values. The sql.bsq script, which is executed when the database is created, sets the size of the **SYS.AUD$** table. It is very important that the audit trail be cleaned up regularly. You should export the data and truncate the **SYS.AUD$** table on a regular basis.

Viewing Audit Trail Information

On most operating systems, special views on **SYS.AUD$** are created when the catalog.sql script (which calls several scripts, including cataudit.sql) is executed. For other operating systems, you can create these views by executing the script cataudit.sql. To remove the audit views, you can execute the script catnoaud.sql.

The following notations are used in the audit trail views:

➤ - Audit is not set.

➤ S Audit by session.

➤ A Audit by access.

➤ / Separates the two settings; the first setting is for **WHENEVER SUCCESSFUL** and the second setting is for **WHENEVER NOT SUCCESSFUL**.

Here are some examples:

➤ -/- No auditing.

➤ A/- Auditing using **BY ACCESS WHENEVER SUCCESSFUL**.

➤ -/A Auditing using setting **BY ACCESS WHENEVER NOT SUCCESSFUL**.

➤ S/- Auditing using **BY SESSION WHENEVER SUCCESSFUL**.

➤ -/S Auditing using setting **BY SESSION WHENEVER NOT SUCCESSFUL**.

➤ A/S Auditing using **BY ACCESS WHENEVER SUCCESSFUL** and **BY SESSION WHENEVER NOT SUCCESSFUL**.

➤ S/A Auditing using **BY SESSION WHENEVER SUCCESSFUL** and **BY ACCESS WHENEVER NOT SUCCESSFUL**.

Several views contain a column called **ses_actions**. The **ses_actions** column is a summary for the actions included in that entry. The **ses_actions** column is an

11-character code with the letters S for success, F for failure, B for both, and None indicates not audited. The character codes are in the following order:

➤ Alter

➤ Audit

➤ Comment

➤ Delete

➤ Grant

➤ Index

➤ Insert

➤ Lock

➤ Rename

➤ Select

➤ Update

The audit views fall into several categories:

➤ General information on auditing performed

➤ Statement audit information

➤ Privilege audit information

➤ Object audit information

There are four general auditing views:

➤ **AUDIT_ACTIONS** Maps audit trail action types to codes.

➤ **STMT_AUDIT_OPTION_MAP** Maps auditing option types to codes.

➤ **DBA_AUDIT_TRAIL** All audit records in the system.

➤ **USER_AUDIT_TRAIL** Audit trail entries relevant to the user.

Table 13.5 provides a description of the data stored in these views.

Column	Definition
Table 13.5	**General DBA data dictionary views for audit records.**

Column	Definition
AUDIT_ACTIONS	
action	Numeric type code assigned by Oracle to the action type
name	Name of the audit action
STMT_AUDIT_OPTION_MAP	
option#	Numeric type code assigned by Oracle to auditing option
name	Name of the audit options
DBA_AUDIT_TRAIL	
os_username	Operating system username for audited user
username	Oracle username for the audited user
userhost	Oracle instance ID number
terminal	User's terminal ID
timestamp	Timestamp for the creation of the audit trail record
owner	Intended creator for the nonexistent object
obj_name	Name of the object affected by the action
action	Numeric type code for the action type
action_name	Name of the action type
new_name	New name for the object in a rename action
new_owner	Owner of the object renamed
obj_privilege	Object privileges granted or revoked in a grant/revoke action
sys_privilege	System privileges granted or revoked in a grant/revoke action
admin_option	The role or system privilege was granted with the ADMIN option
grantee	Name of the grantee in a grant/revoke action
audit_option	Audit option set with the AUDIT command
ses_actions	Session summary
logoff_time	Timestamp when user logged off
logoff_lread	Logical reads for the session
logoff_pread	Physical reads for the session
logoff_lwrite	Logical writes for the session
logoff_dlock	Deadlocks detected during the session
comment_text	Text inserted by an application program for the audit entry

(continued)

Table 13.5	General DBA data dictionary views for audit records (continued).
Column	**Definition**
STMT_AUDIT_OPTION_MAP	
sessionid	Numeric ID code for the Oracle session
entryid	Numeric ID for the audit trail entry in the session
statementid	Numeric ID for the statement executed
returncode	Oracle return code for the message generated (for example, 0 for successful completion)
priv_used	System privilege used to execute the action
object_label	Trusted Oracle label for the object being audited
session_label	Trusted Oracle label for the user session audited

For statement auditing, the following views are useful:

➤ **DBA_STMT_AUDIT_OPTS** Information on current system auditing options across the system and by user.

➤ **DBA_AUDIT_STATEMENT** Audit entries for statements with the **GRANT, REVOKE, AUDIT, NOAUDIT,** and **ALTER SYSTEM** commands.

➤ **USER_AUDIT_STATEMENT** Audit entries for statements issued by the user.

➤ **DBA_AUDIT_SESSION** Audit entries for connections and disconnections.

➤ **USER_AUDIT_SESSION** Audit entries for connections and disconnections for that user.

➤ **DBA_AUDIT_EXISTS** Audit entries created by the **AUDIT EXISTS** command.

Table 13.6 describes the DBA data dictionary views relevant to statement auditing.

For privilege auditing, the **DBA_PRIV_AUDIT_OPTS** view shows the privilege option audit entries. There is one entry for each audited privilege. Table 13.7 describes the columns in this view. The **priv_used** and **admin_option** columns in the **DBA_AUDIT_STATEMENT** view can be used for information on the privileges being audited.

Table 13.6 Data dictionary DBA statement audit views.

Column	Definition
DBA_STMNT_AUDIT_OPTS	
user_name	Username if auditing is by user; null for systemwide auditing
privilege	Name of the system auditing option
success	Audit using BY SESSION or BY ACCESS for tracking the specified action WHENVER SUCCESSFUL
failure	Audit using BY SESSION or BY ACCESS for tracking the specified action WHENEVER NOT SUCCESSFUL
DBA_AUDIT_STATEMENT	
os_username	Operating system username for audited user
username	Oracle username for the audited user
userhost	Oracle instance ID number
terminal	User's terminal ID
timestamp	Timestamp for the creation of the audit trail record
owner	Intended creator for the nonexistent object
obj_name	Name of the object affected by the action
action	Numeric type code for the action type
action_name	Name of the action type
new_name	New name for the object in a rename action
new_owner	Owner of the object renamed
obj_privilege	Object privileges granted or revoked in a grant/revoke action
sys_privilege	System privileges granted or revoked in a grant/revoke action
admin_option	The role or system privilege was granted with the ADMIN option
grantee	Name of the grantee in a grant/revoke action
audit_option	Auditing option set with the AUDIT command
ses_actions	Session summary
comment_text	Text inserted by an application program for the audit entry
sessionid	Numeric ID code for the Oracle session
entryid	Numeric ID for the audit trail entry in the session
statementid	Numeric ID for the statement executed
returncode	Oracle return code for the message generated (for example, 0 for successful completion)

(continued)

Table 13.6   Data dictionary DBA statement audit views *(continued)*.

Column	Definition
DBA_AUDIT_STATEMENT	
priv_used	System privilege used to execute the action
session_label	Trusted Oracle label for the user session audited
DBA_AUDIT_SESSION	
os_username	Operating system username for audited user
username	Oracle username for the audited user
userhost	Oracle instance ID number
terminal	User's terminal ID
timestamp	Timestamp for the creation of the audit trail record
action_name	Name of the action type
logoff_time	Timestamp when user logged off
logoff_lread	Logical reads for the session
logoff_pread	Physical reads for the session
logoff_lwrite	Logical writes for the session
logoff_dlock	Deadlocks detected during the session
sessionid	Numeric ID code for the Oracle session
returncode	Oracle return code for the message generated (for example, 0 for successful completion)
session_label	Trusted Oracle label for the user session audited
DBA_AUDIT_EXISTS	
os_username	Operating system username for audited user
username	Oracle username for the audited user
userhost	Oracle instance ID number
terminal	User's terminal ID
timestamp	Timestamp for the creation of the audit trail record
owner	Intended creator for the nonexistent object
obj_name	Name of the object affected by the action
action_name	Name of the action type
new_name	New name for the object in a rename action

(continued)

Table 13.6	**Data dictionary DBA statement audit views (continued).**

Column	Definition
DBA_AUDIT_EXISTS	
new_owner	Owner of the object renamed
obj_privilege	Object privileges granted or revoked in a grant/revoke action
sys_privilege	System privileges granted or revoked in a grant/revoke action
grantee	Name of the grantee in a grant/revoke action
sessionid	Numeric ID code for the Oracle session
entryid	Numeric ID for the audit trail entry in the session
statementid	Numeric ID for the statement executed
returncode	Oracle return code for the message generated (for example, 0 for successful completion)

Table 13.7	**Privilege options view.**

Column	Definition
user_name	Username if auditing is by user, null for systemwide auditing
privilege	Name of the privilege
success	Audit using BY SESSION or BY ACCESS for tracking the specified WHENEVER SUCCESSFUL
failure	Audit using BY SESSION or BY ACCESS for tracking the specified WHENEVER NOT SUCCESSFUL

For object auditing, the relevant views are:

➤ **DBA_OBJ_AUDIT_OPTS** Auditing options set for all tables and views.

➤ **USER_OBJ_AUDIT_OPTS** Auditing options for the owner's tables and views (corresponds to the **DBA_OBJ_AUDIT_OPTS** view).

➤ **ALL_DEF_AUDIT_OPTS** Default audit options for objects being created.

➤ **DBA_AUDIT_OBJECT** Audit records for all objects in the system.

➤ **USER_AUDIT_OBJECT** Audit trail records for statements concerning objects owned by that user (corresponds to the **DBA_AUDIT_OBJECT** view).

Table 13.8 shows the data you can see using these views.

Column	Definition
Table 13.8 **Object options data dictionary views.**	
Column	**Definition**
DBA_OBJ_AUDIT_OPTS	
owner	Owner of the object
object_name	Name of the object
object_type	TABLE or VIEW object
alt	Alter
aud	Audit
com	Comment
del	Delete
gra	grant
ind	Index
ins	Insert
loc	Lock
ren	Rename
sel	Select
upd	Update
ref	References
exe	Execute
ALL_DEF_AUDIT_OPTS	
alt	Alter
aud	Audit
com	Comment
del	Delete
gra	Grant
ind	Index
ins	Insert
loc	Lock
ren	Rename
sel	Select
upd	Update

(continued)

Table 13.8 Object options data dictionary views *(continued).*	
Column	**Definition**
ALL_DEF_AUDIT_OPTS	
ref	References
exe	Execute
DBA_AUDIT_OBJECTS	
os_username	Operating system username for audited user
username	Oracle username for the audited user
userhost	Oracle instance ID number
terminal	User's terminal ID
timestamp	Timestamp for the creation of the audit trail record
owner	Intended creator for the nonexistent object
obj_name	Name of the object affected by the action
action_name	Name of the action type
new_name	New name for the object in a rename action
new_owner	Owner of the object renamed
ses_actions	Session summary
comment_text	Text inserted by an application program for the audit entry
sessionid	Numeric ID code for the Oracle session
entryid	Numeric ID for the audit trail entry in the session
statementid	Numeric ID for the statement executed
returncode	Oracle return code for the message generated (for example, 0 for successful completion)
priv_used	System privilege used to execute the action
object_label	Trusted Oracle label for the object audited
session_label	Trusted Oracle label for the user session audited

Auditing By Database Triggers

Enabling auditing options may not always be sufficient to evaluate suspicious activity within your database. When you enable auditing, Oracle places records in the **SYS.AUD$** table in accordance with the auditing options that you have specified. One limitation to this type of auditing is that **SYS.AUD$** does not provide you with value-based information. You need to write triggers to record the before and after values on a per-row basis.

Auditing with Oracle supports DML and DDL statements on objects and structures. Triggers support DML statements issued against objects and can be used to record the actual values before and after the statement.

In some facilities, **AUDIT** commands are considered security audit utilities, whereas triggers are referred to as financial auditing utilities. This is because triggers can provide a method to track actual changes to values in a table. Although you can use triggers to record information similar to the **AUDIT** command, you should only customize your auditing by using triggers when you need more detailed audit information.

AFTER triggers are normally used to avoid unnecessary statement generation for actions that fail due to integrity constraints. **AFTER** triggers are executed only after all integrity constraints have been checked. **AFTER ROW** triggers provide value-based auditing for each row of the tables and support the use of "reason codes." A reason for the statement or transaction, along with the user, **SYSDATE**, and old and new values can be inserted into another table for auditing purposes.

Oracle auditing can be used for successful and unsuccessful actions as well as actions such as connections, disconnections, or session I/O activities. With auditing, you can decide if the actions should be by access or by session. Triggers can only audit successful actions against the table on which they are created. If auditing is being performed using a trigger, any rollback or unsuccessful action will not be recorded.

Auditing provides an easy, error-free method to tracking specific actions with all the audit records stored in one place. Triggers are more difficult to create and maintain.

Managing Resources With Profiles

You can set up limits on the system resources used by setting up profiles with defined limits on resources. Profiles are very useful in large, complex organizations with many users. They enable you to regulate the amount of resources used by each database user by creating and assigning profiles to users.

Creation Of Profiles

Profiles are a named set of resource limits. By default, when you create a user, he is given the **DEFAULT** profile. The **DEFAULT** profile provides unlimited use of all resources. The syntax to create a profile is seen in Figure 13.5.

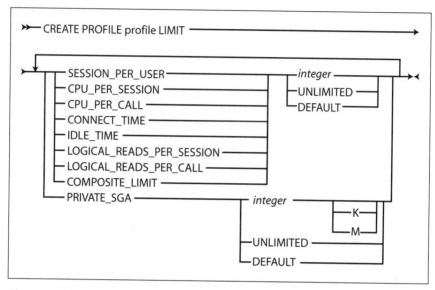

Figure 13.5 Syntax for the **CREATE PROFILE** command.

Here is an example:

```
CREATE PROFILE enduser LIMIT
CPU-PER-SESSION  60000
LOGICAL-READS-PER-SESSION  1000
CONNECT-TIME  30
PRIVATE-SGA 102400
CPU-PER-CALL UNLIMITED
COMPOSITE LIMIT  60000000;
```

You can assign a profile to a user when you create the user or by altering the user.

The syntax to alter the profile for a user is:

```
>-------- ALTER USER  PROFILE  profile ----------------------><
```

Here is an example:

```
ALTER USER sandy
PROFILE appuser;
```

You must have the **CREATE PROFILE** system privilege to create a profile. To alter a profile, you must be the creator of the profile or have the **ALTER PROFILE** system privilege. To assign a profile to a user, you must have the **CREATE USER** or **ALTER USER** system privilege.

Profiles And Resource Limits

The default cost assigned to a resource is unlimited. By setting resource limits, you can prevent users from performing operations that will tie up the system and prevent other users from performing operations. You can use resource limits for security to ensure that users log off the system and do not leave the session connected for long periods of time. You can also assign a composite cost to each profile. The system resource limits can be enforced at the session level, the call level, or both.

The session level is from the time the user logs into the database until the user exits. The call level is for each SQL command issued. Session-level limits are enforced for each connection. When a session-level limit is exceeded, only the last SQL command issued is rolled back and no further work can be performed until a commit, rollback, or exit is performed. Table 13.9 lists the system resources that can be regulated at the session level.

You can combine **CPU_PER_SESSION, LOGICAL_READS_PER_SESSION, CONNECT_TIME,** and **PRIVATE_SGA** to create a composite limit.

Call-level limits are enforced during the execution of each SQL statement. When a call-level limit is exceeded, the last SQL command issued is rolled back. All the previous statements issued are still valid and the user can continue to execute other SQL statements. The following system resources can be regulated at the call level:

➤ **CPU_PER_CALL** Used for the CPU time for the SQL statement.

➤ **LOGICAL_READS_PER_CALL** Used for the number of data blocks read for the SQL statement.

Table 13.9 Resources regulated at the session level.	
System Resource	**Definition**
CPU_PER_SESSION	Total CPU time in hundreds of seconds
SESSIONS_PER_USER	Number of concurrent sessions for a user
CONNECT_TIME	Allowed connection time in minutes
IDLE_TIME	Inactive time on the server in minutes
LOGICAL_READS_PER_SESSION	Number of data blocks read, including both physical and logical reads from memory and disk
PRIVATE_SGA	Bytes of SGA used in a database with the multithreaded server (in kilobytes or megabytes)

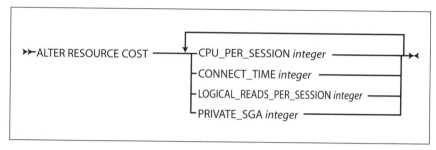

Figure 13.6 Syntax for **ALTER RESOURCE** command.

The assignment of a cost to a resource can be performed with the **ALTER RESOURCE COST** command. Resource limits that you set explicitly for a user take precedence over the resource costs in an assigned profile. The command line syntax for this command is seen in Figure 13.6.

Here is an example:

```
ALTER RESOURCE COST CONNECT-TIME  100 ;
```

Use of resource limits is set in the database initialization parameter **RESOURCE_LIMIT=TRUE**. By default, this parameter is set to **FALSE**. This parameter can be changed interactively with an **ALTER SYSTEM** command.

The **DBA_PROFILES** view provides information on all the profiles and the resource limits for each profile. The **RESOURCE_COST** view shows the unit cost associated with each resource. Each user can find information on his resources and limits in the **USER_RESOURCE_LIMITS** view. Table 13.10 gives a description of these data dictionary views.

Altering Profiles

Provided you have the **CREATE PROFILE** or **ALTER PROFILE** system privilege, you can alter any profile, including the Oracle-created **DEFAULT** profile. You can alter a profile to change the cost assigned to each resource. The syntax to alter a profile is seen in Figure 13.7.

Here is an example:

```
ALTER PROFILE enduser LIMIT
CPU-PER-SESSION  60000
LOGICAL-READS-PER-SESSION  1000
CONNECT-TIME  60
```

```
PRIVATE-SGA 102400
CPU-PER-CALL UNLIMITED
COMPOSITE LIMIT  60000000;
```

To disable a profile during a session, you must have the **ALTER SYSTEM** privilege. A limit that you set for the session overrides the previous limit set by

Table 13.10   Data dictionary views for resources.

Column	Definition
DBA_PROFILES	
profile	The name given to the profile
resource_name	The name of the resource assigned to the profile
limit	The limit placed on the profile
RESOURCE_COST	
resource_name	The name of the resource
unit_cost	The cost assigned
USER_RESOURCE_LIMITS	
resource_name	The name of the resource
limit	The limit placed on the user

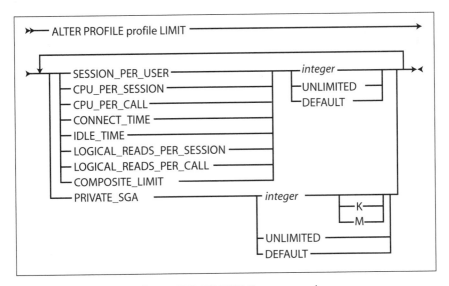

Figure 13.7   Syntax for **ALTER PROFILE** command.

the profile. To reset the profile to the limit originally set by the database, set the limit to **DEFAULT**.

```
>>--ALTER SYSTEM SET RESOURCE-LIMIT = |----TRUE----------|->< 
                                      |----FALSE---------|
```

Here is an example:

```
ALTER SYSTEM SET RESOURCE-LIMIT = TRUE ;
```

Managing The Database Structure

Database creation prepares a set of physical operating system files so they can work together as an Oracle database. Adding tablespaces to your database creates a structure that supports the storage and manipulation of data. Space on the database server is allocated to physical files that make up the database. Placement and naming of the files on which your database is built is important for ease of maintenance and optimum performance of your database.

Physical Database Structures

Each tablespace in the database is made up of one or more physical files. Multiple files (datafiles) can be used for a single tablespace, but each file can only be assigned to one tablespace. The datafiles are the physical storage space on the server. Storage in the datafiles is allocated by blocks to each extent that is used by an object. The block size is operating system-dependent and is determined when the database is created and cannot be changed. The database block size is set in the database parameter file **DB_BLOCK_SIZE**. Typically, a database block is either 2K or 4K. Oracle suggests setting block size to the largest allowed on your operating system.

Each database block consists of a header, table directory, row directory, free space for growth of the data, and row data. Space usage within the blocks is determined by the **PCTFREE, PCTUSED, INITRANS,** and **MAXTRANS** parameters.

PCTFREE sets the percentage of the block space reserved for future updates of the rows inserted into the block. The default setting for **PCTFREE** is 20 percent. If records within a block are rarely updated after they are inserted, you should set **PCTFREE** lower to allow for full space usage. If records within a block are subject to many updates, you should set **PCTFREE** higher to allow for more growth. Once the **PCTFREE** threshold is reached, no additional rows will be inserted until the **PCTUSED** threshold is reached due to deletion of data. If **PCTFREE** is set too low, row chaining and row migration will result because updates to the record will not fit into the block.

PCTUSED sets the threshold for determining when the block is available for more rows to be inserted. The default setting for **PCTUSED** is 40 percent. If data is static, you will be able to set the **PCTUSED** lower and more fully use the space. If large amounts of data are inserted and deleted, you should set the **PCTUSED** higher to prevent block fragmentation.

INITRANS is the initial number of concurrent transactions allocated in each block header when the block is allocated. The default is 1, which is the minimum. The maximum is 255. The size of each transaction entry is operating system-dependent.

MAXTRANS is the maximum number of concurrent transactions for the blocks within the tablespace. The default is 255, which is the maximum. The minimum setting is 1.

When an object is created, there must be sufficient contiguous space for the initial extent. For rollback segments, an initial and at least one additional extent is required during creation. If sufficient contiguous free space is not available, the extent cannot be created and the user will not be able to create the table or rollback segment. When an object needs an additional extent, there must be sufficient contiguous free space to meet the **next_extent** size requirement. If there is not sufficient contiguous space for the next extent to be created, the end user will receive an error message that there is not sufficient space to create the extent.

The settings for objects created take the defaults for the tablespace within which they are created unless you specify otherwise. Table 13.11 shows the extent allocation parameters and the default settings.

There are several data dictionary views that provide information on the settings for each segment and tablespace, as well as for the amount of contiguous free space available. These views are as follows:

➤ **DBA_DATA_FILES** Lists the tablespaces and the physical space allocation for each.

➤ **DBA_TABLESPACES** Provides a description of every tablespace in the database.

➤ **USER_TABLESPACES** Contains information for all tablespaces for which the user has been granted access (corresponds to the **DBA_TABLESPACES** view).

➤ **DBA_EXTENTS** Shows the extents of all segments in the database.

Table 13.11	Extent allocation settings and defaults.
Parameter	**Description**
INITIAL	Size in bytes for the first extent; default is 5 Oracle blocks
NEXT	Size in bytes for the next extent to be allocated; default is 5 Oracle blocks
MAXEXTENTS	Total number of extents allowed; default is operating system-dependent
MINEXTENTS	Total number of extents to be allocated when the object is created; default is 1 for data, except rollback segments, which is 2
PCTINCREASE	Percent the next extent will increase over the current next extent setting; default is 50 percent; recommended setting is 0 percent

➤ **USER_EXTENTS** Shows the extents for objects that belong to this user (corresponds to the **DBA_EXTENTS** view).

➤ **DBA_SEGMENTS** Provides storage allocation information for all segments in the database.

➤ **USER_SEGMENTS** Includes storage information for that user's objects (corresponds to the **DBA_SEGMENTS** view).

➤ **DBA_FREE_SPACE** Shows the amount of contiguous blocks available with one record for each contiguous space in each tablespace.

Table 13.12 describes the DBA data dictionary views for space allocation information.

Table 13.12	DBA data dictionary views for space usage and availability.
Column	**Definition**
DBA_DATA_FILES	
file_name	Physical file name including full path specification
file_id	ID assigned to the datafile
tablespace_name	Name of the tablespace to which the datafile is assigned
bytes	Number of bytes in the datafile
blocks	Number of Oracle blocks in the datafile
status	Invalid or available

(continued)

Table 13.12	DBA data dictionary views for space usage and availability *(continued)*.
Column	**Definition**

DBA_TABLESPACES

Column	Definition
tablespace_name	Name of the tablespace
initial_extent	Default initial extent for objects created in that tablespace
next_extent	Default size for the next extent for objects created in that tablespace
min_extents	Default minimum number of extents for objects created in that tablespace
max_extents	Default maximum number of extents for objects created in that tablespace
pct_increase	Default percent increase for objects created in that tablespace
status	Online, offline, or (if the tablespace has been dropped) invalid

DBA_EXTENTS

Column	Definition
owner	Owner of the segment associated with the extent
segment_name	Name of the segment associated with the extent
segment_type	Type of segment associated with the extent
tablespace_name	Name of the tablespace in which the extent exists
extent_id	ID assigned to that extent
file_id	Name of the file in which the extent is created
block_id	Starting block number for the extent
bytes	Size of the extent in bytes
blocks	Size of the extent in Oracle blocks

DBA_SEGMENTS

Column	Definition
owner	Owner of the segment
segment_name	Name of the segment
segment_type	Type of segment (TABLE, CLUSTER, INDEX, ROLLBACK, DEFERRED ROLLBACK, TEMPORARY, CACHE)
tablespace_name	Name of the tablespace in which the segment resides
header_file	ID of the file containing the segment header

(continued)

Table 13.12 DBA data dictionary views for space usage and availability (continued).

Column	Definition
DBA_SEGMENTS	
header_block	ID of the block containing the segment header
bytes	Size of the segment in bytes
blocks	Size of the segment in Oracle blocks
extents	Total number of extents allocated to that segment
initial_extent	Size of the initial extent for that segment
next_extent	Size of the next extent issued to that segment
min_extents	Minimum number of extents that must be allocated to that segment
max_extents	Maximum number of extents that can be allocated to that segment
pct_increase	Percentage by which the size will increase for the next extent (pct_increase times the next_extent is the size required for the subsequent next extent)
freelists	Number of process freelists allocated to the segment
freelist_groups	Number of freelist groups allocated to the segment
DBA_FREE_SPACE tablespace_name	Name of the tablespace
file_id	ID of the file associated with the free space in that extent
block_id	Starting block number for that extent
bytes	Size, in number of bytes, for that contiguous extent
blocks	Size, in Oracle blocks, for that contiguous extent

Optimal Flexible Architecture (OFA)

Optimal Flexible Architecture (OFA) is Oracle's recommended guideline for database file configuration. The OFA is a method to design your database for easy maintenance and reliability. It deals with how files are distributed on the server and naming standards for database files.

The system requirements of OFA-compliant database servers are:

➤ The file system must be organized for easy administration and provide for future growth.

➤ The server must have sufficient disk space to balance the load and prevent I/O bottlenecks.

➤ Hardware costs should be minimized.

➤ The server should be designed so that it is possible to isolate applications to minimize the impact of hardware failure.

➤ There must be two or more disk drives to accommodate home directories.

➤ The movement of home directories should not impact any programs.

➤ The file system should allow for categorization of files into separate, independent directory subtrees.

➤ The server should support multiple versions of applications to accommodate upgrades.

➤ The structure should support separation of administrative files for each database.

➤ Database files should be named in a way that makes it easy to identify that they are database files and the type of database. Files should easily be associated with the database to which they belong.

➤ Tablespaces can be separated to decrease I/O contention and fragmentation, as well as increase the flexibility of administration of the database.

➤ The system should support tuning the disk I/O load.

➤ Database administration files should be centrally stored and separated from specific administration files that relate to an Oracle instance.

OFA standard databases meet the following criteria:

➤ Each mount point should have a name that indicates it is a mount point and which mount point it is.

➤ Home directories should be named with the following pattern: *mount_point_name/standard_directory_name/directory_owner.*

➤ Explicit path names for files that are normally associated with those path names should be used; explicit path names in all other cases should be avoided.

➤ Each version of Oracle should be stored separately. The file naming standard recommended is *Oracle_login_home_directory/product/version_number.*

➤ Database administration files should be stored in a directory with the following name: *Oracle_login_home_directory/*admin/d. The third-level directory (d) should be organized as listed in Table 13.13.

Table 13.13   Recommended database administration directories.

Directory Name	Contents
adhoc	SQL scripts for the database
adump	Audit trail trace files
arch	Archived redo logs
bdump	Background process trace files
cdump	Core dump trace files
create	Scripts used to create the database
exp	Export files
logbook	Files pertaining to the status and history of the database
pfile	Parameter files for the instance
udump	User SQL trace files

➤ Oracle database files should be placed in a directory with the following pattern: *mount_point/oracle_datafile_indicator/database_name*. The file name should be control.ctl for control files, redo#.log for redo log files, and *tablespace_name#*.dbf for datafiles. (Note that # indicates a number.)

➤ When placing files on disks, separate them according to their life span, I/O request, and backup frequencies for different tablespaces. The following tablespaces should always be created for every database: **SYSTEM, TEMP, RBS, TOOLS, USERS.**

➤ Use eight or fewer characters for the tablespace name.

➤ Standardize on a set of file sizes for easier movement of files when it is necessary to remedy I/O problems.

➤ When using the Oracle Parallel Server, always use one node to be the Oracle administrative home directory.

➤ For the best performance, purchase enough hardware so that each disk drive will only house one application. There should be sufficient disk drives for each database to prevent I/O bottlenecks.

Exam Prep Questions

Question 1

> Which four resource limits are averaged by specified weighting to give a composite limit?
>
> ❏ a. **LOGICAL_READS_PER_SESSION**
>
> ❏ b. **PRIVATE_SGA**
>
> ❏ c. **CPU_PER_CALL**
>
> ❏ d. **CONNECT_TIME**
>
> ❏ e. **IDLE_TIME**
>
> ❏ f. **CPU_PER_SESSION**

The correct answers are a, b, d, and f. A composite limit sets an overall resource limit by user session. It places combined total limits on logical reads, blocks in the private SQL area, connection time, and CPU minutes. Remember, any resource limits that are set by call level cannot be part of a composite limit.

Question 2

> Which privilege is needed to assign a profile to a user?
>
> ○ a. **CREATE USER**
>
> ○ b. **ALTER PROFILE**
>
> ○ c. **CREATE PROFILE**
>
> ○ d. **ALTER USER**

The correct answer is d. Although it is true that you can assign a profile when you create a user, if you look carefully at the question, it implies that the user is already created. Altering or creating a profile will not assign it to a user.

Question 3

> Which data dictionary view would you query to display information related to profiles?
>
> ○ a. RESOURCE_COST
>
> ○ b. USER_USERS
>
> ○ c. DBA_CONSTRAINTS
>
> ○ d. USER_CONSTRAINTS

The correct answer is a. The **RESOURCE_COST** view will provide the name of the resource and the cost of the resource. The **USER_USERS** view will provide the username, user ID, default tablespace, temporary tablespace, and the user creation date, but no information related to profiles. You should immediately eliminate both c and d from your answer because both views would obviously list constraint information that would not be relevant to profiles.

Question 4

> Which script would you run to remove the data dictionary tables and views for auditing?
>
> ○ a. cataudit.sql
>
> ○ b. catnoaud.sql
>
> ○ c. catalog.sql
>
> ○ d. None of the above

The correct answer is b, catnoaud.sql. If you decide to disable auditing and no longer need the audit trail objects, you can delete them by connecting to the database as SYS and running the script file catnoaud.sql. The catalog.sql script, on most operating systems, will call the cataudit.sql script to create the audit trail views. Oracle naming conventions for scripts that reverse what other scripts have created usually include the word "no" with a partial name of the script that created those views. Because the cataudit.sql creates the audit views, the catnoaud.sql would remove the audit views.

Question 5

> Which value for the **AUDIT_TRAIL** parameter in the initialization
> file directs all audit records to the **SYS.AUD$**?
>
> ○ a. **DB**
>
> ○ b. **OS**
>
> ○ c. **NONE**

The correct answer is b. The **AUDIT_TRAIL** is the initialization file parameter that enables or disables the writing of rows to the **SYS.AUD$** table.
Auditing records are not written if this parameter is equal to **NONE**. The **DB**
option enables systemwide auditing and causes the audit records to be written
to the **SYS.AUD$** table in the database. The **OS** option enables systemwide
auditing and causes auditing records to be written to the operating system's
audit trail.

Question 6

> Which object can you audit for the **INDEX** option?
>
> ○ a. Table
>
> ○ b. View
>
> ○ c. Sequence
>
> ○ d. Snapshot
>
> ○ e. Stored procedure

The correct answer is a. Table 13.4 lists object audit options. Notice the only
object you can audit for the **INDEX** option is a table. Most of these options
have common sense options. You cannot place an index on a view, sequence,
snapshot, or a stored procedure.

Question 7

> Which system privilege allows you to disable statement and privilege auditing options with the **NO AUDIT** command?
>
> ○ a. **AUDIT ANY**
>
> ○ b. **AUDIT SYSTEM**
>
> ○ c. **DROP ANY TABLE**
>
> ○ d. **DELETE ANY TABLE**

The correct answer is b. The **AUDIT SYSTEM** privilege allows you to enable and disable statement and privilege audit options. The **AUDIT ANY** allows you to audit any schema object in the database. The **AUDIT SYSTEM** and **AUDIT ANY** are the two system privileges that pertain to auditing. You need to have a solid understanding of the privileges needed to execute each of the commands.

Question 8

> Which information is held in the **SYS.AUD$** data dictionary table?
>
> ○ a. Only records generated by statement auditing
>
> ○ b. Only records generated by privilege auditing
>
> ○ c. Only records generated by object auditing
>
> ○ d. Records generated by statement, privilege, and object auditing

The correct answer is d. **SYS.AUD$** stores all auditing information, including statement auditing, privilege auditing, and object auditing. Oracle provides several views that reflect subsets of the **SYS.AUD$** table. However, all audit records are centrally stored in the **SYS.AUD$** table.

Question 9

Which strategy should you follow when your system contains Oracle and non-Oracle files?

○ a. Store them on separate devices.

○ b. Store them in separate directories.

○ c. Make sure they contain distinct names.

○ d. Remove all non-Oracle files from the system as soon as possible.

The correct answer is a. Whenever possible, it is best to physically separate Oracle and non-Oracle files to simplify maintenance, backup, and recovery processes. This is one of the recommendations in Oracle's OFA.

Question 10

When designing a database, which objects should be stored in the **RBS** tablespace other than the rollback segments?

○ a. User-created objects

○ b. Database triggers

○ c. Temporary segments

○ d. None of the above

The correct answer is d. This goes back to the OFA conventions for separation of files, as well as basic relational database design. Only rollback segments should be placed in the **RBS** tablespace and only temporary segments should be placed in the **TEMP** tablespace, etc. The tablespace names should reflect the type of objects placed in that tablespace.

Need To Know More?

The first place to go for more information is the *Oracle7 Administrator's Guide* and the *Oracle7 Server Reference Manual*.

Ault, Michael R.: *Oracle 7.0 Administration & Management*, John Wiley & Sons, 1994. ISBN 0-47160-857-2. Chapter 4 covers all aspects of user and privilege grants. The Introduction and Chapter 1 cover installation and configuration issues.

Loney, Kevin: *DBA Handbook, 7.3 Edition*, Oracle Press, 1996. ISBN 0-07882-289-0.

Sample Test: Database Administration

14

The sample test that follows covers material likely to appear on Test 2 of the Oracle Certified Database Administrator track, "Oracle7: Database Administration." This test comprises 60 to 70 questions. You are allotted 90 minutes to take the test. The answers to this sample test can be found in the next chapter. You should be reminded that this test covers material discussed throughout this book, and not just material covered in Chapter 13. For test-taking strategy, helpful pointers, and other exam preliminaries, refer to Chapter 11.

Sample Test: Database Administration

Question 1

> To create rollback segments, the system privilege you must have been granted is:
>
> ○ a. **CREATE ROLLBACK SEGMENT**
>
> ○ b. **ALTER ROLLBACK SEGMENT**
>
> ○ c. **CREATE TABLE**
>
> ○ d. **ALTER TABLE**

Question 2

> Which characteristic applies to declarative integrity constraints?
>
> ○ a. Difficult to modify
>
> ○ b. Immediate user feedback
>
> ○ c. Decreased performance
>
> ○ d. Decentralized rules

Question 3

> What is the size of the first extent if the storage parameters are **INITIAL 40K**, **NEXT 10K**, and **PCTINCREASE** of 50?
>
> ○ a. 20K
>
> ○ b. 30K
>
> ○ c. 40K
>
> ○ d. 70K

Question 4

Which database object is a logical repository for physically grouped data?

○ a. Tablespace

○ b. Segment

○ c. Block

○ d. Extent

○ e. File

○ f. Database

Question 5

What is the purpose of the catalog.sql script?

○ a. To create the base data dictionary tables

○ b. To create the system audit tables

○ c. To create the commonly used data dictionary views

○ d. To create the export views

○ e. To create all procedures and packages needed for the procedural option

○ f. To create the grants used for the monitoring views

Question 6

When does a user get assigned the default profile?

○ a. When the user is not explicitly assigned a profile

○ b. When the user first logs in to the database

○ c. When a user exceeds a preset resource limit

○ d. When the initialization parameter **RESOURCE_PROFILES** is set to **TRUE**

Question 7

The session level resource that tracks periods of inactivity is named:

○ a. **LOGICAL_READS_PER_CALL**

○ b. **PHYSICAL_READS_PER_CALL**

○ c. **CONNECT_TIME**

○ d. **IDLE_TIME**

Question 8

Which memory structure is also known as the shared SQL area?

○ a. Library cache

○ b. Data dictionary cache

○ c. Database buffer cache

○ d. Redo log buffer

Question 9

What is the purpose of the SQL*Loader **LOAD** parameter?

○ a. Specifies the number of logical records to load

○ b. Specifies the number of rows to load between commits

○ c. Tells where to place the log file generated during the load

○ d. Sets the size of the array needed during the load

Question 10

Which parameter specifies the percentage of space in each data block reserved for adding rows into a table?

○ a. **PCTUSED**

○ b. **MAXTRANS**

○ c. **INITRANS**

○ d. **PCTFREE**

Question 11

The name of the data dictionary view that displays system privileges that have been granted to all roles and users is named:

- ○ a. **DBA_SYS_PRIVS_RECD**
- ○ b. **DBA_SYS_PRIVS_GVN**
- ○ c. **DBA_SYS_PRIVS**
- ○ d. **DBA_TAB_PRIVS**

Question 12

Which feature describes a row?

- ○ a. Must be contained within one block
- ○ b. Maximum number allowed is 2,000
- ○ c. Uses two bytes in the data block header's row directory
- ○ d. Has at least a five-byte row header

Question 13

Which type of rollback segment is created when a tablespace goes offline?

- ○ a. Private
- ○ b. Public
- ○ c. Deferred
- ○ d. None of the above

Question 14

What is the purpose of the index segment type?

- ○ a. Stores data entries
- ○ b. Increases performance of retrieving data
- ○ c. Allows for the undo of transactions
- ○ d. Allows for implicit sorts

Question 15

What is a disadvantage of using declarative integrity constraints?

○ a. Difficult to get an overview

○ b. Inflexible

○ c. Hard to modify

○ d. Undocumented

Question 16

Which activity might take place in a tablespace created with the keyword **TEMPORARY**?

○ a. Deleting dirty blocks

○ b. Implicit sorts

○ c. Writing to datafiles

○ d. Backups

Question 17

What causes row migration?

○ a. When **PCTFREE** is set extremely high

○ b. When an update requires more space than is currently available on the block

○ c. When a block is chained

○ d. When **PCTUSED** is set extremely high

Question 18

Tablespaces are made up of these database items:

○ a. Extents

○ b. Segments

○ c. Log files

○ d. Control files

Question 19

Which of the following is a function of the **ALTER TABLE** command?

○　a. Removes rows from a table

○　b. Changes data in existing rows of a table

○　c. Renames a column in a table

○　d. Drops a constraint from a table

Question 20

What is the major characteristic of the **PCTFREE** storage parameter?

○　a. Applies to a cluster and not to the individual tables in a cluster

○　b. Controls the maximum number of transactions that can access a block

○　c. Sets the starting size of the transaction portion of the block header

○　d. Sets the size of each extent

Question 21

What is the purpose of the **V$PWFILE_USERS** structure?

○　a. Contains information on the current sessions user

○　b. Contains information about all current active users

○　c. Contains information about all users that have been granted the **SYSDBA** and **SYSOPER** system privileges

○　d. Contains information about all database users with passwords

Question 22

If **PCTFREE** is set at the default value, what could happen if you set a high **PCTUSED** value?

- ○ a. Unused space will increase
- ○ b. Space usage will increase
- ○ c. Processing costs will increase
- ○ d. The need to chain rows will be reduced

Question 23

What is the default value for **PCTFREE**?

- ○ a. 0
- ○ b. 10 percent
- ○ c. 40 percent
- ○ d. 50 percent

Question 24

When could you perform a full database media recovery?

- ○ a. When the database is mounted but not opened
- ○ b. When an instance is started but the database is not mounted
- ○ c. When the database is mounted and opened using the **RESETLOG** option
- ○ d. When the database is mounted and opened using the **ARCHIVELOG** option

Question 25

Which of the following is a purpose of the **ALTER USER** command?

- ○ a. Creates a role
- ○ b. Sets a default role for a user
- ○ c. Creates a user
- ○ d. Sets a role for a session

Question 26

What is the result on blocks of a lower **PCTFREE** setting?

○ a. May require fewer blocks to store data

○ b. May require more blocks to store data

○ c. Will reduce row chaining

○ d. There is no result, the parameter doesn't affect blocks

Question 27

What is the purpose of the shutdown mode **NORMAL**?

○ a. Waits for all users to disconnect before completing a shutdown

○ b. Rolls back uncommitted transactions, logs off inactive users, and then shuts down

○ c. Immediately shuts down the database as fast as possible

○ d. There is no **NORMAL** shutdown mode

Question 28

What role is automatically granted to a user who is created by the Server Manager?

○ a. DBA

○ b. RESOURCE

○ c. CONNECT

○ d. EXPORT

Question 29

What **CREATE ROLE** command keyword requires that the users granted the role are verified by the Oracle server?

○ a. **OSOPER**

○ b. **PASSWORD**

○ c. **IDENTIFIED**

○ d. **USING**

Question 30

> Which view could you query to display users with **ALTER ANY USER** privileges?
>
> ○ a. **DBA_SYS_PRIVS**
>
> ○ b. **DBA_COL_PRIVS**
>
> ○ c. **USER_TAB_PRIVS_RECD**
>
> ○ d. **DBA_USER_PRIVS**

Question 31

> Which privilege is a system privilege?
>
> ○ a. **UPDATE**
>
> ○ b. **ALTER**
>
> ○ c. **DELETE**
>
> ○ d. **CREATE TABLE**

Question 32

> What storage parameter causes extents to be automatically deallocated in an oversized rollback segment?
>
> ○ a. **INITIAL**
>
> ○ b. **NEXT**
>
> ○ c. **PCTINCREASE**
>
> ○ d. **OPTIMAL**

Question 33

> Which of the following steps comes first when establishing an operating systems role management?
>
> ○ a. Create roles in the Oracle server
>
> ○ b. Give each user operating system rights to indicate his database roles
>
> ○ c. Set the initialization parameter **OS_ROLES** to **TRUE**
>
> ○ d. Shut down and restart the instance

Question 34

Which table would not be a good candidate for clustering?

○ a. Frequently updated

○ b. Not often joined

○ c. Primarily queried

○ d. Few distinct values within the columns

Question 35

What is a characteristic of a normal rollback segment?

○ a. Is self-managing

○ b. Records data changed in any tablespace except the
      SYSTEM rollback segment

○ c. Contains sort information

○ d. Contains index entries

Question 36

Which calculation determines the number of rollback segments
to be taken from the private rollback segment pool?

○ a. **TRANSACTIONS/PROCESSES**

○ b. **TRANSACTIONS/
      TRANSACTIONS_PER_ROLLBACK_SEGMENT**

○ c. **ROLLBACK_SEGMENTS/PROCESSES**

○ d. **DB_FILES/ROLLBACK_SEGMENTS**

Question 37

What is the default option for the **MOUNT** clause of the **ALTER
DATABASE** command?

○ a. **SHARED**

○ b. **RETRY**

○ c. **EXCLUSIVE**

○ d. **PARALLEL**

Question 38

What is the purpose of the **PARALLEL** mount option?

○ a. Used when multiple instances will be allowed to access the same database

○ b. Retry startup until successful

○ c. Startup so only one instance can access the database

○ d. There is no **PARALLEL** mount option

Question 39

What is one characteristic of **PCTUSED**?

○ a. Grows from the top down

○ b. Determines when a block is placed on the used list

○ c. Grows from the bottom up

○ d. Determines the number of transactions that can access a block simultaneously

Question 40

Which is a characteristic of the PMON process?

○ a. Recovers failed transactions

○ b. Frees SGA resources allocated to a failed process

○ c. Writes redo buffers to the redo log

○ d. Writes dirty buffers to data files

Question 41

What is one characteristic of a temporary segment?

○ a. Contains permanent data entries

○ b. Contains index entries

○ c. Contains data used to undo transactions

○ d. Must use default storage parameters

Question 42

When is a transaction aborted?

○ a. When a user requests termination

○ b. At the start of a session

○ c. At the end of a previous transaction

○ d. When a user exits normally from the Oracle server

Question 43

When a **SELECT** statement is issued, which memory structure is used to verify the user's privileges?

○ a. Shared pool

○ b. Database buffer cache

○ c. A memory structure is not used to verify a user's privileges

○ d. Redo log buffer

Question 44

What is the purpose of a segment in a tablespace?

○ a. Contains redo information

○ b. Contains records used to synchronize data structures

○ c. Contains cache data

○ d. Contains all the data for a specific structure within a tablespace

Question 45

Which initialization parameter specifies the location where the background process trace files are written?

○ a. **USER_DUMP_DESTINATION**

○ b. **AUDIT_TRAIL**

○ c. **LOG_ARCHIVE_DEST**

○ d. **BACKGROUND_DUMP_DEST**

Question 46

What is the purpose of the **DICTIONARY** table?

○ a. Contains the names of all data files in the database.

○ b. Contains the names of all the sequences in the database.

○ c. Contains the names of all of the data dictionary views.

○ d. There is no **DICTIONARY** table.

Question 47

Which characteristic relates to a tablespace?

○ a. Always have read-write status

○ b. Can only be brought online while database is shut down

○ c. Consists of only one operating system file

○ d. Can be enabled to be read only

Question 48

What is the minimum of extents in a segment?

○ a. 15

○ b. 0

○ c. 1

○ d. 2

Question 49

In what step is the Server Manager invoked during database startup?

○ a. Last

○ b. Never

○ c. First

○ d. Second

Question 50

How often should you check the alert file?

○ a. Weekly

○ b. Daily

○ c. For every error

○ d. Monthly

Question 51

When the data needed by a process is in memory, the process accesses the data by means of what type of hit?

○ a. Cache

○ b. Disk

○ c. Redo segment

○ d. Undo segment

Question 52

What is the purpose of the **LOG_ARCHIVE_DEST** initialization parameter?

○ a. Specifies the location of the user trace files

○ b. Specifies the location for the background process trace files

○ c. Specifies the database name

○ d. Specifies the location where to send archive copies of the redo logs

Question 53

Which of the following is a function of the SMON process?

○ a. Cleans up process-related resources for failed user processes

○ b. Reclaims memory space allocated to sorts

○ c. Writes dirty buffers to disk

○ d. Writes the log buffer to the redo logs

Question 54

What is a characteristic of a cache segment type?

○ a. Contains data entries

○ b. Contains index entries

○ c. Contains information used to redo transactions

○ d. Is self-administered

Question 55

Information from two or more nodes is retrieved with what feature of a distributed database?

○ a. Remote update

○ b. Distributed query

○ c. Remote query

○ d. Distributed update

Question 56

Which data dictionary table holds records generated by statement, privilege, and object auditing?

○ a. **PRIV$**

○ b. **TAB$**

○ c. **AUD$**

○ d. **DUAL**

Question 57

What is a byproduct of frequent deallocation of extents?

○ a. Fragmented blocks

○ b. Nonincremental extents

○ c. Truncated segments

○ d. Fragmented tablespaces

Question 58

The redo log file holds which type of data?

○ a. File synchronization data

○ b. Data segments

○ c. Records used for recovery purposes

○ d. Index data

Question 59

When data is inserted into the database, what type of segment is it placed in?

○ a. Rollback

○ b. Data

○ c. Index

○ d. Temporary

Answer Key To Database Administration Sample Test

15

1. b	18. b	35. b	52. d
2. b	19. d	36. b	53. b
3. c	20. a	37. c	54. d
4. a	21. c	38. a	55. b
5. c	22. c	39. c	56. c
6. a	23. b	40. b	57. d
7. d	24. a	41. d	58. c
8. a	25. b	42. a	59. b
9. a	26. a	43. a	
10. d	27. a	44. d	
11. c	28. c	45. d	
12. c	29. c	46. c	
13. c	30. a	47. d	
14. b	31. d	48. c	
15. a	32. d	49. c	
16. b	33. a	50. b	
17. b	34. a	51. a	

Here are the answers to the questions presented in the sample test in Chapter 14.

Question 1

Don't overthink this one. To create rollback segments you need the **CREATE ROLLBACK SEGMENT** privilege. Therefore, answer a is correct. Answer b is incorrect because that would only allow you to alter a rollback segment but not create one. Answers c and d deal with tables, not rollback segments, and therefore are incorrect.

Question 2

The correct answer is b. When a declarative constraint is violated, the user receives immediate feedback in the form of an error message. Answer a is incorrect because declarative integrity constraints are fairly easy to modify. Answer c is incorrect because declarative integrity constraints can actually increase performance by placing the code into the database engine instead leaving it as application logic. Answer d is incorrect because declarative integrity constraints are centralized in nature.

Question 3

The correct answer is c, 40K. Again, don't overthink the question. The question asks for the size of the first extent. The first extent is sized by the **INITIAL** value, which is set to 40K. The other values listed are not 40K, so they are incorrect.

Question 4

The correct answer is a. A tablespace is a logical construct that is used to hold physically grouped data. Answer b is incorrect because a segment corresponds to a particular object, not a group of objects. Answer c relates to actual physical storage (extents are made of blocks, segments are made of extents, and tablespaces contain segments). Answer d is incorrect because segments are made of extents and only relate to a single object. Answer e is incorrect because a file is a physical construct, and not a logical construct. Answer f is incorrect because a database is made of tablespaces, so it could be considered a collection of groups of logical repositories of physically grouped data.

Question 5

The correct answer is c. The catalog.sql script creates the most frequently accessed data dictionary views. Answer a is incorrect because this is accomplished with the sql.bsq script. Answer b is incorrect because this is accomplished with the cataudit.sql script. Answer d is incorrect because this is accomplished with the catexp.sql script. Answer e is incorrect because this is done through the catproc.sql script. Answer f is incorrect because this is done with the utlmontr.sql script.

Question 6

Answer a is the correct response. If no profile is assigned when the user is created, the user receives the default profile automatically. Answer b is incorrect because the profile must either be explicitly assigned when the user is created or it will default to the default profile at that time. Answer c is incorrect because the profiles are assigned at the time the users are created. Answer d is incorrect because this is how resource accounting is turned on, but the profiles are actually assigned when the users are created.

Question 7

The correct answer is d. **IDLE_TIME**, as its name implies, tracks a user's time spent doing nothing. Answers a and b deal with logical and physical reads, not time, and answer c deals with overall connection duration, not just idle time (periods of inactivity).

Question 8

The correct answer is a. The shared pool section of the SGA and the library caches are one and the same. Answer b is incorrect because the data dictionary cache is a part of the shared pool, but not the shared SQL area. Answer c is incorrect because the database buffer cache is a separate part of the SGA from the shared SQL area. Answer d is incorrect because the redo log buffer is a separate part of the SGA along with the database buffer pool and shared pool.

Question 9

The correct answer is a. The **LOAD** parameter tells the SQL*Loader session how many rows to load before automatically stopping. Answer b is incorrect because this is the purpose of the **ROWS** parameter. Answer c is incorrect because this is the purpose of the **LOG** parameter. Answer d is incorrect because this is the purpose of the **BINDSIZE** parameter.

Question 10

The correct answer is d. The **PCTFREE** parameter reserves space in blocks for future update activity. Answer a is incorrect because **PCTUSED** sets the amount of space that can be used before the block is placed on the used extent list. Answer b is incorrect because this sets the maximum number of transactions that can access a single block. Answer c is incorrect because this sets the minimum size for the block area where transactions are tracked.

Question 11

This is an easy question if you just don't second-guess. The correct answer is c. Answers a and b are incorrect because these views don't exist. Answer d is incorrect because this shows table grants, not system grants.

Question 12

The correct answer is c. The only true statement made is that a row requires a two-byte header. Because this is the only true answer of those shown, it is the correct answer. Answer a is incorrect because the largest detriment to performance in many systems is row chaining, which is when a row is contained in more than one block. Answers b and d are not true descriptions of a row.

Question 13

The correct answer is c. When a tablespace goes offline, a deferred rollback segment is automatically created. Answer a is incorrect because a private rollback segment must be explicitly created. Answer b is incorrect because public rollback segments are also explicitly created by the DBA and are not created when a tablespace goes offline. Obviously because c is correct, d is incorrect.

Question 14

The correct answer is b. An index is used to increase performance for data retrieval. Answer a is incorrect because data segments are used for data storage. Answer c is incorrect because rollback segments (also called undo segments) allow for the undo of transactions. Answer d is incorrect because sort segments allow for implicit sorts.

Question 15

Answer a is correct. Because the data about constraints is spread across several different views, it is difficult to get an overview of them. Answer b is incorrect because declared constraints can be very flexible when compared to programmatic constraints in applications. Answer c is incorrect because declarative integrity constraints are easy to modify. Answer d is incorrect because unless you document any constraint, it is difficult to document.

Question 16

The correct answer is b. Answer a is incorrect; dirty blocks are usually written, not deleted. Answer c is a function of the DBWR process. Answer d is a system function, not usually a database one.

Question 17

The correct answer is b. You will only get row chaining if an update extends a block beyond its allowed size. Answer a is incorrect because **PCTFREE** high prevents row chaining. Answer c is incorrect because a block is not chained, only rows are chained. Answer d is incorrect because a high **PCTUSED** results in the situation where row chaining can occur, but technically only if you exceed an existing row length through update will a row chain event occur.

Question 18

The correct answer is b. A tablespace is made up of segments, whether they be table, index, or rollback segments. Answer a is incorrect because although a segment is made up of extents, an extent has no existence outside of a segment. Answer c is incorrect because log files are not part of tablespaces. Answer d is incorrect because control files are not part of a tablespace.

Question 19

The correct answer is d. Of the functions listed, the only one an **ALTER TABLE** is capable of is dropping a table constraint. Answer a is incorrect because this is a function of the **DELETE** and **TRUNCATE** commands and not the **ALTER** command. Answer b is incorrect because this is the function of the **UPDATE** command, not the **ALTER** command. Answer c is incorrect because there is no way to rename a table column.

Question 20

The correct answer is a. Because all of the other answers have nothing to do with **PCTFREE**, the only answer that is correct is a. In clusters, **PCTFREE** applies to the cluster itself and not the individual tables in the cluster. Answer b is incorrect because this is the purpose of the **MAXTRANS** parameter. Answer c is incorrect because this is the purpose of the **INITRANS** parameter. Answer d is incorrect because this is the purpose of the **INITIAL** parameter.

Question 21

The correct answer is c. The **V$PWFILE_USERS** structure is used to track users who have been granted OSDBA and OSOPER roles. Answer a is incorrect because this is the purpose of the **USER_USERS** view. Answer b is incorrect because this is the purpose of the **ALL_USERS** view. Answer d is incorrect because there is no view strictly for users with passwords.

Question 22

The correct answer is c. Processing costs will increase because the processor will have to spend more time maintaining freelists. Answer a is incorrect because this will happen if **PCTFREE** is set too high. Answer b is incorrect because space usage will actually decrease in this scenario. Answer d is incorrect because a high **PCTUSED** could result in increase row chaining.

Question 23

The correct answer is b. The default value is set to 10 percent, so all of the other answers are incorrect.

Question 24

The correct answer is a. A recovery operation is performed when the database is mounted but not opened. This is the only time a recovery command can be issued. Answer b is incorrect because it states an impossible condition. Answer c is incorrect because how a database is opened doesn't matter. If it is open, you can't perform recovery. Answer d is incorrect for the same reason as answer c as well as there is no **ARCHIVELOG** mode for the **OPEN** command.

Question 25

The answer to the question is b. Of the functions listed, the only one that the **ALTER USER** command is capable of is setting a user's default role. Answer a is incorrect because this is done using the **CREATE ROLE** command. Answer c is incorrect because this is done using the **CREATE USER** command. Answer d is incorrect because this is done using the **SET ROLE** command.

Question 26

The correct answer is a. If the setting of **PCTFREE** is set lower, less space is reserved for future updates. This means that more space can be used for insertion of data; therefore, fewer blocks are required. Answer b is incorrect because this is the result of a higher **PCTFREE** setting. Answer c is incorrect because a lower **PCTFREE** may increase row chaining. Answer d is incorrect because the parameter does affect blocks.

Question 27

The answer is a. A shutdown using the **NORMAL** option waits for all users to log off of the database and then shuts down. Answer b is incorrect because it describes an **IMMEDIATE** shutdown. Answer c is incorrect because this describes the **ABORT** option. Answer d is incorrect because a is correct.

Question 28

The correct answer is c. The CONNECT role is automatically granted to a user created using Server Manager. Answers a and b are incorrect because these must be explicitly granted. Answer d is incorrect because there is no role called EXPORT.

Question 29

The proper answer is c. The **CREATE ROLE...IDENTIFIED BY** command creates roles that must be verified by the Oracle server. Answer a is incorrect because OSOPER is a role, not a command option. Answer b is incorrect because there is no **PASSWORD** keyword for the **CREATE ROLE** command. Answer d is incorrect because there is no **USING** keyword for the **CREATE ROLE** command.

Question 30

The correct answer is a. The **DBA_USER_PRIVS** view is the only view where the data about users with **ALTER ANY USER** privilege would be listed of those given as answers. Answer b is incorrect because **DBA_COL_PRIVS** only shows column privileges. Answer c is incorrect because **USER_TAB_PRIVS_RECD** only shows privileges received by the user. Answer d is incorrect because there is no **DBA_USER_PRIVS** view.

Question 31

The correct answer is d. Any **CREATE** privilege is a system privilege. Answers a, b, and c are object-level privileges, not system privileges.

Question 32

The correct answer is d. The **OPTIMAL** storage option used with rollback segments allows for automatic shrinking of rollback segments by the next transaction that accesses a rollback segment that has extended beyond optimal. Although answers a and b are storage parameters used with rollback segments, they do not allow for automatic shrinkage of the rollback segment. Answer c is incorrect because **PCTINCREASE** is not applied to rollback segments any more and doesn't cause automatic shrinkage.

Question 33

The correct answer is a. The roles must be created before any of the other steps can be successfully accomplished, therefore role creation must come first. Answer b is incorrect because this is the third step. Answer c is incorrect because it is the fourth step. Answer d is incorrect because this is the last step.

Question 34

The proper answer is a. Tables that are frequently updated are not good candidates for clustering because clustering is designed to enhance retrieval but can result in update penalties. Answers b, c, and d are descriptors for good cluster candidates.

Question 35

The correct answer is b. A normal rollback segment records data about transactions in any tablespace except **SYSTEM**. Answer a is incorrect because it describes caches. Answer c is incorrect because this describes sort segments. Answer d is incorrect because this describes index segments.

Question 36

The correct answer is b. All the other answers are invalid calculations that mean nothing to the database.

Question 37

The correct answer is c. If no mode is specified with the **STARTUP** command, the database is started in **EXCLUSIVE** mode. Answers a, b, and d must be explicitly stated.

Question 38

The correct answer is a. The **PARALLEL** mount option is used when the database is to be accessed by more than one instance simultaneously. Answer b is incorrect because this is the **RETRY** option being described. Answer c is incorrect because this describes the **EXCLUSIVE** option. Answer d is incorrect because there is a **PARALLEL** option.

Question 39

The correct answer is c. **PCTUSED** grows from the bottom up. Answer a is incorrect because **PCTUSED** grows from the bottom up. Answer b is incorrect because this is the function of **PTCUSED**. Answer d is incorrect because this is a description of **MAXTRANS**.

Question 40

The correct answer is b. The PMON process is the only process that frees SGA resources used by failed processes. Answer a is incorrect because this describes the RECO process. Answer c is incorrect because this is the purpose of the ARCH process. Answer d is incorrect because this is the purpose of the DBWR process.

Question 41

The correct answer is d. Because a temporary segment is implicitly created, it must use the default storage parameters specified for its tablespace when it is created. Answer a is incorrect because it describes a data segment. Answer b is incorrect because this describes index segments. Answer c is incorrect because it describes an **UNDO** segment.

Question 42

Answer a is the correct answer. A transaction is aborted when a user requests termination or when a user session is abnormally terminated. Answer b is incorrect because there is no transaction at the start of a session. Answer c is incorrect because there is no transaction at the end of a transaction to abort. Answer d is incorrect because it will result in an automatic commit, not an abort.

Question 43

The correct answer is a, the shared pool. The shared pool contains the data dictionary cache that contains the privilege cache. Answer b is incorrect because the database buffer cache is used for data. Answer c is incorrect because a memory structure is used. Answer d is incorrect because redo log buffers are used for transaction entries, not to read privileges.

Question 44

The correct answer is d. A segment can be either an index, table, rollback, or cluster segment. As such, it contains all the data for a specific structure in the tablespace. Answer a is incorrect because this describes redo segments, which are in redo logs. Answer b is incorrect because this describes control files. Answer c is incorrect because this describes cache areas.

Question 45

Answer d is correct. The **BACKGROUND_DUMP_DEST** parameter specifies the location for all background process trace dumps. Answer a is incorrect because this parameter doesn't exist. Answer b is incorrect because **AUDIT_TRAIL** is used to turn on database auditing. Answer c is incorrect because **LOG_ARCHIVE_DEST** specifies the location of archive logs.

Question 46

The correct answer is c. The **DICTIONARY** table contains the names of all of the data dictionary views. Answer a is incorrect because this describes the **DBA_DATA_FILES** view. Answer b is incorrect because this describes the **DBA_SEQUENCES** view. Answer d is incorrect because there is a **DICTIONARY** table.

Question 47

The correct answer is d. The only true statement in the list is that a tablespace can be made read only. Answer a is incorrect because there are read-only tablespaces. Answer b is incorrect because a tablespace can't be brought online when the database is shut down. Answer c is incorrect because a tablespace can consist of many data files.

Question 48

The correct answer is c. Segments must always have at least one extent. Answers a, b, and d are incorrect because they are not the number 1, because a segment has a minimum of one extent.

Question 49

The correct answer is c. The Server Manager is invoked during the first step of the database start-up process. The other answers follow this first step.

Question 50

The correct answer (according to Oracle training) is b. A daily check of the alert log should be sufficient for a production database with low activity; however, for a high activity database, the alert log should be checked more frequently. The other answers are incorrect because they are greater than b or too unspecific.

Question 51

The correct answer is a. The only memory structure that holds data is a buffer cache. Answer b is incorrect because a memory hit is a cache hit, not a disk hit. Answer c is incorrect because there is no such thing as a redo segment hit. Answer d is incorrect because there is no such thing as an undo segment hit.

Question 52

The correct answer is d. The **LOG_ARCHIVE_DEST** parameter tells the Oracle database where to copy filled redo logs to for the purpose of archival.

Answer a is the description of **USER_DUMP_DEST**. Answer b is incorrect because this is the description of **BACKGROUND_DUMP_DEST**. Answer c is incorrect because this is the description of **DB_NAME**.

Question 53

The correct answer is b. Of the functions listed, the only one that applies to the SMON process is that it cleans up memory segments allocated to sorts. Answer a is incorrect because this is the description of the PMON process. Answer c is incorrect because it describes the DBWR process. Answer d is incorrect because this describes the LGWR process.

Question 54

The correct answer is d. Of all the answers specified, the only one that holds true for caches is that they are self-administered. Answer a is incorrect because this describes data segments. Answer b is incorrect because this describes index segments. Answer c is incorrect because this describes redo logs.

Question 55

The correct answer is b. A distributed query is used to get data from two or more nodes in a distributed environment. Answer a is incorrect because update has nothing to do with retrieval. Answer c is incorrect because remote query only applies to a single remote node, not two or more. Answer d is incorrect because it deals with update, not retrieval.

Question 56

The correct answer is c. The **AUD$** table is the root data dictionary table for all audit views. It contains all audit records for all audited actions. Answer a is incorrect because this holds privilege information. Answer b is incorrect because this holds table information. Answer d is incorrect because the table **DUAL** is used for nondirected queries.

Question 57

The correct answer is d. If you are frequently allocating and deallocating extents, this will cause tablespace fragmentation. Answer a is not correct because blocks are the atomic level of storage for Oracle and can't be fragmented. Answer b is incorrect because this has no bearing on deallocation, just allocation of extents. Answer c is incorrect because segments can't be truncated.

Question 58

The correct answer is c. Because the entire purpose of the redo log is for recovery, it only makes sense that it holds data about recovery. Answer a is incorrect because this describes the control files. Answer b is incorrect because data segments hold data. Answer d is incorrect because an index segment holds index data.

Question 59

The correct answer is b. To be placed in a database, information must be placed into a data segment first before it can be placed anywhere else. Answer a is incorrect because only undo data is stored in rollback segments. Answer c is incorrect because only index data is stored in index segments. Answer d is incorrect because sort information is placed in temporary segments.

Glossary

ACCEPT—A SQL*Plus command that enables a SQL program to prompt a user for a variable at runtime and accept an input.

ALTER—A Data Definition Language (DLL) command that is used to change database objects.

analysis—The step in the system development process where the users' needs are gathered and analyzed to produce documentation used to design a program system.

archive log—An archive copy of the redo log. The archive log is used to recover to an earlier point in time or to roll forward from a backup to the present time.

attribute—A detail concerning a thing of significance (entity). For example a *PERSON* entity may have the attributes of name, address, date-of-birth.

audit trail—In Oracle, a defined set of actions that are specified to be audited using system audit tools. For example, you can audit connects to the database.

buffer—In Oracle, a a memory area used to hold data, redo, or rollback information. Usually the buffers are specified using the **DB_BLOCK_BUFFERS**, **DB_BLOCK_SIZE**, and **LOG_BUFFER** initialization parameters.

cache—A memory area that is self-managing and is used to hold information about objects, locks, and latches. The caches are usually contained in the shared pool area of the SGA (system global area) and are preallocated as far as size, based on internal algorithms that control how the shared pool memory is allocated.

cardinality—A term used in relational analysis to show how two objects relate; it tells how many. For example, "A person may have zero or one nose" shows a cardinality of zero or one. "A person may have zero, one, or many children" shows a cardinality of zero to many. And, "A person has one or many cells" shows a cardinality of one or many. In reference to indexes, cardinality shows how many rows in the indexed table relate back to the index value. A low cardinality index such as a person's sex (M or F) should be placed in a bitmapped index if it must be indexed, whereas a high cardinality value such as a person's social security number or employee ID should be placed in a standard B-tree index.

column—Part of a table's row. A column will have been mapped from an attribute in an entity. Columns have datatypes, and may have constraints mapped against them.

COMMIT—A Data Manipulation Language (DML) command. A **COMMIT** marks a transaction as completed successfully and causes data to be written first to the redo logs and, once DBWR writes, to the disk. A **COMMIT** isn't complete until it receives word from the disk subsystem that the redo log write is complete. Committed data cannot be rolled back using the **ROLLBACK** command, and must be removed using more DML commands.

CONNECT—This is a Server Manager (SVRMGRL), SQL*Worksheet, or SQL*Plus command that enables a user to connect to the database or to a remote database.

control file—The Oracle file that contains information on all database files and maintains System Control Number (SCN) records for each. The control file must be present and current for the database to start up properly. Control files may be mirrored; mirrored copies are automatically updated by Oracle as needed. The control file provides for maintenance of system concurrency and consistency by providing a means of synchronizing all database files.

conventional path load—The most used form of SQL*Loader database load. A conventional path load uses DML statements to load data from flat operating system files into Oracle tables.

CREATE—A DDL command that allows creation of database objects.

data dictionary—A collection of C structs, tables, and views that contain all of the database *metadata* (information about the database's data). The data dictionary is used to store information used by all database processes to find out about database data structures.

DDL (Data Definition Language)—A SQL statement used to create or manipulate database structures is classified as DDL. Examples are **CREATE**, **ALTER**, and **DROP** commands.

DELETE—A DML command used to remove data by rows (generally speaking) from the database tables.

DESCRIBE—A SQL*Plus or Server Manager command that is used to retrieve information on database structure. Any stored object (except triggers) can be described.

direct path load—In SQL*Loader, it disables all triggers, constraints, and indexes and loads data directly into the table by prebuilding and then inserting database blocks. It does not use DML commands. There are conventional and direct path loads in SQL*Loader.

discarded records—A record that SQL*Loader rejects for loading based on internal rules for data validation and conversion.

DROP—A DDL command used to remove database objects.

dynamic SQL—SQL used to build SQL. Essentially, queries are issued against data dictionary tables using embedded literal strings to build a set of commands. Usually, dynamic SQL is used to automate a long series of virtually identical commands against similar types of database objects. An example would be creating a script to disable or enable all triggers for a set of database tables using the **DBA_TRIGGERS** table and a single SQL statement.

entity—In relational modeling, a thing of significance. Examples of entities are *PERSON, CAR, EXPENSE*. Entities are singular in nature and are mapped to tables. Tables contain entities.

equijoin—A join between two or more tables using equality comparisons.

ERD (entity relationship diagram)—A pictorial representation using a standard symbology and methodology (such as Chen or Yourdon) of a relational database.

foreign key—A value or set of values mapped from a primary or parent table into a dependent or child table used to enforce referential integrity. A foreign key, generally speaking, must be either **NULL** or exist as a primary key in a parent table.

function—One of several structures. An implicit function is one that is provided as a part of the SQL language. An explicit function is one that is created by the user using PL/SQL. A function must return a value and must be named. As a part of the SQL standard, a function cannot change a database's or package's state, but can only act on external variables and values.

GET—A SQL*Plus command that loads SQL or PL/SQL commands from an external operating system file into the SQL*Plus command buffer.

index—A structure that enhances data retrieval by providing rapid access to frequently queried column values. Indexes can be either B-tree structured or bitmapped. The two general types of index are unique and nonunique. A unique index forces all values entered into its source column to be unique. A nonunique index allows for repetitive and null values to be entered into its source column. Generally speaking, a column with high cardinality should be indexed using a B-tree type index (standard, default type of index), whereas low cardinality values should be indexed using a bitmapped index.

INITIAL—A storage parameter that sets the size in bytes (no suffix) kilobytes (K suffix) or megabytes (M suffix) of the **INITIAL** extent allocated to a table, index, rollback segment, or cluster.

INITRANS—A storage parameter that reserves space in the block header for the transaction records associated with a table's blocks.

INSERT—A DML command that enables users to place new records into a table.

MAXEXTENTS—Sets the maximum number of extents an object can grow into. The **MAXEXTENTS** value can be altered up to the maximum number of extents allowed based on block size.

MAXTRANS—A companion to the **INITRANS** storage parameter. **MAXTRANS** sets the maximum number of transactions that can access a block concurrently.

NEXT—Storage parameter that specifies what the size in bytes (no suffix) kilobytes (K suffix) or megabytes (M suffix) of the **NEXT** extent allocated to a table, index, rollback segment, or cluster. The **NEXT** parameter is used with the **PCTINCREASE** parameter to determine the size of all extents after the **INITIAL** and **NEXT** extents.

object auditing—The specification of auditing options that pertains to database objects rather than database operations.

Optimal Flexible Architecture (OFA)—A standard, authored by internal Oracle Corporation experts, that tells how to optimally configure an Oracle database.

ORAPWD—A generalized term for the Oracle Password Manager that creates and is used to maintain the external password file. The external password file is used to tell the Oracle Enterprise Manager and Server Manager who is authorized to perform DBA functions against a specific database.

OSDBA—A role that is assigned to users who are authorized to create and maintain Oracle databases. If a user is given the OSDBA role, he is also given an entry in the external password file.

OSOPER—A role that is assigned to users who are authorized to maintain Oracle databases. If a user is given the OSOPER role, he is also given an entry in the external password file.

outside join—A type of join where data not meeting the join criteria (that is, the join value is **NULL**) is also returned by the query. An outside join is signified by using the plus sign inside parentheses [(+)] to indicate the outside join value beside the join column for the table deficient in data.

package—A stored PL/SQL construct made of related procedures, functions, exceptions, and other PL/SQL constructs. Packages are called into memory when any package object is referenced. They are are created or dropped as a unit.

PCTFREE—Used in an Oracle block to determine the amount of space reserved for future updates. Too low of a **PCTFREE** can result in row-chaining for frequently updated tables and too high a value requires more storage space.

PCTINCREASE—Determines what percentage each subsequent extent after **INITIAL** and **NEXT** grows over the previously allocated extent.

PCTUSED—Determines when a block is placed back on the free block list. Once used space in a block drops below **PCTUSED**, the block can be used for subsequent new row insertion.

PGA (process global area)—Represents the memory area allocated to each process that accesses an Oracle database.

primary key—In a relational database, the unique identifier for a table. A primary key must be unique and not null. A primary key can either be *natural* (derived from a column or columns in the database) or *artificial* (drawn from a sequence).

privilege auditing—Auditing of what privileges are granted and by and to whom.

procedures—Stored PL/SQL objects that may, but aren't required to, return a value. Procedures are allowed to change a database or package state. Procedures can be placed into packages.

production—The final stage of the system development cycle. The production stage corresponds to normal maintenance and backup and recovery operations against a developed system.

profiles—Sets of resource allocations that can be assigned to a user. These resources are used to limit idle time, connect time, memory, and CPU usage.

PROMPT—A SQL*Plus command used to pass a string out of a SQL script to the executing user. The **PROMPT** command can be used with the **ACCEPT** command to prompt for values needed by the script.

RECOVER—A command used in Server Manager to explicitly perform database recovery operations.

referential integrity—The process by which a relational database maintains record relationships between parent and child tables via primary key and foreign key values.

rejected records—In SQL*Loader, records that don't meet load criteria for the table being loaded either due to value, datatype, or other restrictions.

relationship—A named association between two things of significance. For example, if I say that a wheeled vehicle has one or many wheels, *has* is the relationship, or an employee works for one or more employer, *works for* is the relationship.

resources—The database and system resources that are controlled by use of a profile.

ROLLBACK—A DML command used to undo database changes that have not been committed.

rollback segment—A database object that contains records used to undo database transactions. Whenever a parameter in the database refers to **UNDO**, it is actually referring to rollback segments.

SAVE—A SQL*Plus command used to store command buffer contents in an external operating system file.

SELECT—A DML command used to retrieve values from the database.

Server Manager line mode—The Server Manager has a GUI mode and a line mode. In line mode, all commands are entered at the command line.

SET—A SQL*Plus command used to change the values of SQL*Plus environment parameters such as line width and page length.

SGA (system global area)—Consists of the database buffers, shared pool, and queue areas that are globally accessible by all database processes. The SGA is used to speed Oracle processing by providing for caching of data and structure information in memory.

SHOW—A SQL*Plus command that is used to show the value of a variable set with the **SET** command.

SHUTDOWN—A Server Manager command used to shut down the database. **SHUTDOWN** has three modes: **NORMAL**, **IMMEDIATE**, and **ABORT**. **NORMAL** prohibits new connections, waits for all users to log off, and then shuts down. **IMMEDIATE** prohibits new connections, backs out uncommitted transactions, and then logs users off and shuts down. **ABORT** shuts down right now and not gracefully.

SPOOL—A SQL*Plus command that is used to send SQL*Plus output to either a printer or a file.

SQL buffer—A memory area used to store the last SQL command. The SQL buffer can only store the last command executed, unless it is loaded with the **GET** command. A SQL*Plus command such as **SET**, **DESCRIBE**, or **SPOOL** is not placed in the SQL buffer.

STARTUP—A Server Manager command used to start up the database. A database can be started in one of several modes: **MOUNT**, **NOMOUNT**, **OPEN**, **EXCLUSIVE**, and **PARALLEL**.

statement auditing—Audit actions such as insert, update, and delete.

STORAGE—The **STORAGE** clause is what Oracle uses to determine current and future settings for an object's extents. If a storage clause isn't specified, the object's storage characteristics are taken from the tablespace default storage clause.

strategy—In this step of the system development cycle (usually paired with the analysis step), the overall methodology for the rest of the development effort is mapped out.

SYSDBA—See *OSDBA*.

SYSOPER—See *OSOPER*.

table—The structure used to store data in an Oracle database. Entities map to tables in relational databases.

transition—In this step of the system development cycle, user testing is performed and support of the application moves from development to production personnel.

TRUNCATE—A DDL statement used to remove all rows from a table. Because it is a DDL statement, it cannot be rolled back.

TRUNCATE (functions)—There are both string and date functions called **TRUNCATE**, which are used to shorten the external representations of internal data.

UGA (user global area)—Used to store user-specific variables and stacks.

UID (unique identifier)—Uniquely identifies a row in a table and usually maps to the natural primary key value. Each entity must have a unique identifier to qualify as a relational table.

UPDATE—A DML command that allows data inside tables to be changed.

variable—A user- or process-defined storage area used to hold a value that will probably be different each time a script or procedure is executed.

view—A preset select against one or more tables that is stored in the database and has no physical representation. A view is also known as a virtual table.

virtual table—See *view*.

Index

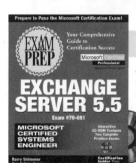